I0814295

PARVA Convivia

IVAN FOLETTI & ADRIEN PALLADINO

BYZANTIUM OR DEMOCRACY?

KONDAKOV'S LEGACY IN EMIGRATION: THE *INSTITUTUM KONDAKOVIANUM* AND ANDRÉ GRABAR, 1925–1952

Viella, Rome • Masaryk University Press, Brno • 2020

Series PARVA Convivia, 8

This book was carried out as a part of the project "The Heritage of Nikodim Pavlovič Kondakov in the Experiences of André Grabar and the Seminarium Kondakovianum" (Czech Science Foundation, Reg. № 18-20666S).

LANGUAGE SUPERVISION • Adriano Hundhausen
EXECUTIVE EDITOR • Klára Doležalová
TYPESETTING & GRAPHIC DESIGN • Petr M. Vronský
PUBLISHER • Masaryk University Press, Žerotínovo nám. 9, 60177 Brno & Viella editrice, via delle Alpi 32, 00198 Rome
EDITORIAL OFFICE • Seminář dějin umění, Filozofická fakulta Masarykovy univerzity, Arna Nováka 1, 60200 Brno

PUBLISHED • 1st edition, 2020
ISBN 978-88-3313-496-3 (Viella)
ISBN 978-80-210-9637-0 (Masaryk University Press)

MUNI ARTS Department of the History of Art Centre for Early Medieval Studies

VIELLA

TABLE OF CONTENTS

INTRODUCTION

Odessa is a charming city on the edge of the Black Sea, laid out by Russian architects during the reign of Catherine the Great.[1] Today, the city belongs to Ukraine and has been modernized in many aspects. The slightly decaying *fin de siècle* architecture, however, still dominates our image of the city, and the curious visitor can go for a walk through the streets of the old Jewish ghetto or have a look at the buildings of the Imperial New Russian University (as it was named when founded in 1865). For those who are passionate about the transcultural spaces of the past, walking through the streets of Odessa is a wistful experience. A century ago, the port city was home to a large, polyglot Russian, Ukrainian, and Jewish community, and attracted many immigrants – Armenians, Bulgarians, French, Italians, Greeks, and others.[2] The city was not only a microcosm of the large, cosmopolitan late Romanov Empire, but also mirrored the multicultural reality of the pre-First World War Mediterranean {1}.

It is in this city, during the spring of 1920, that this book will start. After changing hands several times over the course of the Russian Revolution, Odessa was conquered for good by the Red Army in 1920, and a few last boats sailed away filled with émigrés escaping from one uncertain future to another. Among the last

1• Herlihy 1986.

2• "In the streets one hears Russian, English, Italian, German, Tatar, Polish, Turkish, Greek, Armenian, Moldavian, Bulgarian, Hungarian, Dalmatian, French, Swedish and Spanish, and these are not spoken merely by passing strangers, but by the regular inhabitants; in short, the confusion of tongues which prevails, more or less, all over Russia, reaches in Odessa the true Babylonish extreme", Kohl 1844, p. 420. See also Herlihy 1977.

1) View of the harbor of Odessa, 1902

ships to leave was the *Sparta*. Let us imagine, then, on one of Odessa's splendid spring days, a group of four emigrants reaching the deck of this boat – a man of nearly 50 and his wife, a young lady, and a majestic old professor whose clothing and movements immediately identify him as an intellectual who has dedicated his life to scholarship. The middle-aged man is the future Nobel prize winner Ivan Bunin, accompanied by his wife Vera Muromceva-Bunina. The young lady is Ekaterina Jacenko, and the old man is Nikodim Kondakov, perhaps the most prominent Byzantinist of the age.[3] They look for the last time towards Odessa, and as the ship sails into the Black Sea, they see the coastline getting smaller and smaller. They leave behind, forever as it would turn out, their homes and livelihoods.

It was the beginning of their experience of emigration, one which would deeply affect their existence. Bunin and his wife went to Paris, where he would use his pen to continue his fight against totalitarian regimes. He received the Nobel Prize for Literature in 1933 and died in 1953, still in Paris.[4] The destiny of Kondakov and Jacenko – the latter was working as the aged professor's personal secretary – would be different. After a stay in Bulgaria together with Bunin and his wife, Kondakov and Jacenko moved on to Prague, where

3• Foletti 2017a, pp. 68–70.

4• Guker 1992.

Kondakov would die in 1925, and where we lose track of Jacenko. Kondakov's last years, spent as an exile, would transform him both intellectually and personally.[5] This transformation is, however, only the beginning of the story of this book. After Kondakov's death, his presence in Prague was commemorated by the birth of an entire research institute. For nearly thirty years, the *Institutum Kondakovianum* would be one of the leading institutions in Byzantine studies in the world, drawing in some of the most important scholars and intellectuals of the time. Moreover, a journal, the *Seminarium Kondakovianum*, was inaugurated to promulgate Kondakov's approach and field of investigation. In this sense, Kondakov's legacy in Prague is as impressive as that of any art historian in the world, superseded perhaps only by the legacy of Aby Warburg (1866–1929) in London.[6]

Kondakov's passion for Byzantine art lived on not only in Prague, but also in the careers of his Russian pupils. Dmitrij Ajnalov (1862–1939), his successor at the Faculty of Arts in Saint Petersburg, and André Grabar (1896–1990), one of the most important Byzantinists of the twentieth century, who will figure prominently in the pages of this book.

STRUCTURE, SOURCES, AND METHODOLOGICAL PREMISES

When we began to think about this book project, one of the topics which interested us the most was the link between emigration and art history. For one of us, Ivan Foletti, it was the logical consequence in his interest in Kondakov. For both of us, moreover, the phenomenon of emigration is interesting in itself, both as a key element of European culture and as part of our own personal stories. Albeit in quite different circumstances than those faced by emigrants in the early twentieth century, we have both experienced several phases of emigration, adapted to new societies, and found ourselves obliged to learn a new language in order to integrate. To investigate Russian émigrés was, however, not merely a matter of personal projection for us, but the expression of a deep curiosity. We wished to understand how art historians adapted themselves, and their research

5• Foletti 2014, 2020b.

6• For the bibliography on *Seminarium Kondakovianum*, see *infra*. Concerning Warburg's intellectual legacy, see, e.g., Landauer 1981.

and scholarship, to very different milieus, and especially to investigate how these Russians – while belonging to the former elite of an autocratic state – could find a place for themselves in the academic world of the Western democracies.

This book is rooted in that question and will narrate how Kondakov's legacy affected émigrés in Czechoslovakia and France. These parallel stories are different in many regards. On one hand, we will be analyzing a group, while on the other we will be dealing only with one invidual, André Grabar. In the case of the Kondakov Institute, not only have many publications survived, but we also have the well-preserved archives of the Institute in boxes at the Czech Academy of Sciences in Prague. With Grabar, the situation is more difficult. Of the seventeen boxes of his effects preserved at the Collège de France, the overwhelming majority (sixteen boxes) contain manuscripts of his later publications and official correspondence from his later years. Only one box contains personal letters and other documents, so important for the reconstruction of his personal and intellectual background. Moreover, during the period we are concerned with in this book – corresponding more or less to the years when the Kondakov Institute existed (1926–1952) – Grabar was still a young scholar, yet to reach the apex of his career. We nevertheless believe that our parallel approach, even if based on differing sets of data, is one of the strengths of the volume that the reader now holds in his hands. It will be a book about art history meeting history, both on an institutional level, and through the experience of one exceptional individual.

Our look at the stories of an institution and many individual art historians will cover more than thirty years. Our main task will be to try to understand the context of their scholarly work and how that context affected their research. The history of art history is a field which first bloomed in the 1920s and 1930s, with attention paid to both individual stories of scholars and to overarching philosophical trends.[7] In recent decades, this field has become more sensitive to the ways in which a scholar's national identity can define their research, while an increasing interest has been devoted to the economic and social contexts of the study of medieval art, including some attempts at defining the place of "Byzantine

7 • Waetzold 1921–1924; Venturi 1936; Podro 1982; Kultermann 1990 [1966].

studies".[8] A framework has thus been created for understanding the wider impact of history – economic, social, and political – on scholarship. In this book, we intend to pursue this tradition while adding two hitherto little-explored approaches. One of our innovations will be to consider how art history was transformed by the phenomenon of the "first wave" of Russian emigration (essentially 1917–1923).[9] The other will be the application of a transnational comparative approach, which will help us to avoid the trap of a "Slavocentric" perspective. Furthermore, this comparative approach has already been applied to the first wave of Russian emigration as a whole, but never systematically, as far as we know, to the history of art history.[10] Our work will thus necessarily be interdisciplinary, at the crossroads between art history, history, and the history of scholarship and the social sciences.

Any investigation of the period selected will draw us into some of the most dramatic events of the past century, starting with the Russian Revolution, continuing through the rise of Nazism and Fascism, and culminating in the Second World War, and, for Czechoslovakia, the Communist putsch of 1948. The scholars and institutions we will be following through the pages of this book were often confronted with extreme events, from the economic crisis of 1929 and its effects on the Kondakov Institute, to the collective panic caused in Czechoslovakia by the Munich Agreement, to the daily violence and fear which our "heroes" lived through in occupied Prague and Paris. From this brief introduction the reader will begin to understand our choice of title for this book: "Byzantium or Democracy?" If, in the second half of the nineteenth century, the Byzantine Empire was mainly linked (as we will see) with Russian imperial ambitions, the first wave of Russian emigration proceeded to profoundly transform the very idea of "Byzantium". This will be one of the main hypotheses of our book. In the following pages, we

8• E.g., Moxey 2001; Zimmerman 2003; Born/Janatková/Labuda 2004; Passini 2012; Bartlová 2016. For the historiography of Byzantine studies in art history, see, e.g., Spieser 2007; Gasbarri 2015.

9• It is estimated that between 1 and 3 million émigrés left Russia after the Russian Revolutions and because of the Civil War. See Peeling 2014.

10• The most synthetic systematic approaches to the phenomenon in general are Raeff 1990; for the Russian emigration in Prague, see Chinyaeva 2001; Andreyev/Savický 2004. For the French situation, see, e.g., Johnston 1988; Struve 1996.

will attempt to show exactly how the notion of "Byzantium" was changed by Russian emigration in general, and by émigrés' contact with democratic countries in particular. The rise of Nazism created a new situation wherein former subjects of the Russian emperor, after having experienced twenty years of democracy, were suddenly confronted with a new and more radical kind of authoritarian regime. They were far from being the only ones affected; indeed, all European society was transformed into something unrecognizable by the violence perpetrated by this regime. We will look at how radical transformations in political and social circumstances in those years affected the imaginary island of "Byzantium".

One last point should be mentioned very briefly here. All through this book, we will be dealing with the notion of "Byzantium", even though we no longer believe in its existence – at least not in the way it was understood in the period under study. At that time, the ancient name of Constantinople, Byzantium, was commonly used by scholars and politicians to describe the entire Eastern Roman Empire, the Empire of Constantinople. We now know that this term entered use only when that empire was on its last legs, and was first used by historians in the sixteenth century.[11] But the term inevitably carries with it the negative connotations constructed by Western thinkers in the eighteenth and nineteenth centuries, including Montesquieu, Voltaire, and Didron. We would now prefer to call in, as Charles du Fresne, Sieur Du Cange (1610–1688) did in the seventeenth century, *L'Empire de Constantinople*.[12] Nevertheless, for this book, we will stick with "Byzantium", as that was the term commonly employed by Kondakov, Toll', or Grabar.

The book will be divided into sections dealing with the questions posed above. The first chapter will be biographical, if that is the right word, and will be telling the stories of the Kondakov Institute and of André Grabar in the period in question. It will present historical, economic, and social information, and will show exactly what practical and personal issues confronted the transnational Russian émigré community. The second chapter will be focused, in

11• Spieser 1991.

12• Du Cange 1657, see Spieser 2000; Montesquieu 1838 [1734], p. 179; Didron 1845, see Brisac/Leniaud 1987.

large part, on the writings produced by both the *Institutum Kondakovianum* and André Grabar between the wars. We will concentrate on the relationship between scholarly production – which aims to be objective – and the changing social atmosphere created by political and economic crises. In the last chapter, dedicated to the most tragic years, we will try to understand how the Nazi occupation transformed all of society, especially scholarly research.

Before beginning the book, we should disclose our personal connection with its objects of study, especially with the destiny of the Kondakov Institute and its journal, *Seminarium Kondakovianum*. We are both presently involved in the publication of a journal called *Convivium: Exchanges and Interactions in the Arts of Europe, Byzantium, and the Mediterranean*, the subtitle of which is *Seminarium Kondakovianum Series Nova*. We are therefore consciously attempting to revive the work of the Institute, which was destroyed by the war and the Communist putsch of 1948. This publication was resurrected in 2014 as a collaboration of three institutions: the Department of Art History of the Czech Academy of Sciences in Prague (the formal legatee of the Kondakov Institute), the Faculty of Arts of the University of Lausanne, and the Faculty of Arts of the Masaryk University in Brno. Foletti is editor-in-chief of this journal, and Palladino has been contributing to it since the first year of its existence. We firmly believe that our affection for Kondakov's legacy has not affected the intellectual honesty of our research, but it would only be fair to admit, at this point, that at times we have had the impression, especially when going through the Institute's archives, that we are working on a sort of family history.

• • •

Now that we have reached the end of our work on this book (which was at its most intense in the last three years, but which has its roots as far back as 2004), we would like to express our gratitude to all those who made this effort possible. On the institutional level, we should certainly thank the Czech Science Foundation (GAČR) believing in the project which lies at the heart of this book. This work would be equally impossible without the valuable support of the Department of Art History of the Masaryk University, and especially its two successive heads, Ondřej Jakubec and Radka Nokkala

Miltová, to whom we wish to express all our gratitude. An important stage in our work was completed in the month that we had the privilege to spend in Paris at the Deutsches Forum für Kunstgeschichte. Our thanks for this opportunity go to Philippe Cordez, vice-director of this institution, who was an extremely generous and friendly host. We would also like to thank the Collège de France and its archives in Paris; their kind support and their willingness to make their archives accessible went far beyond what we had any right to expect. Lastly, we must mention the archival department of the Department of Art History of the Czech Academy of Sciences, who welcomed us each time we needed it and provided us with all kinds of support in an extremely friendly atmosphere. Thanks to Jiří Roháček and all his team.

Aside from these institutions, there are, of course, individuals who have supported our writing in many ways. First of all, we would like to mention Anastasia Ivanova, who joined us in this project and worked with us for two years, acting as our assistant and in general helping us very much. *Spasibo*, Nastja. Our gratitude also goes to the students for their support working with the materials at the Academy of Sciences in Prague. In Paris, we had the chance to exchange ideas several times with Ioanna Rapti, to whom we would like to express our all warm wishes and gratitude. We would like to mention that a third scholar, Francesco Lovino, was also involved in this project at its origins, but due to personal reasons, he was forced to cut short his participation. Nonetheless, he remained at our disposition each time we needed his help. We must also thank all the members of the Centre for Early Medieval Studies. They were unconditionally supportive with every manner of task. Moreover, thanks to them, we experience, every day, an atmosphere close to what we imagine it must have been like at the Kondakov Institute in its best years. It would take too long to list all the members of the Centre, but we would like to mention at least Klára Švejdíková, our executive assistant, for her patience in dealing with all administrative tasks linked to the production of this book. We are also grateful to Jana Unčovská and Marie Okáčová for having helped us survive the administrative jungle of the project. Our appreciation goes to the graphic team of the Centre as well, to its head Anna Kelblová, and especially to Petr Vronský, who designed the lavish book you hold in your hands. Furthermore, we are much obliged to Mr. Martin S. Jakubčo, who has provided us with important archival documents from Saint Petersburg and to Nathanael Aschenbrenner, who also facilitated access to precious documents. We must also express our sincere gratitude to Jiří Němec and Giovanni Gasbarri for reading the entire volume and providing many helpful comments. Finally we would like to express our gratitude to Klára Doležalová who helped us during the editing process of this volume.

Beyond the Centre, we had the chance to exchange ideas about topics linked to our research with Michele Bacci, Xavier Barral i Altet, Hans Belting, Klára Benešovská, Nicolas Bock, Armin F. Bergmeier, Valentina Cantone, Chiara Croci, Beatrice Daskas, Francesca Dell'Acqua, Stefano D'Ovidio, Jannic Durand, Allegra Iafrate, Herbert L. Kessler, Klaus Krüger, Alexej Lidov, Anna Magnago Lampugnani, Pierre-Alain Mariaux, Tanja Michalsky, Éric Palazzo, Bissera Pentcheva, Irene Quadri, Serena Romano, Elisabetta Scirocco, Erik Thunø. Thanks to all of you.

We are much indebted to Cecilia Palombelli, the director of Viella, who has agreed to publish this volume as part of the unusual collaborative series *Parva Convivia*. We would also like to thank the editorial board of the series for its support.

Lastly, our month spent in Paris would never have been so productive and pleasant without the generous support given us by Christian Michel. Christian is a genuine intellectual and a true friend. *Merci*, Christian. Throughout the project, one other special person was involved in our research on a daily basis. Moreover, she tolerated our changing moods and our crises during the writing of the book. Finally, she shared with us all her expertise about the first wave of Russian emigration, something which helped us immensely. We are speaking about Karolina Foletti, who can be considered as an integral contributor to this endeavor.

While we were writing this book, we received very sad news from Paris – the death of Xenia Muratova. Xenia was an expert on all questions concerning Russian emigration, a subject which was an integral part of her own story. When we met her for the last time in Paris, she was already at less than full strength, but nonetheless spent an evening talking with us about Grabar, whom she knew personally, and about many other topics. We would thus like to dedicate this book to her memory.

1/ Russian Émigré Byzantinists

If we look at the field of art history in the nineteenth century, and more specifically at Byzantine studies, we cannot help but notice that the study of "Byzantium" was concentrated within the Russian Empire.[1] As was noted explicitly in 1900 by Charles Diehl (1859–1944), and implicitly even as early as 1881 by Anton Springer (1825–1891), this was because Russia considered itself, and was considered by others, as the political and moral heir of the Byzantine Empire.[2] Moreover, many of the most prominent art historians dealing with Byzantine culture – Fëdor Buslaev (1818–1897), Nikodim P. Kondakov, Egor Redin (1863–1908), etc. – directly linked their study of "Byzantium" with medieval Russian art and culture. Russian art was thus presented as a direct successor of Constantinopolitan culture. For these Russians, and Kondakov is as good an example as any, Russia, in a certain sense, *was* Byzantium. One could justifiably claim that in the Romanov Empire, Byzantine studies were considered a patriotic duty.

After the Russian Revolution(s) of 1917, especially the October Revolution, a large part of the Russian intelligentsia left the country. Among them were some of the most important art historians dealing with Byzantine and Russian medieval art, not only Nikodim Kondakov and André Grabar, both protagonists of this book, but also Pavel Muratov and many others. As we will see, some reacted to their new identity as political refugees by searching for new topics to investigate. However, a large majority of them remained faithful

1 • Muratova 2004; Foletti 2017a.

2 • Springer 1886; Diehl 1900.

to their original field of study. For obvious reasons, it was difficult (if not impossible) for them to perceive or present Soviet Russia and the later Soviet Union as the heir of the Eastern Roman Empire. Eastern Orthodoxy had been replaced by Marxism-Leninism, and the autocratic emperor by the General Secretary of the Communist Party.

Within the former Russian Empire, interest in traditional Russian forms of art declined in the 1920s, in favor of increasing interest in modernity and the avant-garde, an interest which, in turn, would be officially cancelled when Socialist Realism was declared the only acceptable aesthetic choice.[3] Moreover, from the beginning, the Communist regime was extremely anti-clerical, and the Byzantine and Orthodox identity was thus progressively marginalized.

But how did these changes in their motherland affect first-wave Russian emigrants' perception of the past?

This question will be one of the threads tying our entire book together, but it is the key to this first chapter, which will mainly be about figures from two different generations – the master Nikodim Kondakov representing the older generation, his pupils from Prague, and André Grabar in Paris, representing the younger. These emigrants were forced to adapt to two new countries, Czechoslovakia and France. However, it would be unfair to mention only these selected figures and those two countries. Indeed, Kondakov and his pupils were part of a much larger social and intellectual network. Moreover, the phenomenon of Russian emigration between the two wars was, by definition, cosmopolitan. The wonderful poetess Marina Cvetaeva (1892–1941) split her time between Prague and Paris.[4] The historian George Vernadskij directed the Prague branch of the *Seminarium Kondakovianum* while living in New Haven.[5] Another characteristic of these Russian emigrants was that they came from an intellectual elite which had been, for at least two centuries, completely internationalized. Often, their mother tongue was not Russian, but French (or even German or English).[6] A glance at the correspondence of any prominent Russian scholar in the decades before the Russian Revolution shows that they were an integral part

3• For an interesting reflection on the subject see, e.g., Reid 2001.

4• See Chinyaeva 2001, pp. 171–172; see also Maritchik-Sioli 2019.

5• Ratchinski 2003.

6• Offord 2015; O'Meara 2019, pp. 34–38.

of a largely homogeneous international network.[7] Emigration always implies a rupture of some sort, but in the case of these Russian intellectuals the rupture was "softened" by the fact that they already knew, and were known by, the rest of the world. This facilitated a certain continuity in their work.[8]

The first part of this chapter will be devoted to Nikodim Kondakov and his entourage in Prague, above all to their place in a global context. The second part will focus on André Grabar, who, after reaching France, became a French citizen while still participating in that same transnational network.

NIKODIM KONDAKOV, THE *INSTITUTUM KONDAKOVIANUM*, AND THE "RUSSIAN ACTION"

NIKODIM KONDAKOV: THE PATRIARCH OF BYZANTINE STUDIES AND RUSSIAN EMIGRATION

Born in 1844 in Khalan' in the province of Kursk, Nikodim P. Kondakov was a perfect example of those who were called, in the second half of the nineteenth century, *raznočincy*: persons from lower social classes who had achieved a higher status as intellectuals.[9] Around 1900, there were approximately 3,200 people in Russia making their livings by writing, whether as journalists, writers, critics, or scholars.[10] Kondakov was one of them. His starting position was even more humble than most, as he had been born a serf, but thanks to the reforms of Alexander II (r. 1855–1881), he had been able to join the intelligentsia {2}.[11] An art historian specializing in Byzantine and medieval Russian art, he began his career as professor at the University of Odessa before reaching, in 1888, the apex of his field: professor at the University of Saint Petersburg and curator of the Medieval and Renaissance Department of the Imperial

7• See for example Medvedev 1995.

8• Foletti 2020a.

9• On the *raznočincy*, see Kimerling Wirtschafter 2006. For Kondakov's biography see the synthesis of Khrushkova 2012a. For more details, see Foletti 2017a.

10• Besançon 1974, p. 125.

11• For the childhood of Kondakov see: Vernadsky 1926, pp. IX–X and Kondakov 1927a, pp. 11–22.

2) Nikodim Pavlovič Kondakov, Florence, 30 October 1882

Hermitage.[12] In this period of his life, he had privileged access to the imperial court, collected Chinese porcelain and Byzantine coins, and had a personal library that must have rivalled many public collections.[13] He owned a splendid apartment in Saint Petersburg and a luxurious villa in Jalta.

Aside from this remarkable story of success, so endearing to the exponents of modern neo-liberalism, Kondakov's intellectual journey is also interesting for how closely it mirrors developments in Russian imperial politics. When Russia was preparing for war with the Ottoman Empire in the 1870s and newspapers were promoting more than ever the idea of Russia as Byzantium, Kondakov published his first book, dedicated to the history of Byzantine art.[14] In this volume, which – strange as it may now seem – was the first monograph ever dedicated to Byzantine art, Kondakov explicitly stated that researching Byzantium meant serving the motherland. A few decades later, Kondakov undertook interdisciplinary research on Macedonia with a clear political intention: to determine

12• Kondakov 1891, 1896.

13• Žebelev 1924.

14• Vzdornov 1986, p. 224; Foletti 2017a, pp. 40–42.

whether the country should belong to Serbia or Bulgaria. Not surprisingly, the conclusion of his book was in perfect harmony with Russia's policy in this region.[15]

We could give more examples of this dialogue between research and politics, but it would be unfair to imply that Kondakov, an international scholar of the highest level, was little more than a political hack. He discovered and described, in the course of his travels around the Mediterranean, innumerable works of art.[16] With interests ranging from Late Antiquity to the Early Modern period, and encompassing every possible artistic technique, he literally constructed, from the ground up, a completely new field of study. One should also notice how modern his approach was in both its geographical range and in the diversity of media it considered. Kondakov explicitly challenged the Vasarian stereotypes that Western art history had been constructed upon and promoted a completely new and original way of looking at art.[17] It is no coincidence that several of Kondakov's exceptional contemporaries showed a similar ability to think in innovative ways about culture. We should mention, by way of example, Vladimir Solovjev (1853–1900). He proposed an innovative approach to Western philosophy starting from the perspective of Russia, a country which (in his view) had never experienced the Renaissance and could therefore offer a completely new intellectual paradigm.[18]

Kondakov was, in short, a remarkable figure – a genuine intellectual, and at the same time a self-made man, with all the accompanying problems linked to this status. At the distance of more than a century, it is easy for us to see the impact of historical events, his personal life, and his destiny on his scholarly work.

When the February Revolution started in Saint Petersburg, Kondakov had already been retired for twenty years, since Russian state employees could retire after only thirty years of service.[19] Kondakov thus retired at the extremely young age of fifty-two, and consecrated the last three decades of his life to the publication of his

15• Vzdornov 2006; Foletti 2017a, pp. 58–60.

16• See, e.g., Kondakov 1881, 1882, 1890, 1902, 1904.

17• For Kondakov as "anti-Vasarian", see especially Kondakov 2011.

18• See, e.g., Gaidenko 2008.

19• Redin 1897, p. 31; Tunkina 1995, p. 12.

most important monographs. Moreover, after 1900, he was involved in a very ambitious project: to save the Russian tradition of panel painting {3}.[20] Contrary to what one might expect of such a retiree, he remained at the peak of his intellectual powers and of his influence on Russian culture.

When the revolution began, Kondakov was dividing his time between Saint Petersburg, Jalta, and long trips undertaken for study and pleasure. He preferred the Mediterranean, and enjoyed long stays in Italy, Greece, the present-day Macedonia, and Syria.[21] When he left Saint Petersburg for Jalta in January 1917, he had no idea that he would never again see the capital of Tsarist Russia.[22] In the nervous half year following the February Revolution, Kondakov rarely strayed from his base in Jalta where he was working on two manuscripts, one devoted to the iconography of the Mother of God, the other to Russian icons.[23] He did travel once to Moscow to check on the ongoing restoration of some medieval Russian panel paintings.[24] Kondakov sensed that his world was under threat, and indeed, the October Revolution meant that within months, his world would collapse. He lost his apartment in Saint Petersburg, then the villa in Jalta. His last few months in Russia were spent in Odessa, where his academic career had started. There he taught one last term and invested his energies in counter-revolutionary politics, writing for the anti-Bolshevik newspaper *Južnoe Slovo* [The Southern Word].[25] By the spring of 1920, he was left with little choice but to escape his homeland with what few personal belongings he could carry with him. From his personal diaries, it is evident that he was living through one of the most difficult moments of his life.[26] Often depressed, having lost almost all his privileges, he felt betrayed and lost. In this same period, he began writing his memoirs. He never completed these memoirs, but nevertheless, they were deemed worthy of posthumous publication in 1927.[27] Like any such

---

20• Kondakov 1901; Foletti 2009.

21• Tunkina 1995.

22• Kyzlasova 2000.

23• *Ibidem*, pp. 20–27.

24• *Ibidem*, p. 28.

25• *Ibidem*, pp. 27–28.

26• Kondakov 1919.

27• *Idem* 1927a.

3) Nikodim Pavlovič Kondakov in front of the icons of the State Russian Museum, Saint Petersburg, 1914

work, they cannot be taken as factual history, and are best read as a sort of dialogue between Kondakov and his homeland. If one reads between the lines, it is clear that Kondakov was gradually losing all hope that things would return to anything like their pre-revolutionary form.[28]

And then, after the final defeat of Pyotr Wrangel's White Army, there was not even time to grieve.[29] As mentioned in our introduction, Kondakov and the future Nobel laureate in literature, Ivan Bunin (1870–1953), a man who had become a close friend of Kondakov's in those last months in Odessa, fled Russia together on the *Sparta*.[30] When they landed at Constantinople,[31] Kondakov

28• For the problem of the understanding of the autobiographies, see Tassi 2007.

29• See Korliakov 2012, esp. pp. 37–46.

30• Muromceva 2002 [1930].

31• Kyzlasova 2000, pp. 46–47.

and Bunin avoided the humiliating disinfection which awaited the other emigrants simply because Kondakov had been awarded membership, many years before, in the French *Légion d'honneur*. The arrival of the Russian émigrés was being overseen by the French army, and Kondakov's status as an *immortel* (i.e. a member of the *Légion d'honneur*) meant that his temporary stay in Constantinople would be more comfortable than the one of other émigrés. But this was nothing compared to Kondakov's reception in Sofia, where he was personally welcomed by Tsar Boris III (r. 1918–1943) **{4}**. Boris gave Kondakov a car with chauffeur, a pleasant flat, and a salaried position that kept him out of poverty.[32] It may beggar the modern reader's belief that a refugee art historian would receive such a regal reception in a foreign country. But it will not seem so strange if we remind ourselves of two factors which were still in play in the 1920s. First, at the beginning of the twentieth century, intellectuals and politicians still belonged to one relatively homogeneous cultural elite, something which certainly is not the case in the twenty-first century. Second, historians played crucial roles in establishing and legitimizing the new nation-states that were formed in the late nineteenth and early twentieth centuries.[33] And Kondakov, as mentioned above, had been deeply involved in the "Bulgarian question". His book about Macedonia had been one of the Russian tsar's tools in his promotion of a powerful Bulgaria in the Balkans.[34] Kondakov's writings, aside from serving Russian political interests, were very supportive of Bulgarian territorial and geopolitical claims, and he had explicitly argued that Macedonia should belong to the Kingdom of Bulgaria.[35] We must therefore see his regal welcome in 1920 as evidence that scholarship had real political importance at that time. Despite this royal welcome, Kondakov did not feel at home in Sofia. The city was too provincial for him, and furthermore, he missed having a proper library.[36] It is no surprise, then, that he gladly accepted an invitation to join the Faculty of Arts at the Charles University in Prague for the autumn semester of 1922.[37]

32• Kyzlasova 2000, p. 49

33• See, e.g., Passini 2012.

34• Kondakov 1909.

35• *Ibidem*, pp. 294–296.

36• Kyzlasova 2000, p. 51.

37• Foletti 2014.

4} View of the city of Sofia, 1923

Just as had been the case in Sofia, Kondakov was very well received in Prague. The university not only paid his travel expenses, but also offered him a relatively high salary for a lecturer, especially one whose scholarly work was, in truth, only tangential to the questions that interested the newly-created Czechoslovak nation.[38] There were, however, more than just professional reasons for Kondakov's warm welcome in Prague. Behind the scenes, one of his personal acquaintances from long ago – Tomáš Garrigue Masaryk (1850–1937) – had been working to bring Kondakov to Prague {5}.[39]

Years before, when Masaryk had begun to favour independence for the Czech lands, he was forced to leave the Austro-Hungarian Empire, and it appears that he requested a professorship at the university in Saint Petersburg. Professor Kondakov personally supported this candidacy. For political reasons, i.e. to maintain good relations with the empire of Franz Josef I, Russia decided not to accept this troublesome refugee, but it was certainly logical for Masaryk to offer Kondakov a helping hand when the tables were turned some years later.[40]

Beyond Kondakov's professional reputation and his personal relationship with Masaryk, a third factor should also be considered. The arrival of this great Russian art historian in Prague was by no

38• The contract is conserved at the PNP/FNK, Korespondence vlastní [personal correspondence], přijatá [received], Zemská zpráva politická, č. 271.231. ai 1924.

39• Houška 2007.

40• Nikolay Andreyev, Material supplied by Dr. N. E. Andreyev, Formerly Student, Fellow and Acting Director of the Kondakov Institute in Prague, CUL/BA/VC, box 158, p. 2.

means an isolated phenomenon. On the contrary, the welcoming of Russian intellectual émigrés and students was a political priority for both Masaryk and the first prime minister of Czechoslovakia, Karel Kramář (1860–1937) {6}.[41] What became known as the *Ruská pomocná akce* [literally, the Russian Relief Action, further referred to as Russian Action] has to be considered one of the most extraordinary examples of the organized reception of refugees ever seen in the last 200 years.[42] The idea – conceived by Kramář and Masaryk, and later pursued by Edvard Beneš (1884–1948) {7}, Minister of Foreign Affairs and future successor of Masaryk as president of the country – was to create, within Czechoslovakia, an entire educational system devoted only to Russian émigrés.[43] Masaryk and Kramář hoped that after training and supporting this Russian intelligentsia, and once the situation in Russia had stabilized, Czechoslovakia would become a natural ally of that enormous nation to the east. Here we can see traces of Kramář's Pan-Slavism, but also the Masarykian dream of Czechoslovakia as a bridge between East and West.[44] The project fell short of its lofty goals, since many of the émigrés would never return to Russia, but rather move on to France, Germany or the United States. Nevertheless, we must admire the initiative of the first Czechoslovak state. Instead of giving in to fear and panic, this newly born state, despite its own significant economic and political problems, decided on a gesture that was not only pragmatic, but truly generous as well.[45] And even if this Russian Action was not a successful model of integration – both Russians and Czechoslovaks considered it a temporary situation – the decision to invest resources into supporting migrants serves as a pioneering model for how a nation can act during a refugee crisis.

When Kondakov arrived in Prague, he was an exceptional émigré, but only one member of a large Russian diaspora in the making. Masaryk also put the old professor in contact with the Crane

41• Lustigová 2007.

42• Sládek 1994; Mchitarjan 2006, 2009. For more, in general, see Raeff 1990. For the Russian action see Tejchmanová 1991; Chinyaeva 1993; Bobrinskoy 1995; Chinyaeva 2001, pp. 41–68.

43• For the general position of Masaryk towards Russian culture see Masaryk 1971 [1913]; for the situation after the revolution see Masaryk 1992 [1922].

44• Lustigová 2007, pp. 101–118.

45• See especially Chinyaeva 1993 and 2001, pp. 41–68; see also Andreyev/Savický 2004, pp. 33–79.

5} Tomáš Garrigue Masaryk

6} Karel Kramář

7} Edvard Beneš

family.[46] This rich family of American industrialists had been sympathetic to Slavic independence since the early twentieth century, and Charles R. Crane (1858–1939) had sponsored the *Slavic Epic* of Czech painter Alfons Mucha (1860–1939).[47] It is not too surprising, then, that Kondakov was invited to live in their Prague residence, the Schönborn Palace, a building which today is home to the United States' Embassy to the Czech Republic.

As celebrated as he may have been, the fact remains that Kondakov had been invited to Prague to teach, and thanks to the archives of the *Památník národního písemnictví* [Museum of Czech Literature], we know very precisely the terms of all of Kondakov's contracts with Charles University.[48] We have already mentioned that Kondakov was best known for his expertise and interest in Byzantine art, as well as in the art and culture of medieval Russia. However, none of these topics were mentioned in Kondakov's contracts. Nor is there a single mention of the Mediterranean. Instead, the focus of the lectures was to be the art of the nomadic peoples, with a special focus on the Slavs. In reality, the courses would also touch on Late Antiquity and Byzantium, but the nomadic tribes were supposed to be the focus of Kondakov's teaching.[49] It was a subject which he had already done research on in the early 1890s when he was asked to publish a significant work with a definitely nationalistic slant to it: *Russkie drevnosti v pamjatnikach iskusstva* [Russian Antiquities and Artistic Treasures].[50] In this series of six volumes, some of them published with the support of Count Ivan Tolstoj (1858–1916), Kondakov constructed an idealized cultural history of Russian art from Antiquity to the Middle Ages. With a clearly imperial point of view, this series presented the medieval art of Crimea, the Southern Caucasus, and Kiev as a single phenomenon.[51] The first volume, moreover, was dedicated specifically to the nomadic peoples who had entered Russia from the East.

46• PNP/FNK, Korespondence vlastní [personal correspondence], přijatá [received], John Crane, č. přír.: 165/42

47• Saul 2013.

48• PNP/FNK, Korespondence vlastní [personal correspondence], přijatá [received], Zemská zpráva politická, č. 271.231. ai 1924.

49• UDU-AV/KI-38, sv. 9, p. 13. See also the master's thesis of Smrčková 2009, pp. 59–66, where the author presents all of Kondakov's teachings in Prague.

50• Kondakov/Tolstoj 1889–1899.

51• Foletti 2016a.

So even if nomadic tribes were not Kondakov's specialty, he knew something about them, and was willing to adapt his teaching to the political priorities of Charles University. More interestingly, it was not just his teaching that Kondakov adapted to this new political reality; he would also dedicate his last published studies to this topic.[52] In these late texts, and presumably in his lectures, Kondakov presented the art of the nomadic tribes, especially the Slavic ones, as a link between Asia and Europe and one of the main vectors of the cultural transfers which would determine the identity of Europe.

One could rightly ask whether Kondakov was simply being obedient to his new patrons, or this kind of thinking was the true result of scholarly reflection. The size of Kondakov's output relating to the nomads is relatively small, but the idea that they linked East and West, Asia and Europe, had been present in his thought at least since the catalogue that he wrote for the Imperial Hermitage in 1891.[53] In that catalogue, Kondakov postulated that Russia and its art were eternally "in between", belonging neither to East nor West, but rather uniting them. This was not atypical at the end of the end of the nineteenth century, when many intellectuals and artists within the Russian Empire considered Russia an exceptional place with a unique soul.[54] Thirty years later, this vision of the Slavs as a link between East and West could be easily resuscitated and applied to the newly born Czechoslovakia. This small country – uniting within its borders Czechs, Slovaks, Ruthenians, as well as Germans, Hungarians, Poles, and Jews – presented itself as a Western democracy, but open to the East thanks to its residents from several Slavic groups.[55] Today, from a purely historical point of view, it is clear that this approach went too far in marginalizing important minorities like the Germans. At the time (as we will presently see), this interest in the Slavic "race" justified the presence of a large number of Russian emigrants, and support for Kondakov's research and thinking.

If the majority of Kondakov's lectures and new publications from his time in Prague revolved around the nomads, he never ceased

52• Kondakov 1924 and 1929.

53• *Idem* 1891; Foletti 2018a.

54• See, e.g., Miller 2008.

55• Kerner 1921; on the general context of interwar Czechoslovakia, see Olivová 1972.

working on two books that he had begun long before. One of these was third and final volume of his monumental *Ikonografia Bogomateri* [The Iconography of the Mother of God], the first two volumes of which had been published in Saint Petersburg in 1914 and 1915.[56] Those first two volumes were dedicated to how the Mother of God had been represented from Late Antiquity to the end of the Middle Ages in the Christian East, and in them Kondakov also emphasized the links between those images and their descendants in Imperial Russia.[57]

For Kondakov, iconography was a methodological tool serving two different purposes. On the one hand, it helped him create an evolutionary tree with its roots in the early prototypes (or models), growing through various intermediate stages until the end of the Middle Ages. In creating such a scheme, Kondakov was applying the evolutionary thinking developed in the second half of the nineteenth century by Herbert Spencer (1820–1903). Such thinking was also applied to the humanities in Russia by the linguist Alexander Veselovskij (1838–1906), who had been a classmate of Kondakov in his early days.[58] On the other hand, showing the close similarities between icons from the fourth, twelfth, and even early twentieth centuries reinforced one of Kondakov's theses about Orthodox religious painting, namely its immutability in time, and thus its fidelity to models.[59] Kondakov's first two books about Marian imagery are also fascinating displays of his incredible erudition. Literally hundreds of objects are mentioned, many of which have since been lost.[60] There is no doubt that Kondakov's scholarship also served a political purpose. While the Romanovs were celebrating the 300th anniversary of their dynasty, and at a time when medieval Russian painting was being promoted at the nation's art par excellence, Kondakov's art history supported the view that Tsarist Russia was the heir of Byzantium and the protector of the Orthodox.[61]

56• Kondakov 1914 and 1915.

57• See, e.g., *Idem* 1914, figs 204–205.

58• Veselovskij 1873; Velmezova 2007; Foletti 2017a, pp. 177–178.

59• Kondakov 1914, p. 4.

60• *Ibidem*, pp. 13–37.

61• For the celebration see Bogdanovič 1913; Roubankov 2009. For the phenomenon of "icons" becoming the Russian "national art", see the catalogue of the exhibition *Vyšlavka* 1913 and its analysis in Foletti 2018b.

The third volume of *Ikonografia Bogomateri* was, however, dedicated to a different subject: the visual representations of Mary in the Latin West, and especially in Italy, from the twelfth to the sixteenth centuries.[62] Like the first two volumes, this book was clearly conceived for a Russian audience, and this was one of the reasons for which Kondakov struggled to get it published once he had left the motherland. Indeed, the book is extraordinary testimony to Kondakov's very Russian mentality, since the reading he proposed for late medieval and Early Modern art in Italy was exactly the opposite of what Western scholars had been saying for centuries. For Kondakov, Giotto represented not the beginning of a rebirth, but the beginning of a decline which reached its nadir with Michelangelo. Kondakov ignores the visual and artistic qualities of the Italian works he studies, concentrating exclusively on the function of the image of Mary, which must be, according to him, exclusively devotional. What emerges from this impressive volume – discovered only recently in Roman archives – is, once more, a very Orthodox perspective on art.[63] The whole book implies that the "iconic potential" of an image is paramount. For Kondakov, Raphael and Bellini are two of the few Western painters who deserve to be "saved" from oblivion because their paintings meet his criterion for "iconicity".[64] It is no coincidence that the manuscript of this book was bought, in 1924, by Pope Pius XI (1922–1939) at a moment when he was pursuing the union of the Roman Catholic Church with the Russian Orthodox Church.[65] There is no doubt that Kondakov perceived this motivation. Indeed, in the dedicatory inscription that Kondakov added to the book, he dutifully expressed his wish that one day the Eastern Orthodox and Roman Catholic churches would be reunited.[66] For the

62• Kondakov 2011.

63• For the discovery of the manuscript see Foletti 2008.

64• *"La meilleure manière de Giovanni Bellini, se manifeste surtout dans ses petites icônes et ses tableaux religieux"*, Kondakov 2011, p. 351.

65• For the life of the pope see: *Ratti* 1996; Broglio 2000. For his unionist politics see Agostino 1991; Wenger 1996, p. 283. In general, see Kondakov 2011, pp. XXXVI-XXXVIII.

66• The text of the dedicatory inscription was: *"À Sa St.eté le Pape Pie XI / Cet ouvrage est dédié comme humble / Hommage, comme traité historique sur les époques sublimes de la foi / Chrétienne et de la haute morale, / Élevée au sein de la vénération / Profonde de la St.e Mère, ayant / Créé la beauté merveilleuse / De l'art italien, et comme témoignage / D'un vœu sincère de l'union Religieuse et Spirituelle de la Chrétienté / Nicodème Kondakov"*, see N. P. Kondakoff, Archivio Vaticano, Segreteria di Stato, Anno 1925, Rubrica 86, Fascicolo 1, p. 42.

8) a) Andrej Rublev, pre-restoration photograph of Andrej Rublev's *Trinity*, with its 17th-century *oklad*, 1904
b) Andrej Rublev, *The Trinity*, state after the restorations of 1904–1906

pope, of course, it was taken for granted that this reunion meant the Eastern churches "re-joining" his Roman Catholic Church. It should also be reminded that this gesture of the pope should be seen against the backdrop of a much larger ambition of the Roman bishops. The idea of such an union was present into the Roman mentality at least since the Council of Florence (1431–1441) and was clearly visible during the entire nineteenth century, but also later, during the Fascist era.[67]

The other book manuscript which Kondakov carried with him from Odessa to Constantinople, then on to Sofia and Prague, was a work about the "Russian icon" which would be published posthumously by the *Seminarium Kondakovianum*.[68] This epic effort – one of the key publications in the formation of Western attitudes towards the Russian *ikona* – must be seen as Kondakov's reaction to the fantastic popularity of Russian panel paintings at the beginning of the twentieth century.[69] After the restoration of Andrej Rublev's *Trinity*, and the subsequent rediscovery of hundreds of medieval paintings – which, for centuries, had been covered by a combination of

67• On this question in general, see Gasbarri 2015; Pettinaroli 2015.

68• Kondakov 1928–1933.

69• Foletti 2016b.

golden and silver revetments called *oklads*, heavy repainting, and smoke – these objects from the past became extremely fashionable **{8a–b}**.[70] It has been argued that icons' popularity, and the resulting periodicals and monographs dedicated to them, must be understood within the context of the avant-garde aesthetics which some artists and viewers, including many Russians, were embracing at this moment in history. It is no coincidence that in 1911, when Henri Matisse (1869–1954) visited Moscow, he was enchanted by medieval Russian paintings, even as his own canvases were causing a stir in Russia.[71] Nor should we forget *Black Square* by Kazimir Malevič (1879–1935), which was hung at the *Last Futurist Exhibition 0.10* (1915–1916), and made explicit reference to Russian devotional images **{9}**.[72] The bibliography concerning the positive reception of Russian medieval paintings by the Russian and European avant-gardes is extensive.[73]

For us, the interesting part of all this is how the new aesthetics transformed old-fashioned and long-hidden objects into extremely popular and "trendy" ones.[74] Kondakov's reaction was not entirely in agreement with the modern approach to icons promoted by those around Pavel Muratov (1881–1950).[75] He found them interesting for completely different reasons, and catalogued them mainly according to their iconographic features, using his traditional evolutionary methodology. There is little doubt that Kondakov's monumental work on Russian icons hit the shelves at the right time, so to speak, after the first wave of Russian emigration had further increased interest in such objects. Aristocrats, rich merchants, and clerics fleeing Russia brought along whatever personal treasures they could, including many "icons", and many of these émigrés were soon forced to raise funds by selling these objects on the Western market.[76] In an art world very much influenced by the aesthetic trends mentioned above, many collectors jumped at the opportunity. It is certainly no coincidence that some of the most

70• Muratova 2004; Martin 2012; Foletti 2017a, pp. 120–139.

71• Rusakov 1975; Leardi 2010.

72• Simmen 1998; Taroutina 2018, pp. 179–182.

73• See for example Lingua 1999; Avtonomova 2004; Labrusse 2007; Taroutina 2018.

74• Foletti 2013.

75• Muratov 1913a; Ščekotov 1914.

76• Kyzlasova 2010, p. 183.

important Czechoslovak collections of panel paintings date to the 1920s.[77] With so many "icons" changing hands, scholarly interest in them also grew, paradoxically making Kondakov's old-fashioned work on icons much more relevant to the wider Western art world than his third book on the Western iconography of Mary.

While Kondakov had conceived these two monographs for a Russian audience, after the Russian Revolution they found their audiences in the West. Were it not for the October Revolution, Pius XI would never have seriously proposed a union of Orthodox with Catholic, and would not have considered Kondakov's work interesting at all. The first wave of emigration out of Russia brought medieval and Early Modern Russian panel paintings to Europe, the USA, Japan, and Southern America, and made the word "icon" and its derivatives among the most common in our modern languages. The Russian word *ikona* was soon transferred to any kind of emblematic image, to the point where we now have "icons of pop" and "desktop icons" on our computers.[78] In art history, the idea has been an obsession at least since the 1990s, with a proliferation of terms such as "iconicity", "iconic", etc.[79]

In 1924, Nikodim Kondakov celebrated his 80th birthday, and the whole year was a special one for him. In April, he attended the first conference in Byzantine studies, and was welcomed by its attendees as the most respected and influential scholar in the field – indeed, its patriarch.[80] An impressive *Festschrift* was written in Kondakov's honor by the large group of friends and pupils which he had assembled around him in Prague.[81] On the day of his birthday, in addition to the personal best wishes of dozens of colleagues, he received letters and telegrams from important institutions all around the world.[82] For Kondakov himself, the highlight of the year must have come when he sold the manuscript of his book on Marian

77• See for example the collections of Girsa and Benešová, mentioned in UDU-AV/KI-II, sv. 6.

78• Foletti 2016b.

79• See, e.g., Mondzain 1996.

80• Marinescu 1925.

81• Aa.Vv. 1924.

82• See the many documents at the PNP/FNK, Korespondence vlastní [personal correspondence], korporace [group], Blahopřejné dopisy k 80. narozeninám N. P. Kondakova [Letters of congratulations on the occasion of the eightieth birthday of N. P. Kondakov], č. přír.: 165/42.

9} Last Futurist Exhibition of Paintings 0.10, Khudozhestvennoe Buro, Petrograd, December 1915 – January 1916

iconography to the pope. The fee that the Vatican had agreed to pay for the work was already impressive, but Kondakov was especially delighted when, once the book had arrived in Rome bearing his special dedication to the pope, an additional sum was sent as well. Kondakov commented that nothing of the sort, i.e. a Roman pope paying more than what had been agreed upon, had even occurred when Raphael completed his commission for Leo X.[83]

Only a few months later, in February of 1925, Kondakov was still writing and reading when, in the middle of night, he suffered a stroke and died early in the morning. His death saddened not only the large Russian diaspora in Prague, but colleagues all around the world, as attested by the large number of obituaries published.[84] In Prague, however, Kondakov's death called forth a tribute which will be one of the main topics of the following pages.

83• *"Mais quand est-ce qu'une chose semblable s'est produite? Même Raphaël n'a pas connu un tel traitement de la part de Léon X!"*, see Kyzlasova 2000, p. 79.

84• PNP/FNK, Výstřižky [clippings], Nekrology [obituary], č. přír.: 165/42.

Before we deal with events after Kondakov's death in February 1925, let us first consider, in retrospect, how the experience of emigration had affected Kondakov. He was not only an authority on Byzantine and Russian art, but had been a full participant in the social, cultural, and political life of the empire. Kondakov was the perfect example of the Russian intelligentsia at the end of the Romanov Empire. All that changed drastically with his emigration. He lost not only his material belongings, but also his audience. In Bulgaria and Czechoslovakia, the international community of scholars and intellectuals – which we are surprised to see included politicians – took good care of him. But how did he deal with all of this on a personal level? His diaries show that Kondakov was sad to the point of depression, and they contain repeated expressions of how Kondakov felt that he had, essentially, "lost his life" along with his motherland. Publicly, however, he put on a braver face. He was forced to delve into a new field of studies, the nomadic tribes, and to think within a completely new context, democratic Czechoslovakia. Kondakov died after less than three years in Prague, and we can only guess at how his thinking might have changed after spending even more time in such a milieu. Nonetheless, there is no disputing that he helped pave the way towards a new identity for Russian émigré scholars and was an important member of the generation of Russian emigrants who brought Russian art and culture to the rest of the world.

By saying that, we do not want to affirm that Kondakov arrived in the West bringing an absolutely unknown know-how or an untouched field of research. Indeed, Czechoslovakia was particularly receptive to his research prior to the First World War. More generally, Byzantine studies were becoming, starting from the eighties of the nineteenth century and all around Europe, an emerging field.[85] In addition to that, the interest in Late Antique and early medieval art was blooming into the Roman milieu of Christian archeology, in the circles of the Vienna School, and more largely in the coeval cultural production.[86] Thus, the personal experience of Kondakov, even if traumatized by emigration, permitted a real

85• See, e.g., Spieser 1991; *Idem* 2007, pp. 7–29; Gasbarri 2015; Foletti 2017a, pp. 171–229.

86• This question is vastly studied, see, e.g., Gasbarri 2015; Labrusse 2018; Lovino 2020; Elsner 2020.

transfer of knowledge towards an already fertile ground. This explains what will follow.

KONDAKOV'S LEGACY IN PRAGUE: THE *SEMINARIUM KONDAKOVIANUM*

SOME PERSONAL STORIES

Within a few weeks of Kondakov's death in April 1925, his pupils, friends, and admirers met and decided to honor him with a scholarly initiative.[87] This initiative resulted in the *Seminarium Kondakovianum*.[88] It is remarkable that in only two and a half years in Prague, Kondakov had left such an imprint on the intellectual and émigré milieu of the city. He considered himself a mediocre teacher, and he did not like formal lectures. And yet we know that in Prague, he enjoyed teaching more than he ever had before.[89] According to Vernadskij, during one lesson he explained teaching by quoting Fustel de Coulanges' maxim: "Years of analysis go into a single day of summary".[90] We think Kondakov may have found teaching in Prague more amenable than elsewhere because of the kind of students he had there. Some of them had already completed a degree in Russia, while many of the Czech students were undergraduates but older than the typical undergraduate student in Russia, where young people typically entered university at the age of seventeen. Lastly, and perhaps most importantly, all of them had experienced, in one way or another, the war, the revolution, and emigration. Between teacher and pupils there was, then, an exceptional link, since they shared much more than just an interest in the history of art. From Kondakov's last diaries we know that even in his darkest moments, Kondakov retained a reason to live – his scholarship.[91] This small Prague

87• Vernadskij/Kalitinskij 1926, p. 297; Beißwenger 2005 [2001], pp. 35–36.

88• For the *Seminarium* in general see Florovskij 1928; Mošin 1935; Ostrogorsky 1936; Sabruk 1971; Hrochová 1972; Rhinelander 1974; Hrochová 1989, 1991; Skálová 1991; Aksenova 1993; Sládek 1994; Hlaváčková 1995; Hrochová 1995; Roháček 1995; Rosov 1995; Beljaev 1996, 2000; Andreyev/Savický 2004; Iberl 2011; Zaoral 2013; Řoutil 2013; Roháček 2014; Lovino 2016a, 2016b, 2017, 2018; Jančárková 2017; Dmitrieva 2018; Jančárková 2019; Lovino 2019.

89• For Kondakov discovering a real passion for teaching, see his diary, Kyzlasova 2000, p. 38. For the Prague lessons, see Vernadsky 1926, p. 6.

90• Vernadsky 1926, pp. XXVI–XXVIII.

91• Tunkina 2001, p. 59; Kyzlasova 2000, pp. 45–48.

10} Georgij Vernadskij and his wife Nina Vladimirovna, Prague, 1925

circle of Russian émigrés, traumatized by the loss of their homeland, must have perceived scholarly research on Russian cultural history to be a sort of intellectual refuge, perhaps even a spiritual one if their research concerned Orthodox religious art. It is not the goal of this book to undertake a full discussion of the psychological reactions of the human mind to the experience of emigration, but this aspect of Kondakov's work cannot be completely neglected. Kondakov's death was a harsh blow to the Prague circle of Russian intellectuals.[92] It would not be long before they decided to turn his death into the beginning of a new story.

Before we deal with the way Kondakov's circle memorialized him and changed the field of Byzantine studies all over the world, we should say a few words about the most important members of that circle. These individuals were, without doubt, extraordinarily gifted, and their individual goals coalesced in a surprisingly effective way.

First, let us mention one of the circle's most prolific (and famous) figures, Georgij Vernadskij (1887–1973) **{10}**.[93] He was the son of Vladimir Vernadskij (1863–1945), the eminent Russian mineralogist and chemist, considered one of the founders of

92• Vernadskij/Kalitinskij 1926; Vernadsky 1926.

93• On the scholar see Halperin 1982, 1985; Soničeva 1995; Ratchinski 2003. His personal archives, with over 200 boxes, are at the Columbia University Libraries, Manuscripts collections, Bakhmeteff Archive, Vernadsky Collection.

modern geochemistry and biogeochemistry, a man whose importance on a global level can be gauged by the simple fact that he invented the notion of the "biosphere".[94] Georgij decided to become a scholar rather than a scientist like his father, and dedicated his earliest research to the history of the medieval nomads of the Eurasian steppes. Later, after moving to the United States, he enlarged the scope of his work, eventually becoming a professor of general and contemporary Russian history and publishing a complete history of Russia from the nomads to Lenin.[95] We would expect an émigré like Vernadskij to be harshly critical of the Soviet Union, yet his work, for the most part, remained rigorous and objective even when he wrote of more recent events. Vernadskij did not meet Kondakov until they were both in Prague, but once there they had much in common, especially an interest in researching the culture of the nomadic tribes.[96] Of all those in the *Seminarium* circle, Vernadskij seems to have been one of the most independent.[97] He was certainly the oldest in Kondakov's circle besides the old professor himself. Vernadskij had been trained by Mikhail I. Rostovcev (1870–1952) in ancient history, and was already involved, to some degree, in an intellectual movement which also seems to have influenced Kondakov himself: Eurasianism.[98] Together with the linguist Roman Jakobson (1896–1982) and the geographer Pjotr Savickij (1895–1968) – the founding figures of the so-called "Prague Linguistic Circle" – Vernadskij was one of the leading figures of this complex movement, which can, however, be understood more easily if we consider the position of the Russian émigré scholars.[99] As shown by Ekaterina Velmezova in 2010, Eurasia was born as a Russian colonial concept, but later attracted the attention of émigrés because it was a geographical space not directly dependent on national boundaries.[100] They had lost Russia, but thanks to Eurasia they

94• Fedoseyev 1976; Lapo 2001.

95• Vernadsky 1931, 1933; Torbakov 2008.

96• Vernadskij 1913.

97• Vernadskij was investigating similar topics before and after his stop in Prague. See *Ibidem*; *Idem* 1927a, 1927b.

98• On Vernadskij and Eurasianism, see Ratchinski 2003; Torbakov 2008. For Eurasianism in general, see, e.g., Dressler 2009. Concerning Rostovcev, see Wes 1990, but also Meyer 2009.

99• Savickij 1927; Trubeckoj 2005. On the Prague Linguistic Circle, see the synthesis by Toman 1995; see also Andreyev/Savický 2004, pp. 135–148.

100• Velmezova 2010.

could continue to research the motherland within a larger context which included other places like Czechoslovakia. Vernadskij's involvement with the *Seminarium* was very important for him, as attested by the dense correspondence pertaining to it preserved in his personal archives at Columbia University.[101] It would, however, be only one of many steps in his brilliant career, and he left Prague for New Haven in 1927. More than a pupil of Kondakov, he should be seen as one of the founding spirits of the *Seminarium*.

The background of Aleksandr Kalitinskij (1880–1946) was entirely different. He had been educated in the natural sciences Russia, and had taught science, mathematics, and geography at secondary school. He later steered himself towards archaeology, perhaps via an interest in geography.[102] It is difficult to find precise information about Kalitinskij, but it seems that he was never formally educated in the humanities.[103] Nevertheless, he had worked at the Archaeological Institute in Moscow. His education and erudition cannot be compared to that of somebody like Vernadskij, and it is not by chance that Kalitinskij's first role with the *Seminarium* was that of executive director, meaning the person in charge of the practical aspects of the Kondakov Institute's work. It was a task that he fulfilled admirably until his psychological collapse in 1931.[104] As we mentioned above, at the core of the *Seminarium* was a passion for material culture, and Kalitinskij shared this passion. He had a particular interest in the art of nomadic tribes and dedicated his research to that area. His interest in archaeology was evident in his studies on fibulas and brooches found on Russian soil.[105] These objects were seen, then as now, as *emblemata* of nomadic cultures. In his analysis of them Kalitinskij adopted an approach directly inherited from his training in the natural sciences. He classified fibulas just as one did butterflies or other species. Such an attitude was typical for that generation of scholars, and scholars in the humanities had been deeply fascinated by biology ever since the late nineteenth century.[106] It is

101 • See Nikolay Andreyev, Material supplied by Dr. N. E. Andreyev, Formerly Student, Fellow and Acting Director of the Kondakov Institute in Prague, CUL/BA/VC, box 158.

102 • Beißwenger 2005 [2001], pp. 70–72.

103 • For the few archival materials see UDU-AV/KI.

104 • Rhinelander 1974, pp. 341–342. Additional details provided by Rosov 1995, p. 6.

105 • Kalitinskij 1928, 1930.

106 • Foletti 2017a, pp. 155, 192–195.

11} **Group photograph with, from front to back, Nikolaj Toll', Nikolaj Andrejev, Dmitrij Rasovskij and Jevgenij Melnikov**

fascinating to observe that both Vernadskij and Kalitinskij were closely and personally linked with the natural sciences, and we can sense how this influenced their methods. Kondakov himself, throughout his career, was also interested in evolutionary theories as well as chemistry and other scientific approaches to the humanities.[107] Each of these key figures in our story of the *Seminarium* saw material culture, history, and sciences as closely related fields.

Kalitinskij and Vernadskij were already well into their professional careers by the time they reached Prague, but the other key figures in our story were all from the generation born around 1900. They all started their education in Russia, had their studies interrupted by the war, and then completed their degrees in Prague, where they came into contact with Nikodim Kondakov. For all of them, therefore, Kondakov was one of the most influential figures in their intellectual training.

The first of these whom we will mention is the archaeologist and future director of *Seminarium*, Nikolaj Toll' (1894–1985) **{11}**.[108] He began his studies in the social sciences in 1915 at the Faculty of

107• Foletti 2017a, pp. 178–179.

108• Drbal 2008; Beißwenger 2005 [2001], pp. 73–77.

12} Natalia Jašvil, *Portrait of Nikolaj Beljaev*, 1931

Philosophy at the University of Kazan. He soon moved to Saint Petersburg, where he became a cadet at the Konstantinov Artillery Academy. After the revolution, he moved to Athens, then Prague, where he enrolled at Charles University in 1922. There, under the direction of Kondakov, he started to investigate Late Antique and medieval textiles, a topic which Kondakov himself was working on at the time.[109] Toll's work soon extended to objects all around the Mediterranean and beyond, and was carried out using an evolutionary approach with a special focus on periods of transition such as Late Antiquity.[110] Later on, Toll' would become interested in decorative elements, such as the so-called "animal style", with a not unexpected focus on the nomadic tribes which had moved from Asia to Europe.[111]

A second important figure from the younger generation was Nikolaj Beljaev (1899–1930) **{12}**. He was, according to Kondakov, one of the most gifted in his last group of students,[112] but he died in a tragic car accident in 1930.[113] Beljaev had attended classes at the historical-philological faculty in Saint Petersburg, but in 1917, he entered the army and became a "junker" at the same Konstantinov Artillery Academy that Toll' attended. Having joined the White Army after the October Revolution, he participated in the "Ice March" as a volunteer in the forces of General Lavr Kornilov (1870–1918).[114] He was therefore evacuated from the Crimea in November 1920 and, after a brief stay in Constantinople, he moved to Prague where he enrolled in Charles University. His dissertation was directed by the Czech scholar Lubor Niederle (1865–1944) and was dedicated to Byzantine fibulae and clothing.

Niederle – an important protagonist who we will encounter again – had been, along with Jiří Polívka (1859–1933), one of the figures responsible for Kondakov's arrival in Prague.[115] Trained as an archaeologist, anthropologist, and ethnologist, he essentially

109• Kondakov 1924.

110• Toll' 1928.

111• *Idem* 1936.

112• Iberl 2011, p. 329.

113• Beißwenger 2005 [2001], p. 44; Iberl 2011, p. 329. For the biography of Beljaev, see also the obituaries by Ostrogorskij 1931; Okuněv 1931; Grabar 1931b.

114• Kenez 1974, pp. 96–130.

115• Hlôšková/Zelenková 2008; Foletti 2014.

13} Dmitrij Rasovskij

founded modern Czech archaeology.[116] Niederle wrote a series of monographs entitled *Slovanské starožitnosti* [Slavic Antiquities], and had long admired Kondakov's work. Niederle was, we believe, responsible for requesting that the old Russian master devote his lectures in Prague to nomadic tribes.[117] Niederle served as a link between the Russian émigrés and Czechoslovak intellectuals.

The brilliant young Nikolaj Beljaev was the result, so to speak, of the combined erudition of Kondakov and of the Czechoslovak scholars who had invited the old master to Prague. Another remarkable thing is that Beljaev was, within the group, the one with the most strictly art-historical approach. Aside from the art of the steppes, he also worked on traditional Russian panel painting and iconography.[118]

The last figure to be mentioned, and one who would play an ambivalent role in the later history of the Kondakov Institute, is Dmitrij Rasovskij (1902–1941) {13}.[119] Rasovskij started his education in Moscow but completed his doctoral dissertation in Prague in 1928. As a historian, he was interested not just in nomadic peoples, but also in the history of the Kievan Rus, Bulgaria, and Byzantium.[120] Like the recently deceased Kondakov, he was convinced that nomadic tribes had played a key part in the formation of Byzantine identity.[121]

Each of these three young scholars, then, were looking into cultural phenomena which linked Asia with Europe. We have already mentioned the Eurasian movement as a possible spur to Vernadskij's and Kondakov's interest in the topic, but we also believe

116• Havlíková 2004.

117• Niederle 1902.

118• Beljaev 1927, 1929, 1930, 1932.

119• Jakobson 1944; Myslivec 1946; Beißwenger 2005 [2001], pp. 82–86.

120• Rasovskij 1927a, 1927b, 1933, 1935.

121• Myslivec 1946, p. 330.

that the very special situation of interwar Czechoslovakia was also a factor. The period of what southern Europeans called "barbarian invasions" was, for Czechoslovaks as well as Russians, a period of great migrations in which their ancestors moved and then settled.[122] Nor was it only Slavs who saw things that way. We should not forget that the idea of the notion of an "age of migrations" seems to have originated in the German-speaking world, where it was called *Völkerwanderung*.[123] Between the wars, the impact of nomadic tribes on European history and culture was a hot topic for many, including Russian émigrés, Czechoslovak authorities, and German intellectuals.

Besides those scholars, one of the pillars of the *Seminarium* was the Princess Natalia Jašvil (1861–1939) **{14}**.[124] Her place in historiography has been neglected not only because she was not a scholar, but because she was also not a man. It took until 2011 for a serious scholar, in the person of Kateřina Iberl, to undertake research on this remarkable figure.[125] Jašvil was a Russian aristocrat fascinated by Russian popular art, and a gifted painter as well. In spite of her tragic destiny – her husband died young, and she buried both of her children – she spent her life supporting many worthwhile initiatives. In Russia, she promoted a revival of traditional culture on her family's lands. The effectiveness of her support was demonstrated when her villagers won a gold medal for artistic creation and craftsmanship at the Paris international exhibition in 1900.[126] Her cultural activities were part of a broader movement in Russia in the late nineteenth century, wherein many prominent artists promoted interest in Russian popular "arts and crafts" (as the English phrase would have it).[127] The Abramcevo artistic colony became the center of this movement,[128] but academic art historians also contributed to the rediscovery of ancient Russian culture.

122• In this sense it is important to see the Czechoslovak position, for example, in the schoolbook by Pekař 1922, pp. 3–6.

123• For this notion in historiography, see, e.g., Springer 2006. For art history, e.g., Michaud 2015, pp. 113–141.

124• Iberl 2011.

125• *Ibidem*.

126• *Ibidem*, p. 326. About the Russian pavilion, in Neo-Russian style, see Kazakova 2014.

127• Salmond 1996.

128• *Ibidem*, pp. 15–45; Paston 2003.

Starting in the reign of Peter the Great (r. 1682–1721), several generations of the Russian elite had dismissed ancient Russian culture for the most part.[129] It was only during the nineteenth century, in a reaction to that attitude, that a Slavophile milieu developed and artists and scholars joined forces to promote traditional Russian arts and culture. This movement eventually found support from the state, starting with Nicolas I (1826–1855), who decided that the official religious architecture of the empire was to be the Neo-Byzantine style, thought at that time to be the traditional Russian style as well.[130] These tendencies became more marked during the reign of Alexander III (1881–1894), when, in a period of crisis following the assassination of his father Alexander II, the tsar decided to re-orient the empire's culture more towards what was thought to be authentically Russian.[131] One of the most important scholarly figures involved in research on Russian medieval art was, of course, Nikodim Kondakov, who aimed his books on Russian antiquities at a large if not general audience. We can see here how the aristocrat and artist Jašvil would feel deep sympathy for Kondakov's work.

After the October Revolution, during which Jašvil's son and son-in-law were shot dead by the Bolsheviks before her very eyes, she left Russia for Prague, where she received the personal support of President Masaryk.[132] She had met him during the war while acting as a representative of the Russian Red Cross in Austria. In Prague, she lived with her daughter, Tatiana Rodzienko (1892–1933), and worked as an artist, but the *Seminarium Kondakovianum* soon became her real life mission.[133] She had already been attending Kondakov's *privatissima*, and her fascination with many of the topics covered by the scholars of the *Seminarium* was real and profound.[134] Věra Hrochová, in her study on the Kondakov Institute, hypothesized that Jašvil was, in fact, a major sponsor of the

129• For a general reflection on the Russian self-perception in dialogue with Europe see Uspenskij 2012. For the reforms of Peter the Great and their impact see Zhivov 2012a. For the following century, see *Idem* 2012b.

130• Foletti/Foletti 2019.

131• Heller 1997, p. 789.

132• Iberl 2011, p. 327.

133• *Ibidem*, p. 326.

134• Vernadskij/Kalitinskij 1926; Rhinelander 1974, p. 335; Beißwenger 2005 [2001], p. 34. On the *seminaria privatissima*, see also Masaryková 1931.

14} Michail Něstěrov, *Portrait of Princess Jašvil*, 1905

15} Natalia Jašvil, *Portrait of Nikodim Kondakov*, 1925

Institute.[135] More recent research calls this into question, but there can be no doubt that her contacts with government authorities and private donors (stemming from her place in the Russian nobility), together with her genuine passion for Russian art, proved of inestimable value to the Institute.[136]

It is likely, even if we lack direct proof, that Princess Jašvil was aware of Kondakov's interest in preserving and promoting traditional Russian panel painting – the art of the "icons" – throughout his career. The indirect evidence includes a trip that Kondakov made in 1900 together with the Count Sergej Šeremetěv (1844–1918) to the region of Vladimir, where he visited the last remaining workshops making artisanal "icons". After returning, he published a book arguing that this ancient Russian craft, threatened by the production of mass-produced metallic devotional images, needed to be saved.[137] With the help of Šeremetěv, he convinced the Emperor Nicolas II (1894–1917) to found a society for the protection of the Russian "icon", and Kondakov himself took on an executive role within the organization.[138] Its goal was twofold. First, Kondakov hoped that political pressure would suppress industrial production (an effort which failed), and second, an effort was to be made to train young artists and craftsmen in traditional "icon" painting. Schools were opened for this purpose, and books were published to share technical knowledge and traditional iconographical patterns.[139] Kondakov himself was the author of one of these books, dedicated to the iconography of Christ.[140] Princess Jašvil, unlike the other founding members of *Seminarium*, must have been primarily interested in Kondakov's activities relating to "icons". She was active in painting "icons" herself and would be the creator of "iconic" post-mortem portraits of Beljaev and of Kondakov himself **{12, 15}**. She was also behind many of the Institute's events celebrating panel painting, some of which attracted large audiences (as will be discussed below).

135• Hrochová 1972, p. 303.

136• Iberl 2011, pp. 326, 329.

137• Kondakov 1901; Foletti 2009.

138• Kondakov 1927a, pp. 77–78.

139• Kovaleva/Šipunova 2014.

140• Kondakov 1905.

Now we have talked about six Russian émigrés who reached Czechoslovakia within a relatively short time and became key figures in the history of the *Institutum*. Five of the six were scholars, and all six shared a passion for the culture of their motherland. This mix of established academics, students, and at least one passionate amateur was not, as one might think, the result of chance. It was brought about by the Russian Action, which we mentioned briefly in connection with Kondakov's arrival in Czechoslovakia.

THE *INSTITUTUM* AS PART OF THE RUSSIAN ACTION

As we have seen, Kondakov was brought to Prague for reasons both professional and personal, with some strings being pulled by academics and others by politicians. This was certainly not the case for the other émigrés who would become members of the Institute, especially the younger ones. And yet, they did not end up in Czechoslovakia by accident. On the contrary, they reached the capital of Czechoslovakia as the result of a clear political decision to welcome Russian refugees.[141] As hinted above, the "Russian Action", organized by the Czechoslovak Ministry of Foreign Affairs, was an impressive and unprecedented project. The idea was to attract Russian students and intellectuals, for whom a parallel educational system would be built up, including secondary schools and the university. As has been noted by Václav Veber, the program was unique in that it had no ambition to integrate the Russian émigrés, instead counting on them maintaining their own Russian culture and identity.[142] This would prepare them for their eventual return to Russia, after which Czechoslovakia and Russia would enjoy a special relationship beneficial to both.[143]

To understand the roots of this project, we need to examine two figures. One was the first prime minister of Czechoslovakia, Karel Kramář.[144] He was married to a Russian woman and was deeply Pan-Slavic and Russophile. He hoped that after the Russian Action,

141• In the very large bibliography see, e.g., Tejchmanová 1993; Veber 1993; Sládek 1994; Veber 1994, 1995, 1996; Sládek/Běloševská 1998; Chinyaeva 2001; Johnson 2007; *Rossijskije učenyje-gumanitarii* 2008; Mchitarjan 2009; *Na rubeže dvuch kul'tur* 2012.

142• Veber 1998, pp. 77–79.

143• Bystrov 1993.

144• Lustigová 2007.

the Slavic world would emerge more powerful and united than ever, with Russia playing a leading role in this bloc. President Masaryk, on the other hand, realized that the situation in Russia was catastrophic, and thought that international help was necessary.[145] He believed that without a stable Russia, there would be no stability anywhere in Europe. Not surprisingly for a Czech, Masaryk thought that the German-speaking lands still posed a threat to Czechoslovakia and the other new Central European states, and hoped that Russia could someday lead a bloc of nations that would serve as a counterweight to the Germans.[146] In 1922, long before the collapse of the new order that had been set up at Versailles, Masaryk expressed his thoughts concerning Russia:

> *“We should help Russia, and by so doing, we will help ourselves. As far as help for Russia is concerned, all countries must work together. No single country by itself can help Russia, even if the others permit it.”*[147]

More directly pertinent to our current discussion is a section towards the conclusion of Masaryk's 1922 text. According to Masaryk, each European country needed to help Russia in its own way, as Czechoslovakia itself had done and would continue to do. Masaryk had a clear plan and hoped that there would be international coordination of the efforts to help Russia. Masaryk saw the role of Czechoslovakia as helping students and intellectuals. He thought that Czechoslovakia, whether by means of the Czechoslovak Legion in Russia or the Russian Action back home, needed to do its part in an international effort to bring Russia through its crisis and back to prosperity. Masaryk's hope, of course, was that democracy would emerge from the chaos of the Russian Civil War, and he seems to have thought that helping and educating émigré students would help to bring about that end.

Masaryk's reasoning seemed less justified once the Soviet regime consolidated its power. He never gave up hope. Twenty years later, his "heir", Edvard Beneš, was still convinced that the effort had been worth the trouble. In 1944, in exile in England, the latter, Minister

145• Masaryk 1992 [1922], pp. 7–8.

146• *Ibidem*, pp. 14–17.

147• *"Máme a musíme pomáhat Rušku, ale zároveň musíme si pomáhat sami sobě. Pokud běží o pomoc Rušku, tedy je třeba součinnošti všech štátů; jeden sám nemůže Rušku pomoci, i kdyby druzí mu to dovolili."*, *Ibidem*, p. 20.

of Foreign Affairs during all of Masaryk's presidency and his successor as President of Czechoslovakia, described the Russian Action in the following terms:[148]

> "*We educated more than 4,000 of these young Russian students, almost all of whom were, a priori, anti-Bolsheviks. Nevertheless, 2,000 of them returned to the Soviet Union as doctors, engineers, etc., to work together on Stalin's five-year plan.*"[149]

In Beneš's view, the goal of the Russian Action was to transform the Soviet Union from inside, and at the same time, to better understand its culture. Masaryk's ambition seems to have been twofold: to save Russia as a fundamental member of the international community, and to build connections within Europe through a shared effort to help Russian émigrés. It is difficult, at this point in time, not to contrast Masaryk's attitude with what we have seen a century later as Europe is again faced with a major wave of refugees. Masaryk's thinking still appears pertinent, especially the idea that Europe will fare better with coordinated action rather than piecemeal action from individual countries.

In order to implement this plan, a Russian section of the ministry was organized by Václav Girsa (1875–1954). He was succeeded in this work by Kamil Krofta (1876–1945), who would later become Minister of Foreign Affairs.[150] Starting in 1921, this section funded émigrés' travels from camps in Constantinople to Czechoslovakia and then supported their education. Those who had interrupted their studies at universities in Russia because of revolution or war (as Toll' and Beljaev had done) were allowed to pick up where they had left off. Others were enrolled in a program corresponding their level of education. Approximately 1,000 students reached Czechoslovakia via Constantinople, while another 600 came directly from the lands of the former Russian Empire. It is worth mentioning that about 40% of all Russian emigrants to Czechoslovakia were students, while less than 5% of the pre-revolutionary Russian

148• Marès 2015.

149• "*Vychovali jsme přes čtyři tisíce těchto mladých ruských studentů, kteří byli téměř všichni a priori proti-bolševiky. Dva tisíce z nich se nicméně vrátilo do Sovětského svazu jako lékaři, inženýři atd., aby spolupracovali na Stalinově pětiletce.*", in Mackenzie 1948 [1947], p. 98.

150• Muratov/Muratova 2011; Morávková 2016.

population had been students.[151] In the same period, from 1921 to 1922, seventy Russian professors were invited to Czechoslovakia in order to create what would be called the Russian Academic Group. As mentioned above, the goal was to eventually create an entire parallel educational system. In reality, only one faculty was ever fully functional (the Faculty of Law), and the Faculty of Arts was never fully staffed.[152] The effort reached its apex between 1923 and 1926, and then rapidly shrank. It is, nevertheless, impressive to note that between 1921 and 1934, the Czechoslovak state, as part of the Russian Action, offered education to 6,818 émigré students.

The project had lost momentum by the late 1920s, and large numbers of émigrés decided to move still further west, whether to other European countries or to North America. Why did they move on, even knowing that no other country offered the same level of support? Zdeněk Sládek has suggested several answers to this question. First, it was difficult to find a job after graduation. In part because of the worldwide economic depression, the Czechoslovak Republic could not offer every Russian a position corresponding to his level of education.[153] Second, direct financial support for the emigrants had also decreased, even though it remained the most generous on the continent. To further complicate matters, there were now pro-Soviet parties in the parliament, blocking support for anti-Bolshevik émigrés. Third, in the early 1930s, political developments in Europe made Czechoslovakia look less secure than other countries further to the west. And finally, starting in 1933, refugees began to arrive from Nazi Germany, competing for any work available. By 1934, according to Veber, the number of émigrés from Germany and Austria was at least five times higher than the number of Russian émigrés living in the country.[154]

This is not the place for a thorough evaluation of the successes and failures of the Russian Action. Its weak points, in retrospect, are obvious, especially its lack of any attempt to integrate Russian émigrés into Czechoslovakia on a cultural or practical level. It was, however, extremely beneficial to those who participated, and those

151• Chinayaeva 2001, pp. 54–57.

152• *Ibidem*, pp. 57–59.

153• We should precise that the great depression did not arrived in Czechoslovakia immediately in 1929, bit quite later, starting in 1930 and touching an apex in 1933. See Sekanina 2004.

154• Veber 1998, pp. 77–79.

students did much for the reputation of Czechoslovakia all over the world.

In light of the above discussion, it is clear that the *Seminarium Kondakovianum* grew out of a larger project and received support for that reason. But the *Seminarium* was also exceptional for a very simple reason: it was supposed, from the start, to be a permanent institution, not just a temporary structure for educating a single generation of Russian emigrants.

THE STORY OF A RUSSIAN ÉMIGRÉ INSTITUTE IN PRAGUE

As we have seen, almost immediately after the death of Nikodim Kondakov, his pupils and friends started to meet regularly in order to honor and continue his life's work. One of the first ideas which emerged from the group was a *Festschrift* in memory of Kondakov. This volume was duly published, in 1926, and contained articles by some of the most prominent Byzantinists of this period, as well as papers by members of the new and still unofficial group in Prague. The book also included a short article describing the activities of the group, noting that seventeen meetings had been held during 1925, and that discussions had begun concerning the establishment of a more permanent organization. In the event, the Institute took shape in 1926, and its first task was to publish those of Kondakov's works that he, for whatever reasons, had not managed to get into print himself, especially the monumental volumes of the series on Russian icons.

It soon became clear, however, that the best way to preserve the master's legacy would be to pursue his research and apply his methodology, and to this end the *Seminarium* began three kinds of public activities. First and foremost, there would be the creation of a periodical. The first volume of *Seminarium Kondakovianum* appeared in 1928, and the journal would be published annually until the war intervened in 1940 {16}. At the same time, two series of books were inaugurated, with each focusing on one of Kondakov's major areas of interest: *Skythika* was dedicated to the arts of nomadic tribes, and *Zōgraphika* dealt with Byzantine and medieval Russian panel painting and iconography. The second category of public activity was essentially a nod to the Arts & Crafts movement: the *Seminarium* organized workshops on the production of enamels, embroidery, and, of course, panel painting. The master painter Pimen M. Sofronov (1898–1973) was invited from Latvia to Prague several times to give courses in panel painting.[155] And third, the scholars of the *Seminarium* did their best to spread knowledge of medieval Russian art to a wider audience. The largest event organized with this end in mind was an exhibition of "icons" held in 1932 in Prague, but we should not forget that the *Seminarium* also held a series of public lectures dedicated to the topics its scholars were researching. During the Second World War, in fact, this desire to educate the public would see the Institute through, with most of its funds coming from the sale of printed images of Russian "icons".[156]

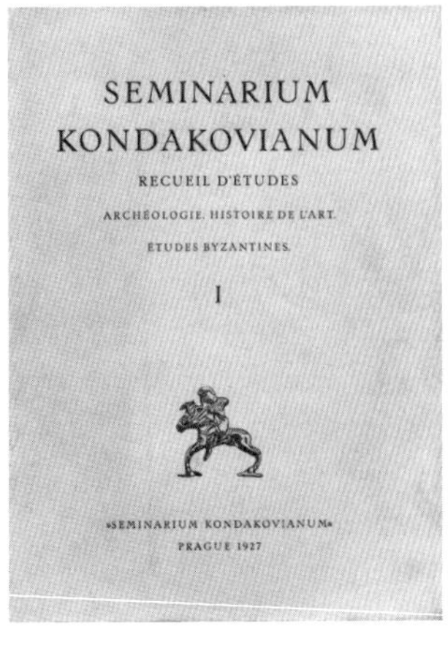

16} Frontispiece of *Seminarium Kondakovianum*, I (1927)

Besides publishing their research, members of the *Seminarium* also did archaeology, and several participated in the excavations at Dura-Europos during the 1930s.[157] This site was one of the most important discoveries ever made for our understanding of Late Antique Jewish and Christian art. The images found at the site's synagogue vanquished for good the myth that all Jews in Late Antiquity forbade images, while the *domus ecclesiae* is probably our most precious evidence of pre-Constantinian Christian visual culture and ritual spaces.[158] The *Seminarium* was present at the site above all in the person of Nikolaj Toll', who was in charge of excavating the Necropolis and authored one of the final reports on the findings.[159] The campaign at Dura-Europos was expensive and politically important,

155• Řoutil 2013, pp. 266–267.

156• For the documents see UDU-AV/KI-1, sv. 9; Nikolay Andreyev, Material supplied by Dr. N. E. Andreyev, Formerly Student, Fellow and Acting Director of the Kondakov Institute in Prague, CUL/BA/VC, box 158, pp. 25–49; Hrochová 1995, p. 34; Zaoral 2013, p. 552.

157• For the historiography of the excavations, see Hopkins 1979.

158• On the intellectual background of these discoveries, see also Olin 2000a.

159• Toll 1943, 1946. On this, see mainly Drbal 2008. In the archives of UDU-AV/KI-47 to KI-50 are also preserved many photographs of the Dura-Europos expedition.

being promoted by Yale University and the French Académie des Inscriptions et Belles-Lettres. The fact that members of the *Seminarium* participated is proof that the institution was held in great prestige around the world. Toll', who worked at the Necropolis, was responsible for objects of green glazed pottery, gold, silver, and bronze jewelry. "Portable", "small", or "minor" art was, in fact, considered one of the specialties of the scholars involved with the *Seminarium*. By this time, Vernadskij was already a professor at Yale, and the Institute also maintained contact with Mikhail Rostovcev, leader of the excavations from 1937.[160] Caspar Meyer has suggested that Rostovcev connected Dura-Europos with his work on Eurasianism, a notion which was also significant in the work of the *Seminarium's* scholars in Prague.[161] We see, then, that the *Seminarium* retained its importance via this international network of Russian émigré scholars working on a variety of interconnected topics.

The year 1930 was a kind of turning point in the life of the *Seminarium Kondakovianum*. Vernadskij had already been in the US for three years, and responsibility for the academic work of the *Seminarium* was being shared by Kalitinskij and Toll'. Given the precarity of the world economy, Kalitinskij and the Princess Jašvil felt the need to stabilize the finances of the *Seminarium*. Kalitinskij had two main ideas on how to proceed. First, the group needed to become a part of the Czechoslovak state education system, and beyond that, Kalitinskij desired to find a partner somewhere abroad and create a branch of the *Seminarium* there.

In 1931, therefore, the *Seminarium* became officially affiliated with the Czechoslovak Ministry of Education. At this time, the intellectual and scholarly aims of the institution were clarified along with its legal status. From the declaration sent to the Ministry of Education, the main purpose of the "Kondakov Archaeological Institute" would be "to publish the works of Kondakov which remained unfinished after his death and to pursue and develop research in the directions indicated by Kondakov in the fields of archaeology and Byzantine studies".[162]

160• Rostovcev was, e.g., the first to be published in the series *Skythika*: Rostovtzeff 1929.

161• Meyer 2009.

162• Ustav Archeologičeskogo instituta, S1; *Report* 1932, pp. 3–4.

The search for a foreign partner also started out well. On a visit to Paris, Kalitinskij met with the Russian artist and philosopher Nicholas Roerich (1874–1947), who now resided in the United States. Roerich was a complex person, to say the least. He was a theosophical mystic who expected the millennium to arrive at any time, and travelled regularly to Asia in order to explore Buddhism.[163] Roerich was active as a publisher, and in 1923 he had set up the Roerich Foundation and Museum in New York. The efforts of Roerich and his wife towards preserving the world's cultural heritage were significant enough for the University of Paris to nominate him for the Nobel Peace Prize in 1929.[164] Roerich was crucial in the promotion of the so-called "Roerich Pact", signed on April 15, 1935 at the White House in Washington. This inter-American agreement was the first international agreement on the protection of cultural property and objects.[165] To sum it up, a powerful and apparently very rich man.

It seems that Kalitinskij, at first, convinced Roerich to create a branch of the *Seminarium* in the US under the "patronage" of Roerich's Institute.[166] Then tragedy struck. According to the documents at our disposal, Kalitinskij suffered a nervous breakdown in Prague and left for Paris to live there with his wife, the actress Maria Germanova (1884–1940).[167] He remained permanently in Paris, where he would be cured. He died in 1946.[168] From correspondence dating to this period between Kalitinskij, Roerich, and other members of the Kondakov Institute, we can see several reasons why the plan to establish a branch in New York did not come to fruition.[169] There were disagreements as to what the vision of the Institute should be, as revealed in a letter from Kalitinskij to the Roerich's son Jurij (1902–1960), whose scholarly work overlapped that of the Institute.[170] Nor was

163• Savelli 2014.

164• "Roerich Nominated for Peace Award", *New York Times*, March 3, 1929.

165• On Roerich's life and activities, see Decter 1989.

166• Not all members of the *Institutum* approved of this initiative, and their positions towards Roerich varied. See Rosov 1996; Beljaev 1995, 2000; the situation is summed up by Skálová 1991, pp. 31–32 and Dmitrieva 2018, p. 186.

167• Chinyaeva 2001, pp. 173–174.

168• Kalitinskij's incident was even reported in the US press: "Kidnapped Russian in Jail; Prague White Leader Found to Be Under Arrest After Hunt", *New York Times*, October 1, 1930.

169• On this failed effort, see mainly Rosov 1995; Beljaev 1996, 2000.

170• UDU-AV/KI-8, sv. 2, letter of Kalitinskij to Jurij Roerich, 01.03.1931. Jurij Roerich had studied with Rostovcev and published a volume in the series *Skythika*, see Roerich 1930.

it clear how independent the branch would be from Roerich's own organization. Kalitinskij's illness certainly did not help, and this is specifically mentioned by Roerich, who became convinced that Kalitinskij was possessed.[171] The disagreements grew to the point where Roerich refused any further contact with the Institute and withdrew all support. Zuzana Skálová believes that Roerich was near bankruptcy at the time and could not have afforded to support the Institute even if he had wanted to.[172]

As if the rupture with Roerich and Kalitinskij's indisposition were not enough, 1930 also brought the tragic death of Nikolaj Beljaev, killed by a lorry on the snowy streets of Prague.[173] In the midst of this crisis, the remaining members of the *Seminarium* turned to Vernadskij, asking him to resume his directorship. Vernadskij declined, citing his busy schedule at Yale and the distances involved, but recommended in his stead a colleague and friend who had studied at the University of Saint Petersburg and was now teaching at the University of Wisconsin. This was the historian Aleksandr Vasiliev (1867–1953), who accepted the offer and became the official director of the *Seminarium*, with Nikolaj Toll' functioning as acting director in Prague until 1938.[174] Toll' was effectively the one in charge of the Institute, doing his best to keep it functioning even as the international political situation becoming less and less stable. It was in the early 1930s, during the first years of Toll's directorship, that the Institute reached its apex in terms of publishing activity, number of subscribers, and number of members. In 1937, the Institute had 111 members all around the world, from Europe to the US and Japan.[175]

The situation within Czechoslovakia, however, was disintegrating. The Ministry of Foreign Affairs had drastically reduced its support, and because of the economic crisis, many Russian émigrés were forced to leave Prague in search of work. Developments in Nazi Germany also affected affairs in Czechoslovakia. As is well known, Czechoslovakia attracted Hitler's attention very early on because of the large number of "ethnic Germans" living there, especially in lands on the borders of Bohemia, later called Sudetenland, where

171 • Rosov 1995, pp. 649–650.

172 • Skálová 1991, p. 32.

173 • Ostrogorsky 1931; Okuněv 1931.

174 • *Report* 1936, p. 3; Beißwenger 2005 [2001], p. 48.

175 • Hrochová 1972, p. 304.

German speakers were in fact the majority.[176] Hitler made no effort to hide his intention of including these people in his Greater Germany, and Beneš had been fighting against the idea for years.[177] German designs on Czechoslovakia made White Russian émigrés nervous, since Hitler and Stalin had a somewhat ambivalent relationship.[178]

It was within this context that the Institute entered negotiations with Prince Paul I of Serbia (1893–1976), regent for Peter II, king of Yugoslavia (1923–1970), about moving operations to Serbia. These contacts were mediated by what seems the most unlikely partner imaginable, Bernard Berenson (1865–1959), the connoisseur and specialist in the attribution of Early Modern art.[179] The initial proposal was to move the Institute and all its property to safety in Serbia. Toll', Rasovskij, and Georgij Ostrogorskij (already teaching in Belgrade), were in favor of this move, but the Princess Jašvil was not.[180] She thought it would show a lack of gratitude towards Czechoslovakia and did not consider Serbia to be any safer from German aggression. History would prove her right.[181] In the end, it was decided to divide the Institute into two. One part, including the research activities and the library, would move to Belgrade, while the other would remain in Prague and continue with some minor activities.[182] What is not clear from our sources is whether the Prague branch was expected to be permanent, or rather to be gradually dissolved. Both possibilities were under consideration.

In any case, the young Nikolaj Andrejev (1908–1982) was appointed secretary of the Prague branch **{17}**.[183] Andrejev was purely

176• On the situation before 1938, see Bruegel 1973; on the Sudeten, see Zimmermann 1999.

177• Cornwall 1992.

178• Lukeš 1996; see also Kvaček 2018.

179• UDU-AV/KI-12 s.v. Berenson, letter from Berenson to Jašvil, 27.06.1938. On Berenson, see Samuels 1979; on this moment in the life of *Seminarium*, see also Jančárková 2005.

180• Myslivec 1947, p. 221; Skálová 1991, pp. 35–36; Beißwenger 2005 [2001], pp. 60–61. On Ostrogorskij see Jančárková 2012.

181• Nikolay Andreyev, Material supplied by Dr. N. E. Andreyev, Formerly Student, Fellow and Acting Director of the Kondakov Institute in Prague, CUL/BA/VC, box 158, p. 8. For Toll's arguments, see p. 9.

182• *Ibidem*, p. 10.

183• On him, besides the published autobiography, Andreyev 2009, see the much more complete document, written in 1968 and discovered in the archives of Vernadskij: Nikolay Andreyev, Material supplied by Dr. N. E. Andreyev, Formerly Student, Fellow and Acting Director of the Kondakov Institute in Prague, CUL/BA/VC, box 158.

17} Nikolaj Andrejev, 1933

18} Prince Karel VI Schwarzenberg

a product of the Russian Action. He had arrived in Czechoslovakia as a child, been educated in Russian rather than Czech, and then entered the *Seminarium* thanks to a scholarship offered to the Institute by President Masaryk in 1928 on the occasion of the tenth anniversary of the creation of Czechoslovakia.[184] Andrejev's fellowship at the *Seminarium* was to be a continuation of his training for his return to Russia, but instead he remained in Prague. He and the Princess Jašvil were to take care of the Institute's affairs in Prague, while all the other prominent members decamped for Belgrade. Toll', who was eager to leave Prague in order to not be drafted into the Czechoslovak army, soon moved on from Belgrade to New Haven, joining his wife Nina (1898–1985), who also happened to be Vernadskij's sister. Before long, Toll' had abandoned the university and become a farmer.[185] The *Seminarium*'s Belgrade branch was left in the hands of Rasovskij, his wife Irina Okuněva-Rasovskaja (1913–1941), and Georgij Ostrogorskij.

184• Kalitinskij 1929, p. 328.

185• Nikolay Andreyev, Material supplied by Dr. N. E. Andreyev, Formerly Student, Fellow and Acting Director of the Kondakov Institute in Prague, CUL/BA/VC, box 229, letter from Toll' to Vernadsky, 25.6.1950; see also Skálová 1991, p. 36, n. 47.

This period of division was a delicate one for the Institute. After the occupation of Czechoslovakia by Nazi Germany, the Belgrade branch asked Andrejev to begin sending the remaining books and property to Serbia. Andrejev refused, however, saying that the newly established Nazi laws forbade this. Indeed, after the annexation of the Sudetenland to the Reich in Autumn 1938, the remainder of the Czech lands had been annexed in 1939. This entity – called the Protectorate of Bohemia and Moravia – would exist until the end of the war in May 1945, and its new legislation did, indeed, prohibit the export of property from the territory.[186] It appears that the reaction of the Serbian branch was quite aggressive, and it may have been fueled by a personal rivalry between Rasovskij and Andrejev. We will return to this period in the last chapter of this book. For now, let us note that the tension may have been related to the Institute's finances, as well. Roman Zaoral has suggested that when the Institute split into two branches, it had not been made clear which of them would receive the income from the international sale of publications. This could have been the cause of the conflict between Prague and Belgrade.[187]

This conflict was resolved in the most catastrophic way imaginable. On April 6, 1941, the German army attacked Belgrade. Rasovskij and his wife were killed in the bombardment, and part of the library and property of the Institute were destroyed at the same time. Princess Jašvil, who had died in 1939, was proven right, and the Belgrade branch of the *Seminarium* was closed. In a stroke of bitter irony, the Wehrmacht brought the Institute's remaining property from Belgrade to Prague, and there the Institute struggled along, its activities much reduced.

After the death of Princess Jašvil in 1939 and during the last months of the conflict with Belgrade, a new board of the Institute was constituted, with its membership as follows: the president was Prince Karel VI Schwarzenberg (1911–1986) **{18}**,[188] who had joined as an honorary member in 1932 and would soon become one of the leading figures of the Institute. The other members were professors Pjotr Savickij and Josef Myslivec (1907–1971), while

186 • See, e.g., Tauchen 2015.

187 • Zaoral 2013.

188 • On Schwarzenberg, see Anderle 1987; Řoutil 2013; Zaoral 2013.

General Vladimir Černavin (1887–1949) was appointed auditor. Nikolaj Andrejev was elected acting director. This board decided that, for the remainder of the war, the Institute would not publish any periodicals or books, and would rather concentrate on the preservation and enlargement of its present collections of books and objects of art. Schwarzenberg made many generous donations to the Institute, but there was little other income, so color reproductions of Russian "icons" were printed on stock paper and sold throughout the Reich. This idea worked so well that by the end of the war, for the first time in its history, the Kondakov Institute was in a strong financial position. Furthermore, the Institute moved to a new and larger building in the center of Prague, on Haštalská Street. The library, which contained 6,500 volumes at the beginning of the war, had reached 10,039 by the end of the war.[189] It was also during the war that Josef Girsa donated his collection of panel paintings to the Institute, greatly enlarging its art collection **{19a–b}**.

The end of the war was the beginning of the end for the Kondakov Institute. The details will be narrated later, but the reader can surely imagine that in a country entering the Soviet sphere of influence, the existence of an institution founded by White Russian émigré scholars would be tenuous at best.

THE PRACTICAL ASPECTS OF DAILY LIFE: ECONOMIC ISSUES, PATRONAGE, AND "DISSEMINATION"

Obviously, one of the main problems faced by the Institute throughout its life was how to finance itself. Since it was not part of any larger institution (such as a university or the Academy of Sciences), it had to raise its own funds, and a look through the accounting ledgers of the Institute in the Prague archives reveals that the money came, essentially, from three sources.[190]

189• Hrochová 1995, p. 34.

190• See mainly UDU-AV/KI-4, where the precise balance of each year is conserved. Moreover, in KI-2, we have all the incomes starting from 1930 and finishing with 1952. In KI-3 is the complete list of all the property of the *Seminarium* and the Institute, including furnishing and collections. In KI-5, there are the balances from the bank account from the 1920s, 30s, and 40s, as well as the recipes from the same bank. Finally, in KI-6, all the documents relative to regular expenses are kept from the years 1937, 1938, 1941–1945.

19} a,b} Kondakov Institute interior

First of all, there was some regular income from the Czechoslovak authorities, namely the Chancellery of the President of the Republic, the Ministry of Foreign Affairs, and the Slavonic Institute. The presidential chancellery gave 10,000 crowns per year, and, from time to time, funded fellowships for young scholars such as Andrejev.[191] The Slavonic Institute gave between 3,000 and 5,000 crowns per year, and, according to Sládek and Běloševská, the Ministry of Foreign Affairs, as part of its Russian Action, gave the Institute a total of 500,000 crowns between 1926 and 1937.[192] These were large sums during the First Republic, but not sufficient for all of the Institute's necessities.

A second source of income was guaranteed by the Institute's publications. The international distributor of these publications was the Verlag Otto Harrassowitz in Leipzig.[193] During the war years, the same firm distributed the printed color reproduction of icons which brought so much income to the Institute.[194] The Princess Maria Teniševa (1858–1928), a friend of the Princess Jašvil who lived in Paris, bequeathed her enamel workshop (with its accompanying library) to the Institute, and once these tools had been brought to Prague, Jašvil and her daughter Tatiana used them to produce panel paintings and enamels which were sold to raise funds for the Institute.[195] According to Iberl, the main distributor of these "Arts & Crafts" objects was Ostrogorskij, who sold them when traveling around Europe for research or to attend conferences.[196]

The third important source of income was "honorary memberships". The cheeky strategy adopted by the directors of the Institute was as follows: first, a potential benefactor received a letter announcing that he had been elected honorary member of the *Seminarium*. Once he accepted the honor, a second letter would arrive asking him to kindly cover the costs of said honorary membership. This strategy was surprisingly successful, and the Institute's network of honorary

191• Hrochová 1995, p. 34.

192• Sládek/Běloševská 1998, p. 190; Zaoral 2013, p. 549.

193• Myslivec 1946; Zaoral 2013, p. 552.

194• UDU-AV/KI-1, sv. 9; Zaoral 2013, p. 552.

195• Was also published posthumously, with *Seminarium Kondakovianum*, a work by Teniševa on enamel and inlaid work, see Teniševa 1930. She also entertained relations with others interested into a "revival" of "Arts & Crafts", as well as with Roerich, see Hardiman 2017.

196• Iberl 2011, p. 329.

members was extensive. They are all present in the extensive correspondence preserved at the archives in Prague. Among them were figures such as the art historian Bernard Berenson (already mentioned above) and the Slavophile American industrialist Charles R. Crane. Also joining from America were Robert W. Bliss, founder of the Dumbarton Oaks research center, Charles J. Connick, painter and designer of neo-medieval stained glass, and Ralph Cram, an architect working in the Gothic revival style.[197] Prominent Czech members included Prince Kolowrat, Alice Masaryková (the daughter of the president), and the printer of all the *Seminarium*'s publications, Václav Neubert.[198] The Institute's correspondence with Neubert illustrates all the steps involved in honorary membership. On January 23, 1932, Neubert received a letter notifying him of his election. The same day, a receipt was issued for his annual membership fee of 1,000 crowns. On February 28, 1933, the Institute sent Neubert the report on its activities during the year 1932, along with a letter explicitly stating that the report was mainly intended for English and American donors. The archives also contain receipts from the years 1934 to 1938 indicating that Neubert's annual contribution in those years was 500 crowns. A letter from October 4, 1939 is much more dramatic: under the Protectorate of Bohemia and Moravia, the Institute is cut off from its normal sources of income and must ask honorary members for further support. Four days later, Neubert's answer arrived accompanied by 500 crowns but also by Neubert's letter of resignation from his honorary membership due to the complicated political and economic circumstances. The Institute's answer, which arrived on October 11, asked Neubert to remain an honorary member even if he would or could not pay the membership fees.[199] The pecuniary side of this correspondence is the most obvious one, but there was often something deeper involved. Sometimes, a letter announcing an honorary membership would, given time, result in a scholarly exchange of information or even participation in a publication. It appears that it was thanks to these honorary memberships that the Institute became one of the world's most renowned institutions for Byzantine studies.

197• UDU-AV/KI-12, Berenson, B.; KI-12, Crane, Ch. R.; KI-12, Connick, Ch. J.; KI-12, Cram, R. A.

198• UDU-AV/KI-13, Kolowrat-Krakovský, J.; KI-14, Masaryková, A.

199• UDU-AV/KI-14, Neubert, V.

Among the honorary members were a few select "charitable honorary members", or patrons as they would now be called.[200] These figures, for instance the Crane and Masaryk families, contributed more than their due. This group of patrons included members of the Czech aristocracy and politicians such as Josef Girsa and Přemysl Šamal (1867–1941),[201] but perhaps the most important of them was the young Prince Karel Schwarzenberg, to whom we will dedicate significant attention in the last part of this book. Schwarzenberg supported the Institute with ever increasing donations, the largest of which was a gift of 65,000 crowns made on September 7, 1940.[202] From the day he joined, he also donated small objects to the Institute's collection and books to its library. During the war, as we will see later, he directed his donations towards very precise and practical ends, such as finding a new headquarters for the Institute.

Although the Institute was often in dire financial straits, its funding and accounting mechanisms were very well organized. Since it drew income from various sources, it managed to survive even disastrous circumstances like the Great Depression and the Second World War. For a long time, the Institute owed large sums to its printer, Neubert, but these debts could finally be paid off during the war thanks to unexpectedly large sales of printed Eastern Orthodox devotional images in Germany, a phenomenon which we are at a loss to explain.[203] A lucky bureaucratic mistake also helped: at the beginning of the war, the members of the Institute had forgotten to declare – to both the German and Czech authorities – their large stock of high-quality ivory paper.[204] The Institute could therefore reproduce its "icons" at a very low cost, since the paper was "free".

Although the *Seminarium* and the later Institute started out as part of the world of the Russian émigrés, over the years the institution became more and more a part of Czechoslovak society. This was partially due to the need for new donors – including Czech scholars such as professors Jaroslav Bidlo or Niederle – but also, we believe,

200• Beißwenger 2005 [2001], pp. 46–48.

201• UDU-AV/KI-13, Girsa, J.; KI-16, Šamal, P.

202• UDU-AV/KI-16, Schwarzenberg, K., letter of the 29.08.1940.

203• See Jančárková/Gagen 2019.

204• Nikolay Andreyev, Material supplied by Dr. N. E. Andreyev, Formerly Student, Fellow and Acting Director of the Kondakov Institute in Prague, CUL/BA/VC, box 158, p. 49.

to the fact that the younger generation of scholars felt an attachment to Czech as well as Russian culture. We have already mentioned how Andrejev, who joined the *Seminarium* in 1928, had been in Czechoslovakia since childhood. From his memoirs it is evident that he considered himself a member of both cultures. This helps explain why, especially from the early 1930s onwards, the activities of the Institute became more and more public, with many events conceived for a general and necessarily Czechoslovak audience.

This was especially true of the 1932 exhibition of icons, the first of its kind in Central Europe and an event which shows, as well as anything, how the scholars at the Institute perceived their mission. We have already mentioned that Russian panel painting was almost unknown in the West before the Russian Revolution, and that the sudden availability of many of these objects on the market changed that situation forever. The Institute's 1932 exhibition was typical in the sense that many private collectors participated, among them Hana Benešová (1885–1974), the wife of the Minister of Foreign Affairs. The growing interest in this kind of art, which fit well with the avant-garde aesthetics of the time, was a Europe-wide phenomenon.

We should remember the monographs which Muratov published in France, of which *Trente-cinq primitifs russes* (1931) was particularly successful **{20}**.[205] The ostensible idea of Muratov's book was to allow comparison of fifteenth-century Russian painting with fifteenth-century Western painting. The Western works were already relatively well known thanks in no small part to the famous exhibitions of "national" fifteenth-century art held in Brussels in 1902 (*"Les primitifs flamands"*) and Paris in 1904 (*"Les primitifs français"*).[206] It has been demonstrated by Enrico Castelnuovo that these exhibitions contributed to the creation of the national myths which led to the First World War.[207] Muratov was certainly nationalist enough to believe that Russian fifteenth-century painting was the equal of Western art from the same era; this is clear in the studies he published between 1914 to 1925, and even more explicit in his introduction to the catalogue for the massive exhibition organized in

205• Muratoff 1931.

206• About the ideological frames of these exhibitions, see Martin 2008; Passini 2010.

207• Castelnuovo 1999, 2004.

1913 to celebrate 300 years of the Romanov dynasty.[208] His *Trente-cinq primitifs russes* would put more evidence for that argument in front of Western audiences.

In our opinion, however, Muratov's intention was more complex. The word *primitif* had entered avant-garde vocabulary thanks to Matisse and to other contemporary artists, and even if Muratov did not directly mention this second meaning of the term, we believe he was perfectly conscious of this semantic slide.[209] The visual values of fourteenth, fifteenth, and sixteenth century Orthodox images, e.g., the paintings of Andrej Rublev, are undoubtedly close to the values of early twentieth-century avant-garde art, and we think that Muratov was encouraging the purchasers of his monograph to see the similarities between Russian *primitifs* and early-twentieth-century *avant-gardistes*.

It was not only in books or galleries that Western audiences could see Russian "icons". In the late 1920s and early 1930s, the Soviet regime began to send Russian medieval panel paintings abroad, initially for sale to raise funds, but later for exhibition as part of the regime's "heritage policy".[210] Large expositions were held in the US and Europe, contributing to the myth of the classic Eastern Orthodox panel painting or "icon".[211] The *Seminarium*'s activities were thus part of a global phenomenon. By exhibiting Russian "icons" in Prague, the Institute hoped to show Czechoslovaks the value, importance, and relevance of the Russian national heritage for European culture in general.

This desire – to advocate for Russian art before Western audiences – was present but not prominent in Kondakov's work. It is more obvious in the work of Muratov and in the work of the scholars of the *Seminarium Kondakovianum* in its later years. A good example is an unpublished lecture given by Karel Schwarzenberg sometime in the 1930s. Written in Czech, and in very descriptive language, this lecture was certainly intended for a larger audience than just the scholars of the Institute.[212] The document is undated,

208• Muratov 1913b, 1914, 1925. On his figure, see Muratova 2008, 2010. On the exhibition, see Foletti 2018b.

209• Leardi 2010.

210• See, e.g., Kyzlasova 2010; Salmond 2010.

211• On the lexicon, see again Foletti 2016b.

212• UDU-AV/KI-28 sv. 5.

20} Virgin of Jerusalem, Novgorod School, 15th century, pl. IV of Paul Muratoff, *Trente-cinq primitifs. Collection Jacques Zolotnizky*, Paris 1931

but must belong to the period following April 20, 1934, when Schwarzenberg became an honorary member of the Institute.[213] As noted above, Schwarzenberg belonged to one of the oldest Bohemian noble families. He was not a trained art historian, but he was very much interested in heraldry and in the Arts & Crafts question.[214] As such, besides offering financial support to the Institute, he actively participated in its activities, including icon-painting workshops and lectures for the public.[215]

The five-page lecture in question begins with a very strong criticism of the murals commissioned by Ludwig II of Bavaria

213• UDU-AV/KI-16, Schwarzenberg, K.

214• Zaoral 2013.

215• Řoutil 2013.

(r. 1864–1886) in imitation of the mosaics of Norman Sicily.[216] According to Schwarzenberg, the result is mediocre, since the Western eye cannot understand the real qualities of Eastern painting. Starting from this point, Schwarzenberg argues that medieval Russian panel painting was the last survivor of Antiquity's tradition of panel painting, of which the most famous examples are the Fayum portraits. This was an idea proposed earlier by Nikodim Kondakov; so far, Schwarzenberg has said nothing too radical.[217] But the interesting part of Schwarzenberg's lecture comes when he says it would be a complete misunderstanding to consider this art "primitive". Once again, that ambiguous term. What kind of "primitivism" does Schwarzenberg mean? Is he reacting to Muratov's recently published book? That is certainly possible, considering the tension between Muratov's followers and Kondakov's – a conflict which was already evident before the Revolution.[218] In the rest of the lecture, Schwarzenberg argues that Russian painting is not a decorative art, but rather, as Henri Focillon and Muratov had argued in their twin introductions to *Trente-cinq primitifs russes,* a true intellectual and spiritual one.[219] The prince considers the masterful use of gold in Russian panel painting as the most perfect example of balance and beauty, elements which survived in Russian art even after Western art had "abandoned" them for the baroque. Schwarzenberg's text is fascinating in many ways. It demonstrates how deeply the study of "icons" had penetrated the milieu of the Institute. In Schwarzenberg's thought we find clear references to Pavel Muratov (at least his early works), to Pavel Florenskij, and, of course, to Nikodim Kondakov.[220] And the emphasis on the poetic and spiritual aspects of art is perfectly in tune with the enthusiasm for religious behavior and devotion so evident in intellectual circles in the 1930s.[221] Thus we are facing here a Czech prince providing a modern interpretation of one of the classic topics in Russian art history.

216• On these images, see Berger 2003; Schellewald 2008.

217• Kondakov 1928–1933, vol. 3, pp. 12–13.

218• See, e.g., the skepticisms of Ščekotov 1914; on the context, see Foletti 2017a, pp. 133–137.

219• Muratoff 1931, for the preface of Focillon, pp. 9–14.

220• On Florenskij, see the collection of essays translated to English in Florensky 2002. See also Strada 1998.

221• For Czechoslovakia see, for example, Med 2004; for France, having an impressive impact on Czechoslovakia see for example Winock 1996, pp. 72–78.

The archives of the Kondakov Institute are full of reminders of the institution's activities aimed at a general audience. We have mentioned the workshops organized by the Princess Jašvil and the regular public lectures given by scholars and enthusiastic laymen. In this sense, *Seminarium* was a very modern institution, which, apart from just carrying out research, considered the sharing of that research with the general public as part of its mission. We must, of course, explain exactly what the term "general public" means when applied to 1930s Prague. While it is true that university-level education was not nearly as widespread then as it is now, we should not forget, either, that during the First Republic, secondary schools took the humanities so seriously that all the elites, even those who received a more technical education (e.g. in medicine or engineering), received a solid grounding in the social sciences, and most educated people remained interested in the humanities long after graduating.[222] In this way, interest in art and culture spread from the capital to the smaller cities, and thence to the countryside.[223] This was the general public that the scholars of the *Seminarium* had in mind for their exhibitions and lectures.

A WORLDWIDE NETWORK

The contemporary reader will be amazed when, upon opening any volume of *Seminarium Kondakovianum*, *Skythika* or *Zōgraphika*, he finds articles by the most important archaeologists, art historians, and historians of the pre-war era, and not only in the field of Byzantine studies. This amazement will only increase if he delves into the correspondence of the Kondakov Institute in the archives of the Department of Art History at the Czech Academy of Sciences in Prague.[224] From East and West, from Japan to the Soviet Union and to the US, scholars corresponded, exchanged ideas, and discussed their research with the members of the *Seminarium*. There are prominent German-speaking scholars, such as Andreas Alföldi, Josef Strzygowski, Friedrich Gerke, Kurt Weitzmann, Oskar Wulff,

222• An interesting reflection about the "technical" intelligentsia and its interest in humanities can be found in Pinto/Lafranconi 2006, p. 233.

223• Emblematic is, e.g., the case of Prostějov, where the intellectual life was in large parts animated by the technical intelligentsia, described in the memoirs of Sergej Machonin, see Machonin 1995.

224• UDU, boxes KI-12 to KI-17.

and Franz Dölger. Charles Diehl, Henri Grégoire, Gabriel Millet, Louis Bréhier, and Paul Perdrizet sent letters from France and Belgium.[225] Ellis H. Minns and David Talbot Rice represent the English-speaking world, and Igor Grabar and Georgij Čubinašvili chime in from the USSR. The Italian Sergio Bettini participated, as did the Armenian émigré Sirarpie Der Nersessian. And, of course, there is a long list of émigrés from the former Russian Empire: André Grabar, Georgij Vernadskij, Mikhail Rostovcev, Aleksandr Vasiliev, etc. There are contacts with the Czechoslovak milieu – for example, with the Byzantinist František Dvorník (1893–1975), as well as with scholars in Bulgaria, Hungary, Serbia, and Romania. This was one of the most impressive scholarly networks established in any field whatsoever between the two wars. The names we have mentioned are just a few of many, perhaps more familiar than the rest for one reason or another. Nearly everybody who was anybody in Byzantine studies or any related field in the years around the Second World War was somehow involved with the Kondakov Institute.

This brings us back to a phenomenon that we mentioned in connection with Nikodim Kondakov. Between the wars, the network of scholars was still small enough that everybody could know everybody else, so that Bernard Berenson could still take a personal interest in promoting Byzantine studies in the US. And supporting a scholarly institution was still considered a prestigious, even aristocratic, activity, so that any scholar with the means was happy to offer financial support as well. The Kondakov Institute benefitted from the fact that it was essentially unique in Europe. Starting in 1924, there would be, of course, the international congresses of Byzantine studies, and other periodicals focusing on Byzantium such as the *Byzantinische Zeitschrift* in Munich, *Byzantion* in Brussels, or the *Vizantijskij Vremennik* in Saint Petersburg (although the latter ceased publication in 1928).[226] These journals, however, were not published by such a large and internationally renowned group of scholars with interests reaching out into every corner of the field.

225• UDU-AV/KI-13 Diehl, C.; KI-13 Grégoire, H.

226• On the role of the first international Byzantine congresses, see Maufroy 2010. On the various journals see e.g. Diehl 1925; Medvedev 1997.

All of this depended on personal ties between Russian scholars who had spread all around the world in that first wave of emigration. Their solidarity – and even family ties, in many cases – played a key role in maintaining the prominence of the Institute. It is no coincidence that Toll' was appointed as head of the excavations at Dura-Europos, even though the campaign was organized by Yale University. His wife Nina, after all, was the sister of Georgij Vernadskij, at that time professor of Russian history at Yale.[227] Moreover, Vernadskij had been the director of the *Seminarium* and a student of the chief excavator at Dura-Europos, Mikhail Rostovcev.[228]

The importance of the *Seminarium* for Byzantinists, and the way it functioned, should now be clear. But why were there so many Byzantinists, and so must interest in Byzantium in the first place? Why was the field so important, in Czechoslovakia and beyond? In the second part of this book we hope to offer some answers to those questions.

ANDRÉ GRABAR, FROM KIEV TO PARIS

André Grabar, born as Andrej Nikolajevič, was one of the most important art historians of the twentieth century **{21}**.[229] An expert in Byzantine, Western, and Russian art, Grabar was considered, in the second half of the century, a sort of "emperor of Byzantine studies".[230] At one point, he was teaching at the prestigious Collège de France and simultaneously held the chair in Byzantine studies at Harvard University.[231] He later abandoned this last post and chose to live out his days in France. His scholarly work, along with that of his many students, remains fundamental in the field. Our present topic, however, is not this post-war Grabar, but rather the young

227• Soničeva 1995.

228• Meyer 2009.

229• In general, on Grabar, see Dufrenne 1990; Maguire 1991; Kitzinger 1990/1992; Dagron 1992; Smirnova 1999a, esp. the various essays from pp. 9–108; Muzj 2005 [1995]; Dagron 2005; Christe 2005; Thierry 2005; Rouillard 2010; Foletti 2012; Serrano Coll 2015; Palladino 2018.

230• This expression is used in the unpublished memoirs of Hans Belting, who met Grabar for the first time in 1959.

231• For Grabar's engagement at Harvard and the decision to leave the chair, see Archives du Collège de France, Fonds André Grabar (FAG) / boîte complémentaire (BC).

21} André N. Grabar

Russian émigré Grabar, who had just escaped the motherland in search of a better life.

Born in Kiev on July 26, 1896 to a family of judges and minor aristocrats, Grabar grew up in the most "Byzantine" city of the Russian Empire.[232] From his memoirs, we know about his fascination for Saint Sophia in Kiev, but when he was a child, the extraordinary church of Saint Michael, built around 1100 and destroyed by the Bolshevik regime in 1932, was still standing as well.[233] The young Grabar was deeply impressed by these monuments and the Orthodox liturgy which was performed there.[234] He finished his standard schooling in 1914, and at first thought of enrolling in the navy, but his eyesight would not permit this.[235] The backup plan was to become a painter, but Grabar soon realized that this would forever remain a hobby, albeit one he would pursue all his life.[236] He finally decided to study art history, first in Kiev, then in Saint Petersburg.

232• For the memoirs of the father, Nikolaj S. Grabar (1852–1924), written in Bulgaria and then in Strasbourg in 1924, see Deligne (n.d.).

233• On the dismantling of Saint Michael's and other monuments of Kiev by the Soviets, see Hewryk 1982.

234• See mainly Grabar 1990. An impression also hinted at by Maguire 1991 and Dagron 2005.

235• ACF/FAG/BC, "Esquisse biographique" (further "Esquisse biographique"), p. 3.

236• *Ibidem*, p. 4.

In the imperial capital, he met Jakov Smirnov (1869–1918) and Dmitrij Ajnalov (1862–1939), students of Nikodim Kondakov.[237] Ajnalov held the chair in Byzantine art at that point, and became one of Grabar's mentors.[238] In Saint Petersburg, Grabar must have also met the old Kondakov, already retired but still very active, and willing to use his home to host private lectures for students and scholars like Ajnalov himself.

We can imagine the general framework of Grabar's education, working his way through Ajnalov's main publications, like his thesis on Late Antique Christian mosaics in Italy, and the influential book that emerged from his second thesis (the equivalent of German habilitation) – *Ellinističeskie osnovy vizantijskogo iskusstva* [The Hellenistic Origins of Byzantine Art].[239] This last volume would become famous in the West two generations later in an English translation by Cyril Mango.[240] Among specialists in Byzantine studies, nearly all of whom could read Russian at that time, Ajnalov's book was one of the key works for understanding Late Antiquity, along with Strzygowski's *Orient oder Rom* (1901) and Riegl's *Spätrömische Kunst-Industrie* (1901).[241] The main thesis of Ajnalov's volume develops one of Kondakov's ideas (which had already been proposed by the Frenchman Jules Labarte in the 1860s): there was clear continuity between the art of Antiquity and Byzantine artistic production.[242] One of the hidden goals of Ajnalov's book was to promote a positive vision of Byzantine art even in circles that only valued art in the "classical" tradition. We can imagine how Grabar, who was already enamored with medieval Russian architecture, absorbed these ideas about Byzantine art.[243]

After the February Revolution, Grabar decided to move to Odessa, a city which would remain in the hands of anti-Bolshevik forces for another three years. There he continued his education at the Imperial New Russian University and attended the lectures of Kondakov,

237• On Ajnalov and Smirnov, see the notices of Khrushkova 2012b, 2012c.

238• Jakubčo 2020.

239• Ajnalov 1900.

240• Ainalov 1961 [1900].

241• Strzygowski 1901; Riegl 1901; on the context, see, e.g., Olin 2000b; Leardi 2002; Elsner 2002, 2020; on the Russian milieu, see also Lidova 2020.

242• Kondakov 1876; Labarte 1864–1866. On Labarte, see Tomasi 2008, 2009.

243• Smirnova 1999b; see also Medvedkova 2016.

who had also found refuge in Odessa. In 1918, Grabar published his first article, dedicated to the topic of his thesis, namely the church of Saint Sophia in Kiev.[244] From documents preserved at the archives of the Collège de France, we know that in 1919 Grabar received permission from the rector of the Imperial New Russian University to leave Odessa for a study trip abroad **{22}**.[245] Officially, therefore, Grabar was not "emigrating", but was only leaving temporarily. This was not unusual. Whenever they could, scholars left the country with similar documents, and some sought to prolong their "research trips" as long as possible in order to keep their options open if and when the political situation in Russia turned in their favor.[246]

Like many émigré scholars, Grabar never returned (except for a brief visit to the Soviet Union after he had become a French citizen), and from 1920 on was forced to construct a new life abroad.[247] On reaching Sofia, Grabar found a job as one of the curators at the local archaeological museum, headed by Bogdan Filov (1883–1945), and carried out research on local "Byzantine" painting from the Middle Ages.[248] In Sofia, he crossed paths once more with Kondakov, who had obtained a teaching post in Bulgaria thanks to Tsar Boris III (and Grabar, in turn, may have obtained his position at the museum through the intervention of his old master). Grabar stayed in Sofia for more than two years, sharing a flat with his friend Konstantin V. Močulskij (1892–1948), another émigré, who later became an eminent professor of theology in Paris.[249] While in Sofia the young Grabar also met his future wife, the medical student Julia Ivanova (?–1977).

During his time in Bulgaria, Grabar travelled through the country with a photographer, making approximately two hundred photographs and gathering enough information for several articles and a bilingual French-Bulgarian book dedicated to the Bojana Church (published in 1924).[250] We will return to Grabar's art-historical

244• Grabar 1918, reprinted and translated to French in Grabar 1968a.

245• ACF/FAG/BC.

246• For the similar cases of Kondakov and Muratov, see Foletti 2017a, p. 69 and Muratova 2010, p. 69.

247• "Esquisse biographique", pp. 13–14.

248• On Filov, see Basciani 2010.

249• "Esquisse biographique", p. 15.

250• Amongst the articles, see, e.g., Grabar 1921, 1921–1922; for the monograph, *Idem* 1924. On this period of Grabar's life, see especially Palladino 2020.

МИНИСТЕРСТВО
НАГО ПРОСВѢЩЕНІЯ

РЕКТОРЪ
оссійскаго Университета.

Дек 1919 года.

№ 3400

Одесса.

БИЛЕТЪ.

Предъявитель сего оставленный при Новороссійскомъ Университетѣ для приготовленія къ профессорскому званію Андрей Николаевичъ Грабар.

командированъ за границу съ научною цѣлью

почему благоволено будетъ въ проѣздѣ г. А. Н. Грабарю чинить свободный и безпрепятственный пропускъ.

Въ удостовѣреніе изложеннаго данъ ему, г. Грабарю сей билетъ за надлежащею подписью и съ приложеніемъ малой университетской печати.

За Ректоръ Новороссійскаго Университета [signature]

Секретарь Совѣта [signature]

22} Travel permission of André Grabar, 1919

politics later, but here we should mention that Grabar's work was perceived (and this is clear in Bogdan Filov's introduction to the book on the Bojana Church) as supporting the idea that Bulgaria was an heir to Byzantine artistic traditions, just like Kondakov's earlier work.

By the time that book came off the press (1924), Grabar was no longer in Bulgaria. He had left in 1922 in search of a job further west. His journey took him first to Czechoslovakia, where he had the pleasure of meeting Kondakov yet again, and then to Germany.[251] In Berlin, he met Adolph Goldschmidt (1863–1944) but did not secure any position.[252] Grabar then decided, in the summer of 1922, to accept an invitation – offered to him by André Mazon (1881–1967) at the encouragement of Grabar's former flatmate Močulskij – to become a lecturer in Russian at the University of Strasbourg.[253] Grabar's fiancée, Julia, as well as his parents, joined him in Strasbourg, but he was never really satisfied by his situation there.[254] From a letter sent to Ajnalov asking for a recommendation, we know that he still hoped to obtain a position teaching art history, something that was nearly impossible given his legal status as a Russian émigré.[255] Around the same time, he was given a function that had little to do with his academic training, but which would have, we believe, great significance for his future: he was elected administrator of the Orthodox community in Strasbourg. In practical terms, this meant that he was in charge of organizing the Orthodox liturgy, each month, for the émigré community, in a space rented from the local Protestant community.[256]

At the end of 1927, his wish to return to the field of art history was finally fulfilled. He was appointed substitute professor of modern art history at the University of Strasbourg. The university was forced to do this because professor Albert Gabriel (1925–1941) was incessantly travelling to Turkey instead of holding his lectures.[257]

251• "Esquisse biographique", p. 45; see also Kyzlasova 1999.

252• "Esquisse biographique", p. 45. On the figure of Goldschmidt, see, e.g., Seidel 2018 with bibliography.

253• "Esquisse biographique", p. 17.

254• *Ibidem*, pp. 19–20.

255• Archives Saint Petersburg, letter from Grabar to Ajnalov, 03.01.1927, see Palladino 2020.

256• "Esquisse biographique", pp. 23–24.

257• Chatelet 1989.

While modern art was not Grabar's specialty, this position allowed him to stabilize his financial situation and to get a foot in the door of the French university system in the precise field that he wanted to work in. New professional possibilities were opened to Grabar when he and his wife became French citizens on April 25, 1928; this had been facilitated by a 1927 change to French naturalization laws.[258] Now his wife could practice medicine in France, and Grabar could be appointed to a more prestigious position at the university. From 1933, then, he gave special lectures on the archaeology and art history of the "European East" – a term which encompassed Byzantium, all Orthodox countries, and those Catholic countries usually ignored by Western scholarship.[259]

In this same period, Grabar was working under the direction of the great Byzantinist Gabriel Millet (1967–1953) on his doctoral dissertation (*thèse de doctorat ès lettres*) and complementary thesis (*thèse de doctorat complémentaire*), both of which were published in 1928, when Grabar was 32 years old {23}.[260] Grabar would later succeed Millet as head of the Department of Byzantine Art and Archaeology at the École Pratique des Hautes Études in Paris. The second great influence on Grabar in this period was Paul Perdrizet (1870–1938), professor in Strasbourg, who was remembered by Grabar as one of his most influential teachers and as a true friend.[261] A letter from Millet to Perdrizet shows that both of them hoped Grabar would remain in France.[262] At this point in his life, Grabar had received a complete education in both Russian and French. Moreover, throughout his career he would benefit from the fact that his education was what we would now call "interdisciplinary". Kondakov and Ajnalov were art historians but with extensive experience in archaeology, and if Millet was an art historian in the traditional sense, Perdrizet had been trained as an archaeologist

258• Archives nationales, BB/11/10719, dossier 50225 X 28. Grabar and his wife took advantage of law of August 10, 1927. See also "Esquisse biographique", p. 24.

259• Études byzantines 1935.

260• Grabar 1928a, 1928b.

261• *Idem* 1938; on Perdrizet, see Provost 2016.

262• *"Si l'on attend mon retour, cela fera novembre, un peu tard, si Grabar veut chercher un enseignement. – À propos, ne pourrions-nous le retenir en France? Ce serait une force pour notre pays si l'on réussissait à lui trouver une maîtrise de conférence dans une Faculté."*, Archives Paul Perdrizet, Université de Lorraine, Nancy, PP. 717, letter of Millet to Perdrizet, 18.04.1925.

specializing in Hellenistic and medieval French objects.[263] At the completion of his doctoral studies, Grabar was, by education and experience, as well prepared for a career in Byzantine studies as anyone could possibly be.

Grabar's very fruitful period in Strasbourg lasted for twelve years. In this time, Grabar was obviously working within the French milieu, but also maintained strong links with the Russian émigré community. He was a member of the *Seminarium Kondakovianum*, regularly contributed to that institution's journal, and also wrote a monograph on the *Sainte Face* of Laon for the *Zōgraphika* series (1931).[264] This book is important, and not only because it is still, to this day, the only monograph about this absolutely crucial object.[265] Grabar produced a book using an extremely advanced methodology, combining an iconographical approach with deep knowledge of historical sources and a particular interest in what we now call "cultural mobility".[266] The book was an important professional milestone for Grabar for another reason: the *Sainte Face* is a "Russian" object which "emigrated", probably in the thirteenth century, to France, where it got an enthusiastic and well-documented reception. Grabar details the welcome the object received within the French kingdom and the history of the *Sainte Face* itself, but also focuses on important details such as the way Western scholars, starting in the seventeenth century, attempted to understand the object's Old Church Slavonic inscriptions. This type of research was particularly suited to Grabar's very specific skills, and it is also tempting to see in Grabar's attention to this particular object a kind of psychological projection: like Grabar himself, the *Sainte Face* had started out in Russia and "made" a home for itself in France. Grabar's book was published not in France, but in Prague, in French and Russian. The book's topic, author, and even place of publication were all balanced between Eastern and Western cultures.

263• *"Scientifiquement, presque tout ce que j'ai porté en moi, à travers toute ma vie, avait pour origine l'enseignement du groupe de savants de Petrograd, et la formation de mon esprit par Paul Perdrizet: le champ de mes intérêts iconographiques et les pensées relatives aux liens entre la vie religieuse et l'art."*, "Esquisse biographique", p. 6.

264• Grabar 1931a.

265• On this historiography of the object since Grabar, see, e.g., Sansterre 2008.

266• See, e.g., Somerset/Watson 2015.

RÉPUBLIQUE FRANÇAISE.

Diplôme de Docteur ès Lettres

Le Ministre de l'Instruction publique,
Vu le Certificat d'aptitude au grade de Docteur ès Lettres accordé le 20 juin 1927
par les Professeurs de la Faculté des Lettres de Strasbourg, Académie de Strasbourg
à M. Grabar André
né à Kiev, département de Russie, le 26 juillet 1896.
Vu l'approbation donnée à ce Certificat par le Recteur de ladite Académie;
Ratifiant le susdit Certificat;
Donne par les présentes, à M. Grabar le Diplôme de Docteur ès Lettres, pour en jouir avec les droits et prérogatives qui y sont attachés par les lois, décrets et règlements.

Fait sous le Sceau du Ministère de l'Instruction publique, le 7 MAI 1929
MINISTÈRE DE L'INSTRUCTION PUBLIQUE
Pour expédition conforme
Le Directeur de l'Enseignement supérieur,

Le Ministre de l'Instruction publique,
Signé: Pierre Marraud

Délivré par le Recteur de l'Académie de Strasbourg le 10 JUIN 1929

Signature de l'impétrant: A. Grabar

23} **Doctoral diploma of André Grabar delivered by the University of Strasbourg, 1929**

The late 1920s saw another important event in Grabar's life – the birth of his two sons, Oleg (1929) and Nicolas (1932). From the unpublished French version of Grabar's memoirs, we get the impression that his years in Strasbourg were calm ones, despite his low salary and occasional struggles with his national identity.[267] Grabar was deeply shaken by the assassination, in May 1932, of the president of the French Republic, Paul Doumer (1857–1932), by the Russian émigré Paul Gorgulov (1895–1932), an event which caused much of France to be suspicious of all Russian émigrés.[268] In a letter to Perdrizet, Grabar reacts to the assassination with both pain and fear, sympathizing on the one hand with the Russian émigré community, but on the other hand writing as a citizen of the French Republic.[269] In the early 1930s, Grabar

267• "Esquisse biographique", pp. 24–25.

268• On the context, see Foshko 2009.

269• *"Vous me connaissez assez, pour avoir deviné les sentiments d'horreur et de honte dans lesquels m'avait plongé la nouvelle du crime abominable. D'ailleurs, la dizaine de Russes que je connais à Strasbourg et qui sont venus me voir hier et aujourd'hui, sont aussi abattus et consternés que moi-même, et la comparaison avec Brest-Litovsk s'imposa à plusieurs d'entre eux. Le sort ne nous épargne aucune épreuve."*, Archives Paul Perdrizet, Université de Lorraine, Nancy, PP. 336, letter of Grabar to Perdrizet, 08.05.1932.

wrote one of his most important books, *L'empereur dans l'art byzantin.* Published in Paris in 1936, this volume is a complex reflection on the visual representation of imperial figures in the Byzantine world.[270] Grabar's thinking about this topic goes beyond his predecessors' in many ways. For one thing, he compares imperial imagery with representations of Christ.[271] Moreover, he also constructs a very precise "evolutionary" theory of Christian art, where images of Christ are direct descendants of Late Antique imperial portraits. Here we clearly sense Kondakov's influence, since he, too, believed that iconography could help explain the development of Mediterranean art. Besides the iconography of the emperor, Grabar talks about how the ruler "performed" his role. Decades before the invention of "performance studies" in art history, Grabar's emperors act both as living individuals and as images. Here again, Grabar is standing on the shoulders of Kondakov, who had been nearly obsessed with the *De Ceremoniis* of Constantine Porphyrogenites.[272]

We believe that this interest in the ritual surrounding the emperor and visual representations of him is one of the most important contributions of Kondakov's school of art history. Grabar developed this line of thought even further: for him, rituals and bodies cannot be dissociated from spaces. Some parts of *L'empereur dans l'art byzantin* even remind us of the work of modern scholars like Alexej Lidov and Bissera Pentcheva.[273] In the last fifteen years, both have written extensively about a new conception of the sacred space as a constant interaction between images, rituals, human bodies, objects, architecture, etc. It is intriguing to try to understand why Grabar was working in that same direction, even if his vocabulary is very different. It is likely no coincidence that Grabar, Lidov, and Pentcheva are all from countries with their cultural roots in Eastern Orthodoxy. Unlike in post-Tridentine Roman Catholicism, where believers are mainly passive spectators of the liturgy, sitting in pews in almost military formation, the Orthodox liturgy supposes the continual movement of the believers, sometimes in coordination with the clergy. Moreover, in the Orthodox liturgy, sacred liturgical

270• Grabar 1936.

271• See Muzj 2005 [1995].

272• Kondakov 1924.

273• E.g., Lidov 2006; Pentcheva 2010.

action is not limited to what is happening around the altar and the ambo, but also includes visual and physical contact with sacred images in various places around the church. During the liturgy, believers touch these images and pray before them. On special occasions, such as during Lent, devotional images take on the role of Christ, and the assembly enters the sepulcher "with him". Those with an experience of the Orthodox liturgy, even its twentieth-century variants, may have a different sensibility towards Christian art in general, and medieval art in particular.[274]

Grabar's approach in *L'empereur dans l'art byzantin*, a book which revitalized the study of Byzantine and medieval art, was rooted in his Orthodox and Russian background. The structure of the book and the space it devotes to Western art, on the other hand, reflect the French milieu in which Grabar was writing. The book's effect is still felt today, and in our last chapter we will discuss it further.

Thanks not just to the inherent qualities of *L'empereur dans l'art byzantin,* but also to the very positive reception it got – nearly thirty reviews of it were published in scholarly journals within months of its release – Grabar was called to teach, starting in 1937, at the École Pratique des Hautes Études, and then to occupy the chair in Byzantine art and archaeology of the most prestigious scholarly institution in France, the Collège de France.[275] In 1938, he moved to Paris to succeed his mentor Gabriel Millet at the École Pratique des Hautes Études, but the promotion did not come at an ideal time. Since the mid-1930s, Europe had been heading for a catastrophe which would not leave Grabar untouched. Grabar served in the French army as an interpreter for the officers' corps from 1939 to 1940.[276] After the French army was defeated in 1941, he attempted to return to "normal life".

Grabar lived, nevertheless, in a city and country occupied by the Nazis, and had to drastically curtail his activities. There is no trace in the archives of him making any research trip between 1941 and

274• Dagron 2005.

275• A list of the reviews can be found in the Archives du Collège de France, with twenty-eight reviews, among them by some of the most famous Byzantinists and scholars of the period. See *infra*, pp. 111–112.

276• "Esquisse biographique", p. 27.

1945, a troubled period which we will analyze more deeply in the last chapter of this book. It seems that, like many other intellectuals under the Nazi occupation (and like Kondakov during the Russian Revolution), Grabar hunkered down, found refuge in his research, and waited for better times to share his ideas with colleagues around the world. It is not as if Grabar ceased entirely to publish his work during the war. Indeed, we have eight articles from those years, on highly varied subjects, from iconographical research on theophanies, to Late Antique architecture, to Egyptian Christian painting. But most of these articles are really reports from talks given at conferences, rather than major efforts of scholarship.[277] During the war Grabar also supervised the publication of several facsimile versions of important manuscripts.[278]

Once France had been liberated, however, Grabar and his peers opened the floodgates. The year 1945 saw a monumental event in the historiography of Byzantine and medieval studies: the inauguration of the *Cahiers archéologiques: Fin de l'Antiquité et Moyen Âge*, with Grabar as the series' editor. Work on assembling the first issue apparently did not commence until after the liberation of Paris in August of 1944, but Grabar notes that it was the fruit of work carried out during the long, dark years before that.[279] Grabar himself published six new articles in 1945 alone.

Then, in 1946, Grabar published a book which revealed what he had been thinking about during the war: *Martyrium. Recherches sur le culte des reliques et l'art chrétien*, published in two large volumes.[280] This may be Grabar's most impressive work, but its reception would be mixed. In the first volume, which was dedicated to architecture, Grabar postulated that architects used a fixed, shared syntax when they erected buildings for the cult of martyrs. Architecture was never at the center of Grabar's thought, and the book was criticized by some specialists in medieval architecture who considered

••••••••••••••••••••••••

277• Grabar 1942, 1944.

278• *Idem* 1943.

279• "[...] *j'ai préparé et mis en marche une collection de recueils qui, sous le titre de Cahiers Archéologiques, offriront des études sur l'archéologie paléo-chrétienne, byzantine et latine du haut Moyen Âge, avec l'accent porté sur des problèmes comparatistes et sur les recherches d'archéologie religieuse et 'idéologique'. Le premier Cahier paraîtra en Octobre; le 2e est en composition.*", Grabar 1944–1945, p. 438: letter of Grabar of 1945 added as a note by Henri Grégoire.

280• Grabar 1946.

his approach too general and therefore imprecise, arguing that the time for big "syntheses" was past.[281] This debate overshadowed the second volume, a masterful reflection on the cult of martyrs, images, spaces, and what we would today call "performance". Here Grabar once again stressed the role of the face to face encounter with images. The fundamental question, which Grabar had touched on in *L'empereur dans l'art byzantin* and now brought to the foreground, was this: why did Christianity renounce three-dimensionality – whether in sculpture or illusionistic painting – in favor of the bidimensional image? Grabar suggested that the answer lay in their way of perceiving images, one which emerged and was developed in the neo-platonic milieu around figures such as Plotinus. Grabar had already dedicated an article to the interaction between philosophy and visual culture, and even though he did not believe in any overarching "theory of images", he did think that mentalities and modes of visual representation were complementary.[282]

We know very little about Grabar's personal life or thoughts during his first years in Paris. His archives in Paris contain only scholarly documents and correspondence, plus a few pictures, so we can only guess at how his personal feelings affected the direction he took his professional life in. His memoirs concentrate on his youth, so we have little to go on for his years in Paris. Grabar's humility also works against us. Even in an article dedicated to French Byzantinology during the occupation, he gives us no personal information.[283]

It would be nice to know what Grabar was thinking during the war, because just as soon as it ended, he assumed the leadership of an astonishing revival in the study of Byzantine and medieval art, a movement by no means limited to France. The *Cahiers archéologiques* played a major role in this revival. From the very inception of this journal, its goal was to unite two fields that had almost always been considered separate: Byzantine studies, and scholarship on Western culture from Late Antiquity to the end of the Middle Ages.

It is difficult not to see, in this focus, a continuation of the work of the *Seminarium Kondakovianum*. As we have noted, Grabar had been

281 • See the positive review by Krautheimer 1953 and the later reception by Ward-Perkins 1966. Grabar responded to some of the criticism, see Grabar 1968b. See also Wharton 1990.

282 • Grabar 1945; on this text, see Palladino 2018.

283 • Grabar 1944–1945.

deeply involved in the *Seminarium*, and had even written an article for the last issue of the *Annales de l'Institut Kondakov* published in Belgrade in 1940.[284] He must have been aware, too, of the decline of the Kondakov Institute after the disaster in Belgrade and the situation in Prague after 1945, a dramatic moment which we will describe at length later.[285] The first *Cahiers archéologiques* were published in October 1945, at a moment when almost no one expected a rebirth of the *Annales* of the Kondakov Institute. It would appear, then, that Grabar's *Cahiers* were his attempt to continue Kondakov's legacy, only now, the project went far beyond the international community of Russian émigrés. Grabar, of course, was an émigré, but his new team of colleagues were not. From 1952, the French archaeologist Jean Hubert (1902–1994), a specialist in Western medieval art – particularly from the period of the migrations – would join Grabar in his efforts.[286] The project had become truly European, even in the composition of its editorial board, and the fact that the journal focused on the "long-neglected" period bridging Late Antiquity and the Middle Ages was duly remarked in reviews of the first issue.[287]

André Grabar's life up to the end of the Second World War makes a fascinating comparison with the lives of the émigrés who settled in Prague and shows that the first wave of Russian emigration to the West took many different forms. Unlike the scholars of the *Seminarium*, who were supported as part of the Russian Action, Grabar was on his own. Moreover, while the aim of the Russian Action was to preserve Russian culture, the French authorities expected integration and assimilation. In Grabar's case, the result was magnificent. His legal "move" from East to West, i.e. his requesting French citizenship, was mirrored by the shift in his scholarly interests, where "Byzantine" topics were soon joined by Western ones. Grabar started as a Russian scholar dealing with the Eastern Orthodox heritage, but became a medievalist investigating both the eastern and western parts of the Mediterranean. This change is evident if we compare *L'empereur dans l'art byzantin* (1936) with *Martyrium* (1946). The earlier work still treats the lands of the Eastern Orthodox Church as something separate, but in the later book, Grabar treats the entire

284• Grabar 1940.

285• See *infra*, pp. 141ff.

286• On Hubert, Erlande-Brandenburg 1995.

287• Courcelle 1946; Rolland 1946.

Christian Mediterranean as a single historical and cultural space. One could argue that the experience of emigration and acculturation caused Grabar to perceive medieval art differently. It is not that he suppresses his Eastern origins, but he enlarges and enriches them in a way that no Russian scholar had done before.

Grabar's experience of emigration enabled him to understand that many historical divisions were, in truth, little more than historiographical constructions. Grabar's vision would not be an easy one for scholars or intellectuals to accept once the world had been divided anew by the Cold War. Many preferred to see the historical East and West divided, like the Soviet bloc and the West.

2/ BYZANTIUM AND DEMOCRACY

This second chapter will focus on the scholarly work of both the Kondakov Institute and André Grabar between the wars. We will try to understand how these scholars' flight to democratic countries may have influenced their research on Byzantium. This question arises as soon as we remember that, as we have shown in the first chapter, Byzantium played a large part in the self-definition of the Russian imperial identity, and that culture and history unabashedly served that empire's rulers. The relevance of the cultural history of the Eastern Roman Empire to the culture and politics of democratic countries such as Czechoslovakia or France, on the other hand, was not entirely clear when Russian émigrés first arrived in those countries.

Before continuing, let us describe our methods for this chapter. Considering the very nature of the books and periodicals published by the Kondakov Institute, one would not expect to find an absolute consistency in their historiographical orientation. Scholars from all around the world contributed, representing different nations and varied intellectual and political perspectives. Moreover, even within the membership of the Institute, there were specialists in different fields, and some prominent members living far from Czechoslovakia, as we have seen with Vernadskij and Ostrogorskij. We will therefore look only at the journal *Seminarium Kondakovianum* and the later *Annales de l'Institut Kondakov*. Moreover, we will look not at individual contributors, but rather at the general vision of the editors and the themes of the work published. We will also consider the way the Institute presented itself to the public and to the scholarly world, especially in the regular reports published for its American scholars and supporters. We thereby hope to see where the Institute's intellectual activities fit in the Czechoslovak and global context.

André Grabar's work will be approached differently. Here we only need to evaluate the writings of one Russian émigré scholar who became part of the French academic world almost immediately. He stayed in contact with other Russian émigré scholars, but compared to the members of the Kondakov Institute, he was much more isolated, since there was no equivalent institution for Russian émigrés in France. The backbone of the present chapter will be Grabar's most important interwar monographic, *L'empereur dans l'art byzantin*. We will examine where Grabar's interaction with French politics and society is reflected in his writing, and where his Russian and Orthodox background. We will then be in a position to compare the way emigration affected this individual with the way it affected an entire institution for Russian émigrés, the Kondakov Institute.

THE *SEMINARIUM KONDAKOVIANUM* AND INTERWAR CZECHOSLOVAKIA

If we thumb through the pages of the *Seminarium Kondakovianum*, a periodical which would later change its name to the *Annales de l'Institut Kondakov*, the first thing that strikes us is the publication's deep debt to Kondakov himself. Some of his unpublished work was immediately printed, and soon his memoirs made their appearance.[1] But long after that, there was an extremely consistent editorial policy: with very few exceptions, the journal concentrates on subjects closely related to Kondakov's work. A large portion of the work published is thus dedicated to Russian medieval art and painting, while Byzantine history and Byzantine cultural history receive much attention as well.[2] There are also many articles linked with the nomadic tribes of the steppes and their art and culture.[3] The leitmotiv of these latter texts is the influence of the art of these tribes

1 • See Kondakov 1931; this includes individual reports of Kondakov's lectures in Prague, e.g., Masaryková 1931.

2 • See, e.g., Ostrogorskij 1927; Ajnalov 1928; Wulff 1929; Beljaev 1930; Diehl 1931; Born 1932; Myslivec 1932a; Ostrogorsky 1933; Grabar 1935; Weitzmann 1936; Vasiliev 1937; Dvorník 1938; Grabar 1940.

3 • See, e.g., Kalitinskij 1928; Beljaev 1929; Rasovskij 1933; Anderson 1937.

on cultures from Asia to Central Europe, and thence to the south and west, ultimately linking Nomadic art with the Byzantine Empire. Noteworthy is the attention paid to many different techniques and media, not just "art" in the Vasarian tradition, but also textiles, jewelry, enamels – or what we still sometimes call the "minor arts".[4] All of these characteristics of the journal mirror Nikodim Kondakov's areas of interest and methodology.[5]

In the preceding chapter we discussed the general reorientation of Kondakov's scholarship once he reached Czechoslovakia, a tendency which carry over into the pages of the publications of the Institute founded in his memory. Two obvious factors pushed Kondakov and his circle towards the study of the nomadic tribes, the strongest of which was the political and ethnic identity of the new Czechoslovak state. The Austro-Hungarian Empire, from which Czechoslovakia emerged, had supported research into imperial art and imagery. Margaret Olin and others have examined the *fin de siècle* writings of Alois Riegl and Franz Wickhoff, who seem to have subconsciously projected their Austro-Hungarian political surroundings into their investigation of the late Roman art.[6] Most Czechoslovaks – whose state was based on democratic values – had no interest in this kind of work. Moreover, the Czech, Moravian, and Slovak lands had never truly belonged to the "Byzantine world", so there was no obvious reason for interest in Byzantine or Russian medieval art. One of the main aims of Czechoslovak art history was to help build a proper national narrative,[7] and in the preceding chapter we discussed how Kondakov was explicitly asked to teach about nomadic Slavic tribes.[8] It was taken for granted that these common roots in the age of the nomadic tribes could be used to promote Slavic unity in the twentieth century, within the borders of Czechoslovakia and beyond.

We have also mentioned Eurasianism, an intellectual movement which was born before the Revolution in Russia but reached its apogee in first-wave émigré communities around the world. The idea

4• For the notion of the "minor arts" in general, see the volume by Hourihane 2012; for these topics in *Seminarium Kondakovianum*, see, e.g., Kalitinskij 1928; Beljaev 1929.

5• Foletti 2017a, pp. 171–229.

6• On the Viennese situation and Late Antiquity, see, e.g., Olin 2000b; Elsner 2002, 2020.

7• Foletti/Palladino 2019, with further bibliography.

8• See above, pp. 32–33.

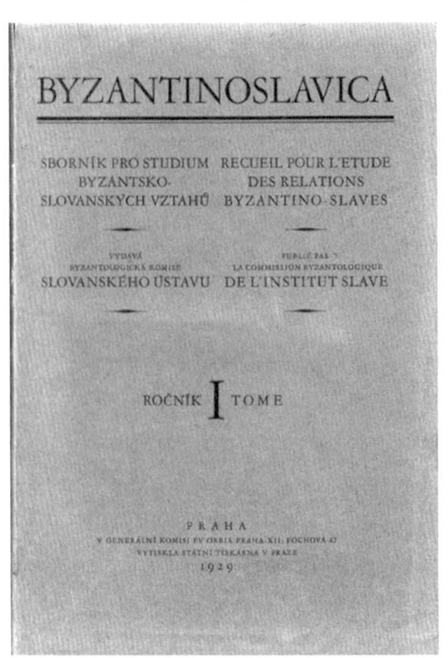

BYZANTINOSLAVICA

SBORNÍK PRO STUDIUM BYZANTSKO-SLOVANSKÝCH VZTAHŮ

RECUEIL POUR L'ETUDE DES RELATIONS BYZANTINO-SLAVES

VYDÁVÁ BYZANTOLOGICKÁ KOMISE SLOVANSKÉHO ÚSTAVU

PUBLIÉ PAR LA COMMISSION BYZANTOLOGIQUE DE L'INSTITUT SLAVE

ROČNÍK I TOME

PRAHA

V GENERÁLNÍ KOMISI FY ORBIS PRAHA-XII, FOCHOVA 62

VYTISKLA STÁTNÍ TISKÁRNA V PRAZE

1929

24} Frontispiece of *Byzantinoslavica*, I (1929)

was especially popular in Prague, where art historians, historians, linguists, and philologists aspired to a transnational identity which could replace the old and quickly disappearing Russia.[9] It is worth remembering that three of the key figures in the founding of the *Seminarium Kondakovianum* were Vernadskij, Toll', and Kalitinskij, all of whom were involved in Eurasianism to some degree.

But what of the continuing study of Byzantium itself? Articles about Byzantium continued to be published in the pages of *Seminarium Kondakovianum,* and this would be so regardless of Czechoslovak politics, since many of the contributors were not resident there. A glance at the list of contributing scholars shows Germans, Austrians, Frenchmen, and of course Russian émigrés from all around the world.[10] The journal managed to remain essentially untouched by the simmering German-vs.-Slavic tensions which infected interwar politics in Czechoslovakia and elsewhere.[11] The *Seminarium*'s harmony and goodwill are all the more remarkable when we consider that Kondakov himself had become polemical when dealing with Germanic and Slavic nomads.[12]

9• See above, pp. 43–44.

10• E.g., Wulff 1929; Diehl 1931; Born 1932; Myslivec 1932a; Grabar 1935; Weitzmann 1936; Dvorník 1938; Grabar 1940.

11• Němec 2017.

12• Kondakov 1929, p. 61.

It may also be surprising that of the scholars who contributed articles about Byzantium to the *Seminarium Kondakovianum*, several were Czechs. The nomadic tribes may have been a trendier topic in Czechoslovak academic circles in the 1920s, and one that more obviously fit with efforts to establish a national identity, but if we probe deeper, we find that interest in Byzantium persisted. In fact, so many scholars in interwar Czechoslovakia were studying Byzantium that the Czechoslovak government created its own journal dedicated to the history, art, and culture of the Eastern Roman Empire: *Byzantinoslavica: Recueil pour l'étude des relations byzantino-slaves* **{24}**.[13]

SEMINARIUM KONDAKOVIANUM, BYZANTINOSLAVICA, AND THE CYRILLO-METHODIAN TRADITION

Whereas Czechoslovaks' enthusiasm for the nomadic tribes is easy to explain, why would they care about Byzantium? As it turns out, their interest in Byzantium was related to the Pan-Slavic tradition that had taken root in the Czech and Slovak lands. It was in Prague, in the mid-nineteenth century, that the first Pan-Slavic congress took place,[14] and belief in the common Christian heritage of all Slavic nations, begun by the missionary activities of Cyril and Methodius, was widespread in the Czech lands in the late nineteenth and early twentieth centuries **{25}**.[15] For Czechoslovakia and Great Moravia, the Cyrillo-Methodian tradition had a special value, since it was believed that Great Moravia had united the ancestors of modern Czechs and Slovaks. Thus, in 1925, we read, in the first volume of the periodical *Morava*:

> "*At the founding of the Czechoslovak Republic, a proposal was made that our new state should be named, for historical reasons, Great Moravia, since from the geographical point of view it almost renewed the borders of the Great Moravian realm of Rastislav and Svatopluk.*"[16]

---

13 • Lovino 2018, pp. 46–50.

14 • Haselsteiner 2000.

15 • Lustigová 2007, pp. 101–118. Moreover, on this tradition, see Mareš 2000; Malíř 2016.

16 • *"Při založení Československé republiky vyskytl se návrh, aby nový náš stát byl pojmenován z historických důvodů Velkou Moravou, poněvadž se v něm zeměpisně skoro obnovily hranice staré Velkomoravské říše Rastislavovy a Svatoplukovy."*, *Morava*, 1 (1925), p. 142.

25} *Dědictví otců zachovej nám, Pane!* [Lord, preserve the heritage of our fathers!], postcard from Velehrad in nine Slavic languages, Methoděj Melichárek publisher, 1920s

It was commonly believed that Great Moravia had largely overlapped with the territories of Czechoslovakia, and the Cyrillo-Methodian tradition meant that the new state could be seen as a kind of spiritual heir to the Eastern Roman Empire.[17] For scholars like Jaroslav Bidlo, Miloš Weingart, and František Dvorník – all with connections to the Kondakov Institute – Byzantium was the catalyst for the Christianization and acculturation of the "Slavs".[18] Starting long before the collapse of Austria-Hungary, and continuing through the two decades of the First Czechoslovak Republic, the Byzantine heritage was perceived as a fundamental part of the identity of the Slavic nations. In retrospect, this sounds dangerously similar to the ideas of Charles Diehl (1859–1944), who, in his *Byzance: Grandeur et décadence* (1920), took a "colonial" view of the Byzantine Christianization of the Slavic "nations":

> " *With its powerful hands, Byzantium kneaded all these barbarian tribes into nations. It was Byzantium which 'from these Slavic, Bulgarian, Magyar, and*

17• E.g., Pekař 1922, pp. 12–14.

18• See, e.g., Bidlo 1917; Weingart 1922–1923; Dvorník 1926, 1933. See also Jančárková/Gagen 2017.

Varangian hordes made Christian Serbia, Croatia, Bulgaria, Hungary, and Russia'. [...] *Without Byzantium, these peoples would be ignorant of almost all their past, just as they would be completely ignorant of civilization.*"[19]

For Czech scholars, of course, the tone of this was all wrong, but they implicitly agreed that Byzantium had been fundamental for the creation of Slavic civilization. Their emphasis on the Byzantine heritage of Slavic civilization was also part of their efforts to distinguish Slavic culture from German culture, and to put the former on a level with the latter. This is what Jaroslav Kadlec (1911–2004) was getting at when he wrote:

"*Other Slavic tribes were luckier. They entered the Latin Church, thus joining the Western cultural milieu. But they maintained their nationality. To this group belong all the Western Slavs, such as Czechs, Slovaks, and Poles. The Christianization of the Czechoslovak tribes was attempted in the ninth century by many missionaries. They arrived, according to the Old Slavic Legend of Cyril, 'from Germany, Italy, and Greece'. In the end, however, our ancestors joined the Christian faith thanks to the brothers from Thessalonica, Cyril and Methodius. The golden key to the heart of the prince of Great Moravia, Rostislav* [...] *was a great novelty introduced by the apostles, that is, the use of the Slavic language in the liturgy.*"[20]

The story of Cyril and Methodius and their impact on the Slavs was significant to parts of the Czechoslovak intelligentsia, including some Catholics like Dvorník and Kadlec, who both happened to be Catholic priests. It was also, in theory, something which should have interested Russian émigrés as well. But if we search for the topic in the pages of *Seminarium Kondakovianum*, we find no explicit reference to the tradition, not even in the text which Dvorník published

19• *"De ses mains puissantes, Byzance a pétri toutes ces tribus barbares pour en former des nations. C'est elle qui 'de ces hordes slaves, bulgares, magyares, varègues, a fait la Serbie, la Croatie, la Bulgarie, la Hongrie, la Russie chrétiennes'.* [...] *Sans Byzance, tous ces peuples ignoreraient presque tout de leur passé, comme sans elle ils auraient longtemps tout ignoré de la civilisation."*, Diehl 1920, pp. 293, 295.

20• *"Jiné slovanské kmeny byly šťastnější. Vstoupili sice do církve latinské a dostaly se tak do kulturní oblasti západní, ale svou národnost si zachovali. Do této skupiny patří všichni ostatní západní Slované, totiž Češi, Slováci a Poláci. O pokřesťanění kmenů československých se pokoušeli ve stol. 9. četní misionáři, přicházející, jak praví staroslovanská legenda Cyrilova, z 'Němec, Vlach i Řek', ale vnitřně přilnuli naši předkové ke křesťanské víře zásluhou soluňských bratří sv. Cyrila a Metoděje. Zlatým klíčem k srdci velkomoravského knížete Rostislava* [...] *byla velkolepá novota sv. věrozvěsty zavedená, užívání slovanského jazyka v bohoslužbě."*, Kadlec 1946, p. 10.

in the journal.[21] This can be partially explained by the fact that the original Pan-Slavic movement, created and developed in Central Europe, did not put Russia at the centre of the Slavic world.[22] What is more, by the time of the First Republic, there were actually two competing visions of what Russia's role in the new world should be[23] – Masaryk's vision was a pragmatic one, as against Kramář's more idealistic vision with its basis in the Pan-Slavic movement.[24] We know in retrospect that the pragmatic variant won the day.

What, then, was the position of the *Seminarium* regarding the importance of the Cyrillo-Methodian heritage and Pan-Slavism? In order to give a good answer to this question, it will be useful to look more closely at the local "competition" in the field of Byzantine studies, namely the Slavonic Institute and its journal *Byzantinoslavica*. Lubor Niederle, the director of this institute, had been one of the scholars behind Kondakov's invitation to Prague in 1922 **{26}**. Later, the institution even became one of the financial sponsors of the Kondakov Institute, and the two institutions often worked together.[25] In April 1933, for example, members of the Kondakov Institute sent their publications to an event organized by the Czechoslovak Union of Slavonic Societies in Mladá Boleslav.[26] But the journal created by the Slavonic Institute had a different purpose from the *Seminarium Kondakovianum,* and the difference is announced in the publication's name. In the first issue of *Byzantinoslavica*, published in 1929, the editors clearly expressed the thesis that it was impossible to understand Slavic cultures without a proper analysis of their relationship to the Byzantine and post-Byzantine world. In the introduction to that first issue, we read that:

> "*In 1928, the president of the Czechoslovak Republic, T. G. Masaryk, who had thoroughly investigated, in his own scholarly works, the Byzantine elements in the mentality of the Slavic world, gave impetus to the creation, in Prague, of a special organization for Byzantino-Slavic studies. The latter was set up not*

21• Dvorník 1938.

22• Heimann 2009, pp. 20–47.

23• See above, p. 30.

24• Lustigová 2007, pp. 101–118, 184–208.

25• The regular support of the Slavonic Institute is attested in all the reports of the Kondakov Institute published for the American public, see *Report* 1932–1937.

26• *Report* 1934, p. 4.

26} Lubor Niederle

only to gather and support Czech scholarship in this field, but also to facilitate cooperation between Slavs and non-Slavs."[27]

This is, without a doubt, a political statement. *Byzantinoslavica* was to develop Masaryk's ideas of the relationship between Byzantium and the Slavs. The project was also firmly rooted in the Czech academic world (or "Czechoslovak" as the First Republic would have it), with four of the seven founding members being Czechs.[28] It was to be printed at the "national printing house".[29] For Masaryk, then, investigating the relationship between Byzantium and the Slavs was a patriotic duty for scholars in the new country, just recently born out of the ashes of the Austro-Hungarian Empire. Ethnic Germans, of course, were left out of this effort, and this is just one more manifestation of an attitude that turned out to be one of the weaknesses of the First Republic.[30] Czechs and Slovaks, if taken

27• "*R. 1928 president Republiky československé T. G. Masaryk, jenž se ve svých vědeckých pracích hluboce zabýval studiem byzantských prvků v myšlenkovém světě slovanském, dal podnět k tomu, aby byl v Praze vytvořen orgán pro studia byzantsko-slovanská, který by nejen sdružoval a podporoval českou vědeckou práci v tomto směru, nýbrž získával také součinnost odborníků slovanských i neslovanských.*", Bidlo *et al.* 1929, p. I.

28• Jaroslav Bidlo, František Dvorník, Karel Kadlec, Aleksandr Kalitinskij, Mathias Murko, Nikolaj Okuněv, Miloš Weingart. After the death of Kadlec, he was replaced by Theodor Saturnik. For the "Czech" identity of multicultural Czechoslovakia, see Němec 2017.

29• Bidlo *et al.* 1929, p. II.

30• Heimann 2009, chap. 3.

together, did indeed constitute a majority of the inhabitants, but large minorities – Germans, Hungarians, Poles, and Ruthenians – felt marginalized.[31] Few Czech intellectuals saw any problem with the "Slavic" domination of the country, or indeed with the idea that membership in their "nation" should coincide with membership in the Slavic "race". Before the Second World War, however, this would be still part of the nineteenth-century national liberal legacy. Such a situation would be radically transformed during the years of the Protectorate, when, reacting towards the Nazi racism, Czechoslovakia would react formulating nationalistic theories as well. This would lead, in 1945, to the expulsion of the German components of the population. It was, however, not long before the "Slavic" Slovaks and Ruthenians began to resent the prominence of Czechs in the country.[32]

While generous in his support for such overtly "Slavic" scholarship, Masaryk was aware of the dangers it brought. The complexity of his thought is evident in the fact that besides *Seminarium Kondakovianum* and *Byzantinoslavica*, he also backed a journal called *Germanoslavica*.[33] The delicacy of the situation in Central Europe was obvious to any keen observer, and Masaryk, before the collapse of the Habsburg state, had even proposed a federal model for the empire (with the leading role played by the Slavs, of course).[34] Concerning Czech history, we should, however, observe divergent tendencies: Masaryk's reading of the "Czech idea" is constructed around a local and national tradition, starting with the Hussite revolt and going through the Protestant tradition until the nineteenth century "Czech National Revival". On the contrary, Josef Pekař (1870–1937), one of the most prominent scholars of the interwar period, was proposing a much more transcultural framework.[35] In his *Smysl českých dějin* [The Meaning of Czech History], Pekař argued that, unlike the previous generation with its strongly Pan-Slavic bent, his generation understood the history of the country as one of "positive"

31• Heimann 2009, pp. 48–86; Němec 2017.

32• Heimann 2009, pp. 48–86.

33• On the purpose of the journal, published from 1931–1939, and rekindled in 1994, see Měšťan 1994.

34• For a general reflection by the future president, and the diverse "options", see Masaryk 2016 [1918/1920].

35• Hanzal 2002.

foreign influences.[36] One of those influences in the early history of the country, he notes explicitly, was Byzantium. Pekař was very influential in shaping the historical identity of the new country, especially through his school textbook entitled *Dějiny československé* [Czechoslovak History] (1922). The part dedicated to contacts with the "Byzantine" world is brief and factual, but Pekař's position is coherent. Even if Masaryk and Pekař were not agreeing on this topic, it is evident that both understood the necessity of seeing Czechoslovakia in a more complex way.[37] Unlike Kramář, they understood Czechoslovakia as something more complex than a simple "Slavic" nation-state.[38]

Byzantinoslavica was not, then, as ethnocentric as one might expect. Its purpose, at least in Masaryk's mind, was to publish research into Slavic culture and identity from a broader, transcultural perspective. This research would not only help justify the existence of Czechoslovakia but would also lend intellectual support to the idea that the country had a special role to play in Europe – that of mediator between cultures. Seen from this perspective, the two journals of Byzantine studies published in Prague complemented each other. That is the way scholars seem to have perceived them at the time, since there were many who participated in both projects. One of the most important figures in the Kondakov Institute, Kalitinskij, was also a founding member of *Byzantinoslavica*,[39] and Kondakov Institute members such as Marija A. Andrejeva or Beljaev contributed to *Byzantinoslavica* as well.[40] Andrejeva, in fact, was directly involved in editing *Byzantinoslavica*.[41] In the other direction, two of the leading contributors to *Byzantinoslavica*, František Dvorník and Nikolaj Okuněv, also had articles published in *Seminarium Kondakovianum*.[42]

A look at the articles published by each of these journals will give us a firmer idea of their editorial policies and how each responded to the political and intellectual context around them.

36• Pekař 1929, pp. 8–9.

37• *Idem* 1922, pp. 12–14.

38• Lustigová 2007, pp. 184–208.

39• Bidlo *et al.* 1929, p. II.

40• Andreeva 1929; Beljaev 1930.

41• Burgmann 2001, p. 29.

42• E.g., Okuněv 1929, 1936; Dvorník 1938. On the relationship between the two periodicals and their contributors, see Lovino 2018.

Between 1927 and 1940, *Seminarium Kondakovianum* published 150 articles. The greatest number, 63, were devoted to Byzantium itself, about 40 to interactions between the Byzantines and the Slavic world, and 30 to the nomadic tribes. A majority were written in Russian – 89, to be precise – with the remainder mostly in French and German (about 25 each) or English (13). There was, in this whole period, but one article in Czech, written by Josef Myslivec.[43] Between 1929 and 1946, *Byzantinoslavica* published 106 articles. Ninety-three were dedicated to interactions between the Slavic and Byzantine worlds, only eleven to "Byzantium" proper, and the other three to Moravian topics. As for the languages of these articles, almost half were written in Russian, and a bit more than a quarter in Czech or Slovak. The remainder were in French (11), German (8), or other Slavic languages – Bulgarian, Polish, and Serbian (13 in total). We can see from this overview that the target audience and the topics of the two journals overlapped less than one would expect, given the fact that many of the same scholars were involved in both.

On the whole, *Seminarium Kondakovianum* had a very "transcultural" approach, covering topics from a wide swath of Asia and Europe, from Mongolia to the Western Roman Empire, with the "Empire of Constantinople" and the art of the nomadic tribes as its twin nuclei. Byzantium was perceived and presented as a transcultural entity, and the tribes are presented as a physical and cultural link between Asia and Europe. This approach guaranteed that *Seminarium Kondakovianum*, and the Institute in general, would be known all over the world, and their fame is confirmed by the large number of scholars from all around the world who contributed to the journal. The impressive international visibility of the Institute is emphasized in the reports of the Institute printed for its supporters from the United States of America. Besides the numerous international members mentioned into the first chapter of the present book, there is a list of 60 institutions with which the Kondakov Institute was exchanging publications in 1932.[44] That number would increase by another 10 by 1937.[45]

••••••••••••••••••••••••

43• Myslivec 1932a.

44• *Report* 1932.*

45• *Report* 1933–1937.

In his correspondence with the Institute from the late 1920s and early 1930s, Wolfgang Born (1893–1949), a pupil of the Austrian Josef Strzygowski, made clear that he perceived *Seminarium Kondakovianum* to be a journal of what would now be called "transcultural studies".[46] Strzygowski himself even had one article published in it, something which goes to show how *Seminarium Kondakovianum* enabled scholars of diametrically opposed approaches to engage in discussions within its pages.[47] Jaś Elsner sees Strzygowski as a sort of pioneer of this kind of transcultural studies, and regards him, despite his subsequent flirtation with Nazi ideology, as a precursor of the scholars who adopt a "transcultural" approach today.[48] If we accept this classification, then we are looking at a scholarly institution for Russian émigrés that was in the vanguard of research in the humanities, as well as one that gave scholars an outlet for ground-breaking and sometimes competing theories.

This wide geographical coverage and relatively radical approach was, we think, the result of the way the *Seminarium Kondakovianum* focused on what we now call "material culture", i.e. the study of archaeological finds and artistic objects such as fibulae, textiles, but also painted panels **{27a–c}**. There were, obviously, purely historical articles in *Seminarium Kondakovianum* as well, but research into visual and material culture predominated, mirroring the type of scholarship advocated by Nikodim Kondakov himself.

Byzantinoslavica was quite different. The thematic focus was quite narrow, but topics were studied using many different approaches, from philology to art history, history, literary studies, and codicology. Even pioneering linguists like Trubeckoj and Jakobson contributed to *Byzantinoslavica*.[49] We have already mentioned the political purpose of founding *Byzantinoslavica* and have noted its implicit "philo-Slavism". But, paradoxically, the journal was not simplistically nationalistic. Its approach was more subtle, presenting the Slavic identity as a dominant element in medieval cultures. One other thing to notice about *Byzantinoslavica* is that, at least in the beginning, most of its articles were published in Russian. During the

46• UDU-AV/KI-12, Born, W., e.g., the letter of the 08.08.1931, see Palladino 2019.

47• Strzygowski 1928.

48• Elsner 2001, 2020. Regarding Strzygowski and his legacy, see Foletti/Lovino 2018.

49• E.g., Jakobson 1932.

филигранью, на перекрестьи (рис. 26). Фибула имѣетъ поперечную перекладину, на которую намотана пружина, съ двумя гранеными головками.[306] Наконецъ послѣдняя, происходящая оттуда же, отличается отъ предыдущей тѣмъ, что ея пластинка не заканчивается у пружины, а проходитъ далѣе и нѣсколько расширяется, благодаря чему фибула пріобрѣтаетъ форму креста съ расширенными концами (рис. 27).[307] Сравнительно тонкая работа, украшеніе шлифованными камнями и примѣненіе зерни и филиграни, позволяютъ считать эти фибулы византійскими, тѣмъ болѣе, какъ мы видѣли, въ предѣлахъ имперіи фибулы этой конструкціи были въ ходу.

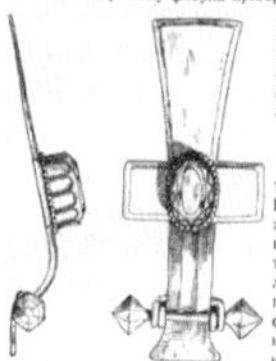

Рис. 27.

*

Остается группа фибулъ двупластинчатаго типа, который несомнѣнно существовалъ въ Византіи и который мы знаемъ и по изображеніямъ, однако, не вполнѣ яснымъ, обосновывать какія либо сужденія на которыхъ очень трудно. Поэтому ограничусь только ихъ бѣглымъ перечнемъ. Такъ, на упоминавшейся уже пластинкѣ слоновой кости Трирскаго собора, фибулы нѣкоторыхъ фигуръ, напр. придворныхъ свиты императора (рис. 28, b) или кучера на повозкѣ (рис. 28, c) несомнѣнно передаютъ двупластинчатый типъ,[308] а фибула самого императора нѣсколько напоминаетъ фибулу т. наз. „готскаго" типа (рис. 28, a).[309] Возможно, что подобныя же фибулы изображены и на монетахъ Ираклія съ подвѣсками (табл. XIII, 1, 2), и Льва Мудраго, безъ подвѣсокъ (табл. XIII, 3).[310] На одной изъ дощечекъ ящичка собора въ Troyes, на изображенныхъ конныхъ императорскихъ фигурахъ мы довольно ясно видимъ типъ двупластинчатой фибулы, приближающійся къ т. наз. „готскому", т. е. симметричный по одной оси. Фибула состоитъ изъ полукруглой передней пластинки и закругленной ножки (рис. 28).[311] Сопоставляя это съ монетой Льва VI (табл. XIII, 3)

[306]) Отч. Арх. Ком. за 1904 г., стр. 130.

[307]) См. статью А. П. Калитинскаго, въ S. K. I, стр. 209—210 и табл. XVIII. Также его статью въ Mélanges-Uspensky.

[308]) Въ формѣ симметричной по 2-мъ осямъ, примѣръ хотя бы фибула изъ Charnaye, Cabrol, V, 2. fig. 4450. Фибулы такого типа извѣстны и изъ Италіи, см. N. Aberg. Die Goten und Langobarden in Italien. Объ устройствѣ и развитіи типа двупластинчатой фибулы см. статью А. П. Калитинскаго въ S. K. II, стр. 279—308.

[309]) B. Delbrueck, Cons. D., № 67. Датируется она началомъ VII вѣка, что, однако, м. б. оспариваемо. Объ этомъ въ слѣд. очеркѣ.

[310]) Wroth, I pl. XXIII, 13; II pl. LI, 8.

[311]) Dalton: East. Ch. art. pl. XXXVIII. Обычно относятъ этотъ памятникъ къ XI в., см. Ch. Diehl, Manuel II f. 650, хотя несомнѣнно онъ старше. H. Peirce et R. Tylor, o. c. относятъ его къ серединѣ X в. Отмѣтимъ, что тѣ же фибулы повторяются и на всей группѣ памятниковъ (створка диптиха въ Дрезденѣ, триптихъ въ Harbaville, триптихъ въ Берлинѣ) ibidem, pl. XVII,2, 3, XVIII, 2, XIX, 2.

XVI

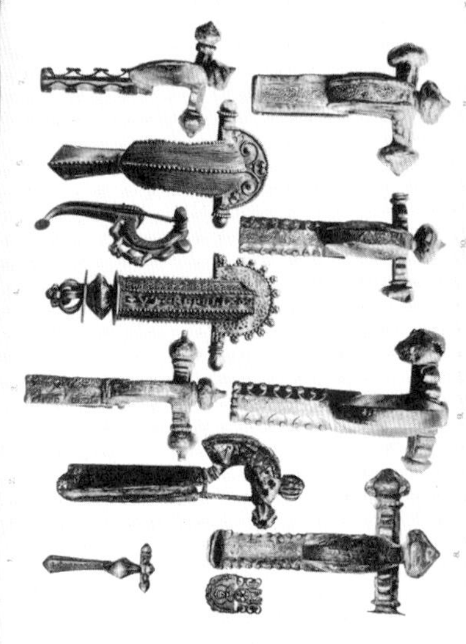

XXI.

1.

2.

XIV.

27} a} Page from Nikolaj M. Beljaev, "Ocherki po vizantiiskoj arkheologii, I. Fibula v Vizantii" [Essays on Byzantine Archaeology, I. Fibulae in Byzantium], *Seminarium Kondakovianum*, III (1929)
b} Page from Nikolaj P. Toll', "Sasanidskija tkani s izobraženiem Bahrama Gura" [Sassanid Textiles with Representations of Bahram Gur], *Seminarium Kondakovianum*, III (1929)
c} Page from Nikolaj P. Toll', "Ikona Tihvinskoj Božiej Materi" [The Icon of the Holy Virgin of Tikhvin], *Seminarium Kondakovianum*, V (1932)

first four years of the journal's existence, almost 40 articles were written in Russian, most of them by Russian scholars but some by Czechs. Then, starting in 1933–1934, the number of articles written in Czech and Slovak would increase, with the number in Russian decreasing in equal measure. This was no accident. After its apogee in the 1920s, the effects of the Russian Action started to fade in the aftermath of the economic crisis of 1929, with more and more Russians leaving Czechoslovakia for other destinations.[50] More importantly, Czechoslovakia gave diplomatic recognition to the Soviet Union in 1934, drastically altering the status of the Russian émigrés on Czech soil. Since Imperial Russia no longer existed, nor even the official hope that it would be re-established, there was far less justification for supporting the activities of Russian émigrés.[51]

This does not completely explain why Czech scholars writing for *Byzantinoslavica* switched from Russian (or other international languages) to Czech or Slovak, something which greatly restricted their audience.[52] After all, the same switch did not take place in the *Seminarium Kondakovianum*. The timing of the shift appears to hold the key here: Czech becomes prevalent in the issue of *Byzantinoslavica* for the years 1933–1934. This is exactly the time when Hitler rose to power in Germany and began his rhetorical attacks on Czechoslovakia.[53] These attacks centered on the status of the German-speaking minority in Czechoslovakia, which was, in fact, the majority of what will be called after 1938 the "Sudetenland", i.e. the Germanophone lands mainly on the borders of Czechoslovakia.[54] Czechoslovakia also irritated the Nazis with its insistence on being a progressive, Western-oriented democracy.[55] And last but not least, the Nazis' disdain for the "Slavic race" is well-known.[56] From the mid-1930s onwards, the fear of war with Germany grew within Czechoslovak society in general and amongst the country's political elite in particular. In the face of increasing pressure from a neighbor both anti-Slavic and anti-democratic, the natural reaction was to

50• Chinyaeva 2001, pp. 157–160.

51• Lustigová 2007, pp. 203–205; Chinyaeva 2001, pp. 154–156.

52• E.g., Dvorník 1929; Myslivec 1932b.

53• In general, see Lukeš 1996, pp. 113–172.

54• Zimmermann 1999; Brandes 2008; Němec 2018.

55• Hazera 2018.

56• For an overarching overview of the topic, see Schaller 2002.

celebrate the Czechoslovak Republic all the more.[57] It is hard to not see the linguistic changes in *Byzantinoslavica* as a reflection of these political circumstances.

Things were different for *Seminarium Kondakovianum*, a journal with a large international circulation edited by Russian émigrés. In spite of the changing world around it, *Seminarium Kondakovianum* remained consistent in its topics, authors, and approach; it also continued to publish its articles in international languages. As we showed in the first chapter of this book, the Institute was not immune to the economic crisis which began in 1929, and its financial difficulties are a recurring theme in its annual reports from the 1930s.[58] These financial problems, however, did not result in any dramatic changes in its scholarship. Logically enough, these Russian émigrés had adopted a transnational, "Eurasian" perspective and had little reason to change their work to make it more relevant to the political situation in Czechoslovakia. The winding down of the Russian Action may have contributed to a sense of isolation, which was only exacerbated when Czechoslovakia recognized the USSR.[59] At the same time, the financial situation of the Institute remained more or less stable thanks to its international prestige. Whereas *Byzantinoslavica* was dependent on Czechoslovak state, the Kondakov Institute was supported by a worldwide network of Russian émigrés, who, together with the many libraries and private scholars who had subscribed to *Seminarium Kondakovianum*, ensured that the Institute did not have to depend on the Czechoslovak government for support.[60]

On a continent girding itself for war, amidst a rise in animosity between nations, these two journals, both published in Prague, reacted to the politics of the era in markedly different ways. Let it be said that our analysis of their politics does not mean that we would denigrate the scholarship of either publication. The contributors to both applied valid methodologies and, for the most part, resisted the pull towards explicitly political scholarship.

57• A great example is certainly the burial of Masaryk himself; see the pamphlet published at this occasion. The legacy of Masaryk weighed heavily on Czechoslovak democracy. Cf. Svačina 1937, sp. p. 60.

58• *Report* 1932–1937.

59• Dejmek/Kováč 2018, p. 55.

60• For the accounting, see *Report* 1932–1937.

Nevertheless, from a purely historiographical perspective, it is interesting to note how the Russian émigré community, spread around the world and deprived of any participation in a "national" discourse, focused on transnational topics and published works for an international audience. The Czechoslovak journal, meanwhile, became less international in its outlook. This is not totally unlike the situation in our own times, where part of the academic world focuses on transcultural topics, presenting them to a global or "globalized" audience, while society at large is ever more fragmented by nationalistic rhetoric.

ANDRÉ GRABAR, BYZANTIUM, AND FRANCE

André Grabar faced different circumstances than his compatriots who settled in Czechoslovakia. He had only his immediate family with him, not all of whom were Russian. He met few other émigrés, instead undergoing a process of acculturation. As he recalls in his memoirs, the French were not always extremely welcoming:

> "[...] *as is known, the xenophobia of the French, devoid of any violence, consists in ignoring the presence of a stranger when the time comes to invite people to one's home. Our native French acquaintances in Strasbourg were always friendly as far work is concerned, but never went so far as to invite us into their homes.*"[61]

Despite these difficulties, André Grabar decided to become a French citizen, and we have already mentioned that this was necessary in order for him to obtain a permanent position at the university. But circumstances forced Grabar to integrate into French society in ways that went far beyond that legal step.

This integration is not reflected in his first publications, something which is not surprising since the cycles of academic research always lag behind the events in a scholar's life. During his first

61• "[...] *comme on sait, la xénophobie des Français, dépourvue de toute violence consiste à ignorer la présence d'un étranger parmi les gens qu'on invite à la maison. Nos connaissances à Strasbourg d'origine proprement française nous ont été toujours très favorable, aussi longtemps qu'il s'agissait de nos travaux en commun, mais n'allaient pas jusqu'à nous inviter dans leurs familles.*", "Esquisse biographique", p. 23.

decade in France, Grabar was still summarizing and publishing the results of his Bulgarian experience. This will change, in the 1930s, with the preparation of his seminal monograph on images of the emperor: *L'empereur dans l'art byzantin. Recherches sur l'art officiel de l'Empire d'Orient*.[62] In the meantime, the emigrant Grabar's notions of Byzantium were being transformed. This is already evident in his writing on Bulgaria and the Balkans in general:

> "*There would be no point in establishing, in Balkan painting, as many schools as there are Christian nations in the peninsula. For one thing, the fusion of religious and social conceptions, together with political and military events and, of course, the instability of frontiers, have deeply unified Balkan art. What is more, painters, who moved themselves and their ateliers at the call of the founders of churches or monasteries, did not stop at political or ethnic borders. Passing from one town to another, they founded no permanent schools attached to specific places.*"[63]

In this text we see a clear shift away from the "imperial perception" of Byzantine culture promoted by Russian scholars around the year 1900. The Russian conception of Byzantium was not terribly different from the real-life Russian Empire – multi-ethnic but dominated by one nation. Grabar's description of Balkan painting seems to have been transformed by his experience of emigration. For Grabar, just as for the members of the Kondakov Institute and for many other Russians around the world, Byzantium now seems like something closer to their own fragmented and yet still culturally unified reality. National borders lose their importance, and art, workshops, and culture all function irrespective of "ethnic boundaries", and art, rather than being national, is Slavic and Orthodox.[64] Although Grabar was already living in France at this point, he shared the kind of Russian internationalist perspective we have already

62• Grabar 1936.

63• *"Il serait vain de chercher à établir, dans la peinture balkanique, autant d'écoles qu'il y a de nations chrétiennes dans la péninsule. D'une part, la fusion des conceptions religieuses et sociales, les évènements politiques et militaires, l'instabilité des frontières ont profondément unifié l'art balkanique. D'autre part, les peintres, qui se déplaçaient, avec leurs ateliers, à l'appel des fondateurs d'églises et de monastères, ne s'arrêtaient pas aux limites politiques ou ethniques d'un pays, et, en passant d'une localité dans une autre, ils ne fondaient guère d'écoles durables, attachées à un lieu précis."*, *Idem* 1928a, p. IV.

64• Foletti/Palladino 2020.

examined in the work of Kondakov's circle in Prague. Soon, however, Grabar's perspective would change yet again.

BECOMING A FRENCHMAN AND A DEMOCRAT: GRABAR AND *L'EMPEREUR DANS L'ART BYZANTIN* (1936)

Before we begin this section, let us make a few disclosures. First, we will be discussing the intellectual development of a man from whom we have no personal letters, diaries, or any other documents that would allow us direct access to his inner life. Only Grabar's professional correspondence made it into the archives of the Collège de France at Paris. There are, in those archives, a few documents concerning Grabar's involvement in the French army, but we have no direct evidence of how Grabar perceived the rise of the Nazi regime in Germany, the defeat of the French army in June 1940, or life in occupied Paris.[65] Grabar's brief autobiography, written in 1981–1982 (i.e. at the very end of his life), contains but a few lines about this period of his life.[66] We will therefore have to work exclusively from his printed scholarly works, texts which offer us no explicit help at all. We will have to try to read between the lines to see how Grabar's outstanding work was impacted by his new surroundings. The focus of our analysis in this chapter will be Grabar's most significant publication from before the Second World War, main publication produced by Grabar during the pre-war period, *L'empereur dans l'art byzantin.* Grabar's work on this book was done entirely in France, and it was published in Paris in 1936.[67] We will start by looking at where this book fits in Grabar's personal history and how it compares with other scholar's work from those years.

IN SEARCH OF A "BYZANTINE" IDENTITY: BETWEEN EVOLUTIONARY THEORIES AND RELIGIOUS STUDIES

It was thanks to *L'empereur dans l'art byzantin*, a pivotal publication in Grabar's career, that he became a scholar of international renown. We have already mentioned the more than three dozen book reviews

65• In general, see Azéma/Bédarida 2000; Laub 2010. See also, from a cultural perspective, Debray 2005.

66• See chapter 1, pp. 77–91.

67• Grabar 1936.

which the book received in international journals, guaranteeing him international status, but it was also an important step in his intellectual journey **{28a–b}**.[68] The book would be fundamental to Byzantine studies for decades, and Grabar's conclusions remained unquestioned until 1993, when Thomas F. Mathews finally raised some objections worth taking seriously.[69] Despite gaps in Grabar's research that appear obvious to us now, modern scholars still agree that his analysis was ground-breaking.[70]

The book's first part starts by looking at monuments and at the iconography of imperial portraits and depictions of imperial victories, goes on to examine images of the emperor with his subjects, and concludes by comparing the figure of the emperor with the figure of Christ.[71] The second part is entirely dedicated to historical research, divided into the main eras of Byzantine history.[72] The third and last part, which would have the greatest impact on later scholars, is devoted to the development of "imperial" imagery in Christian art from the fourth century to the Middle Ages.[73]

A first look at Grabar's methods in the book gives one the impression that he makes very orthodox use of iconography to shape and construct historical discourse.[74] In this he follows Kondakov, whose methods we discussed earlier. Even though Grabar is applying these methods to a different set of images, we are reminded of Kondakov's last books, especially his study of the iconography of Christ and the two volumes on how the Mother of God was depicted.[75] Grabar makes no mention of Kondakov in his introduction to *L'empereur dans l'art byzantin*, even though the whole project at times seems like the completion of a triptych begun by the older scholar. Kondakov's legacy is present throughout *L'empereur dans l'art byzantin*, and Grabar often quotes directly from Kondakov, especially his

68• A complete list of the book reviews includes prominent international scholars, such as, to name only a few, Charles R. Morey, Franz Dölger, Louis Bréhier, Percy E. Schramm, Georgij Ostrogorskij, Bogdan Filov, Aleksandr Vasiliev, or Guillaume de Jerphanion.

69• Mathews 1993, pp. 16–22.

70• For approaches "indebted" to the one of Grabar, see, e.g., Andaloro 2006; Sena Chiesa 2009; Foletti 2017b.

71• Grabar 1936, pp. 1–122.

72• *Ibidem*, pp. 123–188.

73• *Ibidem*, pp. 189–262.

74• This is the main focus of Muzj 2005 [1995], pp. 93–121.

75• Kondakov 1905, 1914, 1915; on Kondakov's method, see Foletti 2017a, pp. 171–229.

28} a} Frontispiece of André Grabar, *L'empereur dans l'art byzantin. Recherches sur l'art official de l'Empire d'Orient*, Paris 1936
b} Plate VI. of André Grabar, *L'empereur dans l'art byzantin. Recherches sur l'art official de l'Empire d'Orient*, Paris 1936

articles about the representation of Russian aristocracy in the Middle Ages or his large-scale studies on the antiquities of Southern Russia.[76] Grabar also refers to research on the nomadic tribes carried out by Kondakov or his followers at the Kondakov Institute.[77]

And yet, the further we dig into Grabar's book, the more we are forced to admit that although Grabar's methods have their roots in Kondakov's way of analyzing the evolution of standard visual patterns, Grabar has also radically transformed Kondakov's methods. Grabar's book is structured very differently. For one thing, after presenting the book's main themes and art objects, he goes on the talk about them in the terms of traditional history, not just art history. But in Grabar's approach to the meaning of the monuments, we can also sense the reception of Erwin Panofsky (1892–1968) and a hesitant step in the direction of "iconology", even if the latter's studies are not quoted from directly.[78] The field of art history was rapidly expanding in those years. German scholarship played a key role in that expansion, and Grabar was clearly attuned to developments in the field.[79] German-speaking scholars

76• Kondakov 1906; see Grabar 1936, e.g., in the notes pp. 23, 28.

77• *Ibidem*, notes pp. 72–73.

78• See, notably, Panofsky 1932; on the origins and development of the method, see, e.g., Elsner/Lorenz 2012.

79• For an overview of the expansion of the field in these specific years, see Kultermann 1990 [1966], pp. 201–215; Passini 2017, pp. 109–207.

did much to expand "Byzantine studies" to include new topics of study, and Grabar quotes from Andreas Alföldi (1895–1981), Oskar Wulff (1864–1946), Richard Delbrueck (1875–1957), and Percy E. Schramm (1894–1970).[80] Some of this work, such as that carried out by Alföldi and Delbrueck, consisted mainly of archaeological studies of items from both the early and late Roman Empire. While focusing on "material culture" and symbols, these scholars took a historical – one could almost say philological – approach to their research.[81] Grabar got hold of Schramm's study on the symbolism of images of rulers only when his own text was near completion, and mainly refers to Schramm's work when their interpretations are different. Nevertheless, it is clear that both were thinking in terms of the link between visual symbols and political rituals,[82] and Grabar himself acknowledges his debt to historians like Schramm.[83] Grabar also took into account the work of francophone archaeologists and historians of Antiquity such as Franz Cumont (1868–1947) and Grabar's mentor and friend from his Strasbourg days, Paul Perdrizet.[84] The result could not help but be "interdisciplinary", as we would say today. The very topic of *L'empereur dans l'art byzantin* encouraged this, since it had already been touched on by several of the above-mentioned scholars from a purely historical point of view.

The most fascinating innovation of the book, and the one which shapes its last part, is the way Grabar connects imperial images with Christian images. We see the first hint of this in the first section of the book, in the chapter entitled "*L'empereur et le Christ*".[85] There Grabar explicitly compares the images and the authority of the Byzantine *basileus* to the figure of Christ. According to Grabar, imperial images lend Christian images some of their key symbols of authority, and Grabar sees images of Christ mainly as depictions of imperial prestige. In the third section of the book, entitled "*L'art impérial et l'art chrétien*", Grabar makes his reasoning explicit:

80• See Grabar 1936, pp. VII, 5, 6, 10, 12, 13, 54, 64–66, 75–78, 85, 86, 99, 104, 106, 114–115, 127, 144–146, 148, 151–153, 168, 190, 199, 200, 206, 209, 214, 215, 226, 229, 232–234, 237, 255, 257, 276.

81• See, e.g., the abundantly quoted Alföldi 1934 and Delbrueck 1929.

82• Schramm 1924.

83• Grabar 1936, pp. VI–VII.

84• See, e.g., Cumont 1932 and Perdrizet 1922. On Cumont, Motte 1999; on Perdrizet, see, once again, Grabar 1938, and more recently Gallo/Provost 2018.

85• Grabar 1936, p. 98.

“*We already know that these two aspects* [imperial and Christian] *of Byzantine art existed side-by-side from the foundation of Constantinople and until the fall of the Eastern Empire* [...] *It would have been surprising if, under these conditions, contact had not been established between the two branches of Byzantine art. And already, while examining imperial imagery throughout the centuries, we noticed several typical traits shared by Christian and imperial works from the same era.*”[86]

The language Grabar uses to describe Byzantine images owes much to evolutionary theories. Terms like “branches” and their “evolution” are clearly indebted to Darwinian discourse, which was often imported from biology into art history starting in the mid-nineteenth century.[87] The important thing to note about Grabar's application of that discourse in this book is how he essentially posits that there were two separate visual patterns – imperial and Christian, and then describes exchanges and interactions between these two “species”:

“*But so far we have not dealt with the essential question of the relationship between Christian and imperial art in Byzantium. We are thinking, as one might guess, about whether imperial art influenced Christian art. Was the art of the Church conquered by the official art of the emperors?*”[88]

On the basis of previous research – Charles Bayet (1849–1918), Gabriel Millet, Oskar Wulff, Hayford Pierce (1883–1946), and Royall Tyler (1884–1953) are the names mentioned – Grabar proposes trying to understand the relationship between the two realms by using a sort of comparative research. For Grabar, the thing that yokes the two realms together is what today's scholars could call an “anthropological constant”:

86• *“Nous savons déjà que ces deux aspects de l'art byzantin ont existé côte à côte, depuis la fondation de Constantinople jusqu'à la chute de l'Empire d'Orient* [...] *Il aurait été étonnant que, dans ces conditions, un contact ne se fût pas établi entre les deux branches de l'art byzantin. Et déjà, en observant l'évolution de l'imagerie impériale à travers les siècles, nous avons pu relever plusieurs traits typiques qui rapprochent les œuvres contemporaines, chrétiennes et impériales.”*, Grabar 1936, p. 189.

87• On this shift between disciplines, see notably the contributions in Larson/Flach 2013.

88• *“Mais le problème essentiel qui touche au rapport des arts chrétiens et impérial, à Byzance, ne nous a pas occupé jusqu'ici : nous songeons, on le devine, au problème de l'influence de l'art impérial sur l'œuvre artistique chrétienne. L'art de l'Église a-t-il subit l'ascendant des œuvres de l'art officiel des empereurs ?”*, Grabar 1936, p. 189.

“*Lastly, a conception of monarchy which is essentially a religious one, which we could recognize as the basis of all the themes of imperial imagery, better justifies the power it could exert over Christian art* [...] *This argument seems particularly important since we already know, on the one hand, the origins of most of the themes in the repertoire taken from the official art of the emperors of the late Roman Empire into Byzantium, and on the other hand, we know about the later attempts to adapt this pagan monarcho-religious iconography to the notion of a Christian empire in the early Middle Ages.*”[89]

Grabar's hypothesis is that imperial and Christian imagery are part of the same world, properly belonging to the history of religion. From this perspective, elements are shared because certain religious and para-religious experiences are essentially identical. These similarities are more typically the terrain of scholars of religion, but Grabar may have had special insight thanks to his own childhood: in an article explaining what inspired him in his work, he mentioned seeing, as a child, the religious and imperial rituals performed at the church of Saint Sophia in Kiev **{29}**.[90] Thus, personal experience and scholarly theory converge in Grabar's approach.

More specifically, Grabar believed that a greater “migration” of themes from one realm to the other took place at two important moments of Byzantine history: at the birth of the Christian empire in Late Antiquity and during the period after what Grabar calls the iconoclastic crisis, (which we would now call the “struggle over images”).[91] It is at these two moments that, according to Grabar:

“[...] *artists must have looked to the images of official imperial art for compositional models and iconographic schemes that they could adapt to Christian themes.*”[92]

....

89• *“Enfin, la présence d'une idée monarchique d'essence religieuse, que nous avons pu reconnaître à la base de tous les thèmes de l'imagerie impériale, justifie mieux l'ascendant qu'elle a pu prendre sur l'art chrétien* [...] *Cet argument nous semble particulièrement important, depuis que nous connaissons, d'une part, les origines de l'écrasante majorité des thèmes du répertoire transmis à Byzance par l'art officiel des empereurs du Bas-Empire, et d'autre part, les essais d'une adaptation ultérieure de cette iconographie de la religion monarchique païenne aux idées de l'Empire chrétien du haut moyen âge.”*, Grabar 1936, p. 191.

90• *“Je la voyais tous les jours et elle* [Sainte Sophie] *était au centre d'événements réguliers et importants: fêtes religieuses, anniversaires de l'empereur, etc.”*, *Idem* 1990, p. 115.

91• On this term, see the synthesis by Brubaker 2012.

92• “[...] *les artistes ont dû demander aux images de l'art officiel des empereurs des modèles de composition et des schémas iconographiques, qu'ils adaptaient ensuite aux données des sujets chrétiens.”*, Grabar 1936, p. 191.

29} Cathedral of Saint Sophia, Kiev, c. 1911

At this very point in the book, without a wholesale change in terminology, Grabar switches to a very different approach. Now it is the workshops which seek out traditional patterns and reuse them out of necessity, and here Grabar implicitly accepts a characterization of Byzantine visual culture which had been around at least since Adolphe-Napoléon Didron (1806–1867) proposed it in the mid-nineteenth century. According to Didron, Eastern Christian images are the result of loyal adherence to traditional schemes.[93] But now, what was for many Western scholars a criticism of Byzantium becomes, for Grabar, an advantage:

> “*No-one can ignore the dignified majesty of the Byzantine style, which is reflected even in the most mediocre recent productions of the Orthodox church, saving them from vulgarity.*”[94]

Here we see echoes of Kondakov, who made similar statements in his last publication (completed in 1924 but not published until 2011)

93• Didron 1845; on the figure of Didron, see Brisac/Leniaud 1987; Belting 1990, pp. 28–30; Foletti 2013.

94• *“Nul n'ignore en effet la grave majesté du style byzantin qui se reflète jusque dans les plus médiocres et les plus tardives productions de l'Église orthodoxe, et les préserve de la vulgarité.”*, Grabar 1936, p. 191.

about the iconography of the Mother of God in the Latin West.[95] Grabar, too, sees value in Eastern Orthodox traditions.

While *L'empereur dans l'art byzantin* is a book which follows up the work of Kondakov and the early-twentieth-century French Byzantinists, its emphasis on historical research and Grabar's willingness to adopt a fundamentally interdisciplinary approach make the book a very modern work indeed. Grabar's main thesis in the book – that imperial and Christian imagery are the result of a similar religious or para-religious frame of mind – pushes it towards the field of comparative religious studies, even though Grabar's comparison was not between two different religions as such.

INVENTING SACRED SPACE THROUGH PERSONAL EXPERIENCE

We have mentioned how deeply Grabar was affected by his Orthodox upbringing. He was profoundly touched by the rituals he witnessed as a child in the church of Saint Sophia in Kiev, and later, he was responsible for the liturgy of the Russian Orthodox community in Strasbourg. Rituals must have played a crucial role in his perception not only of religious experience, but also of the religious images that are so important in the Orthodox world. We also discussed the idea that a certain kind of majestic authority was characteristic of Eastern images from Late Antiquity to Grabar's own times.[96] But there is a much more radical suggestion in Grabar's description of how Christian and imperial art interacted:

“*One could have derived this immanent majesty of Byzantine art from the liturgical ceremonies of the Church, where we find the same solemn rhythm.*”[97]

Here Grabar is talking about the how Byzantine art is part of the performance of ceremonies. The popular modern term for this is "performativity".[98] Grabar did not have the term, but he certainly understood the concept, for he refuses to dissociate images from

95• Kondakov 2011; Foletti 2008.

96• See pp. 71–74.

97• *"On aurait pu faire dériver cette majesté immanente de l'art byzantin des cérémonies liturgiques de l'Église, où l'on retrouve le même rythme solennel."*, Grabar 1936, p. 191.

98• For an introduction to the term "performativity" in visual studies, see Gillgren/Snickare 2012.

rituals and spaces. We believe that this connection is fundamental to his scholarship, in this text and elsewhere. Consciously or not, Grabar perceived visual culture as only one part of what is presently called the "sacred space" and of the religious ritual taking place in and around that space.[99] Although Grabar never used the term "sacred space", he went a long way towards defining it. We think that his emphasis on this "performativity" – something explored more recently by scholars such as Alexej Lidov and Bissera Pentcheva – was a result of his own direct experience of rituals, sacred spaces, and devotional images.[100] This is how personal experience can influence scholarly research. Another characteristic of Grabar's work is his thorough self-criticism:

"[…] *but I don't think that this explanation, as correct as it may be, really gets to the bottom of things. We will come closer, we believe, by tracing the style of Byzantine ecclesiastical art and the allure of Byzantine liturgical rites back to a common source, namely the ceremonies and art of the imperial palace. Both seem to have kept the memory of their 'imperial' origins alive forever.*"[101]

The common origins of both rituals, a sort of original prototype, justify Grabar's methodological framework. The search for a common prototype was a standard procedure in nineteenth-century Russian scholarship, whether in philology or art history. Kondakov and Aleksandr Veselovskij investigated iconography and language from a similar perspective and with a similar methodology, seeking original prototypes.[102] Grabar, however, was seeking something more, something extending beyond his own culture, and showed a remarkable capacity for self-criticism:

"*Admittedly, this is only a hypothesis – which I am not the first to adopt – but it is one that we believe we can support with facts by showing that most*

99• For a synthesis about the use and meaning of this notion, see Bacci 2020.

100• Lidov 2006; Pentcheva 2010.

101• "[…] *mais pareille explication, sans être erronée, ne nous semble pas toucher au fond des choses. On s'est rapproche davantage, croyons-nous, en faisant remonter le style de l'art ecclésiastique byzantin et l'allure des rites liturgiques byzantins à une source commune, à savoir aux cérémonies et à l'art du Palais impérial : l'une et l'autre semblent avoir conservé pour toujours le souvenir de leurs origines 'impériales'.*", Grabar 1936, p. 191.

102• Foletti 2017a, p. 178.

post-Constantinian Christian images in the sumptuous, solemn style were inspired by similar imperial compositions. ”[103]

For Grabar, a hypothesis should always be supported by facts. And these should be sought in the art objects themselves, especially in their iconography and the way they were produced. The meaning of images and how they were produced will confirm or refute the scholarly hypothesis.

Grabar was much ahead of his time, both in his attention to sacred spaces, and in the importance he gave to material culture. Both tendencies seem to be intrinsically linked to his personal experience and to his training in Russian scholarly and religious culture. Grabar seems to be aware of the limits of his approach, which he systematically deconstructs in his search for "objective" proof of his hypotheses. It is remarkable to see how he intuitively anticipated so many of the tendencies that lie at the heart of art history today. Without a doubt, Grabar is one of the scholars responsible for the fact that medieval studies – in any case since the appearance of Hans Belting's *Bild und Kult* (1990) – have been one of the driving forces for the methodological renewal of art history as a field.

IMPERIAL FIGURES BETWEEN AUTHORITARIANISM AND DEMOCRACY

In 1993, Thomas Mathews penned a thoroughgoing critique of *L'empereur dans l'art byzantin*, in which Mathews accused Grabar of entertaining a "nostalgia for lost empire".[104] Mathews was led to this conclusion by a historiographical analysis of the backgrounds of the principal interwar scholars who investigated imperial imagery. According to Mathews, all of them had an "imperial" past, meaning that they had been born in countries ruled by an emperor at that time. What is more, all had belonged to the elites of these countries under their imperial regimes. Mathews posited that they had projected their nostalgia for their respective empires into their scholarly work. Since these scholars were all raised in countries

103• *"Certes, ceci n'est qu'une hypothèse – que nous adoptons après d'autres – mais que nous croyons pouvoir appuyer par des faits, en montrant que la plupart des images chrétiennes où dès la Paix de l'Église apparaît le style somptueusement solennel, s'inspirent de compositions impériales analogues."*, Grabar 1936, p. 191.

104• Mathews 1993, p. 19.

featuring a cult of personality around their leaders, they were fascinated by the very idea of the imperial authority figure.

Mathews' book – *The Clash of Gods: A Reinterpretation of Early Christian Art* – has been widely criticized since its publication, and Mathews' discussion of Grabar's writing, because of its highly polemical tone, has been called "politically incorrect". As Anne-Orange Poilpré pointed out in an article written to summarize the reception of this book, Mathews' tone was extremely polemical, especially considering that Grabar had died just a few years before. Poilpré concludes that because of this tone, some of the important achievements of Mathews' book have simply been ignored, and that the field of art history is the worse for that ignorance.[105]

We agree that one should not reject Mathews' analysis merely because of the tone of his writing, without any attempt at a detailed analysis of his ideas. At first glance, Mathews' thesis seems logical. Between the wars, those fascinated by emperors were, in fact, either former subjects of an emperor or enthusiasts for the emerging totalitarian regimes.[106] But is Grabar's *L'empereur dans l'art byzantin* really an exercise in nostalgia for imperial times?

If we work through Grabar's book, we find that Grabar puts a surprising distance between the Byzantine emperors and images of them. Or rather, Grabar presents his emperors more as links in an iconographical chain of evolution than as individual personalities:

> "*The emperor does not exist at all as a theme of portraiture apart from his rank and his social and mystical function. The first task of the 'portrait' is simply to make apparent that a certain man is the 'true' basileus. This is achieved by showing his obligatory nobility and dignity, the prescribed majestic allure, the consecrated gesture, the right clothing and insignia.*"[107]

Grabar's emperor is thus anything but an individual, and Grabar's focus throughout the book is on the attributes that make a man the "lawful" emperor. In other words, Grabar's emperor is not

105• Poilpré 2005; see also Russo 2005.

106• Gundle 2013; Chapoutot 2017; Lerner 2017.

107• *"L'empereur n'existe guère en tant que thème de l'art portraitique, en dehors de son rang ou de sa fonction sociale et mystique à la fois, et la première tâche du 'portrait' est précisément de faire sentir qu'un tel est le 'vrai' basileus, en montrant qu'il en a les traits nobles et graves obligatoires, l'allure majestueuse prescrite, le geste consacré, les vêtements et les insignes réglementaires."*, Grabar 1936, p. 10.

a charismatic figure, as the name of his book may have led some to believe, but rather the representation of a public and civic function which is quite constant across the "Byzantine" centuries. This does not correspond at all to the accusations made by Mathews.

If we are going to analyze a scholar's politics, we should also remember Grabar's life story. As we detailed above, he arrived in France at the age of 26. Six years later, he would become a French citizen, and would go on to serve in the French army at the beginning of the Second World War. It may be true that Grabar never forgot his Russian origins, but he became French in every aspect of his practical life. His education was also just as French as it was Russian. Kondakov was, of course, an important source, but some of other inputs reached Grabar through Gabriel Millet and Paul Perdrizet. Millet, who was Grabar's French mentor, maintained an extensive correspondence with Kondakov. Millet also contributed to the first *Recueil* in honor of Kondakov in 1926.[108] Perdrizet, Grabar's other important professor and friend from the Strasbourg period, knew Kondakov's works well and later contributed articles to the *Seminarium Kondakovianum*.[109]

One could even wonder which generation of scholars to place André Grabar with. He was born at around the same time as the philosophers Alexandre Koyré (1892–1964), Alexandre Kojève (1902–1968), or Emmanuel Lévinas (1906–1995), all of whom are now essentially considered French philosophers, albeit Frenchmen whose special contributions to French culture were made possible by their Eastern roots.[110] More importantly, perhaps, these men perceived themselves as French. According to Olga Medvedkova, Grabar's situation was very similar to theirs, and we should see him as one of many Russians who emigrated to Western Europe, transforming Western European academic life with their individual contributions.[111]

If we consider both Grabar's life and the actual content of *L'empereur dans l'art byzantin*, Mathews' accusation does not appear to be very well founded. Grabar's biography is that of a young émigré

108• Millet 1926; see Medvedev 1995.

109• Perdrizet 1932.

110• For an overview, see, e.g., Shashlova 2020.

111• Medvedkova 2016, p. 99.

who, over time, became French through and through, and his book shows no trace of nostalgia for a charismatic emperor. The wisdom and honesty with which he served his new country during the Second World War, demonstrated by the honors he received, are proof enough of his acculturation.[112] Nor was his case unique; the French policy of "forced acculturation" was apparently rather effective.

30} Frontispiece of Ernst Kantorowicz, *Kaiser Friedrich der Zweite*, Berlin 1927

But why, then, would Grabar devote an entire book to the figure of the Byzantine emperor – in the mid-1930s, no less? We have mentioned Kondakov's interest in the topic, manifested in his publications about the ruling families of medieval Russia and his later "obsession" with the *De Ceremoniis* of Constantine VII Porphyrogenites.[113] Kondakov had produced monographs about the iconography of Christ and Mary in the Byzantine world, but that left a gaping hole in the field of Byzantine studies – a study of the iconography of the emperor, a figure who was more or less omnipresent in the Byzantine world. Seen in this light, Grabar's decision to devote a book to the emperor seems to be more a consequence of his education and the logic of the field of Byzantine studies than a reflection of any particular ideological or political bent.

Grabar's book is, nevertheless, surprising, and to show just how it stands out from its historical context, we will compare it with an almost contemporary publication – Ernst Kantorowicz's (1895–1963) *Kaiser Friedrich der Zweite*, published in 1927 and devoted to the figure of Frederick II of Hohenstaufen **{30}**.[114] In this work, the emperor is represented as an ideal ruler. His likeness and his character are precisely described, as are his mores. His Germanic identity is not omitted. Not surprisingly, this book was either loved or hated when

112• ACF/FAG/BC.

113• Kondakov 1906, 1924.

114• Kantorowicz 1927; in the "ocean" of bibliography on Kantorowicz, see the biography of Lerner 2017; cf. also Boureau 1990.

it was released. French scholars were extremely critical, noting not only the book's almost total absence of bibliographical references (a choice that Kantorowicz later justified and corrected in a supplementary volume), but also its personal and celebratory tone.[115] For this book, Mathews' accusations are more pertinent. Mathews notes that Kantorowicz belonged, in the 1920s, to several circles of German mystics – such as the one centered on the poet Stefan George (1866–1933) – before turning into an active German nationalist.[116] His book was, of course, received much more positively in Germany, especially by nationalists and, later, by the Nazis themselves. It is another irony of history that this book by the Jewish Kantorowicz should become (according to Robert Lerner, at least) the bedside reading of Heinrich Himmler, and later be presented by Hermann Göring to Benito Mussolini.[117]

While both Grabar and Kantorowicz devoted their books to emperors, their approach is totally different. The difference becomes clear if we consider that Grabar decided to use the singular *L'empereur* instead of the plural, emphasizing the office rather than the men who held it. Earlier French research on imperial figures had portrayed the men themselves in an almost romantic light, emphasizing their lives, deeds, and legends. A good example are Charles Diehl's biographies of "Byzantine" emperors or empresses.[118] Even if Diehl was too young to have lived during the Second Empire (1852–1870), he may have felt nostalgia for the France of Napoleon III.[119]

In this context, Grabar was certainly an outlier; both his methods and his approach differed markedly from those of predecessors and contemporaries who wrote about the Byzantine emperors. And even taking into account what we have added to our knowledge since the 1930s, one must admit that, on the whole, Grabar's conclusions

115• For the supplementary volume, Kantorowicz 1931. For the reviews, see, e.g., Verlinden 1932.

116• Mathews 1993, pp. 16–17. On George and Kantorowicz, see Grünewald 1982; Raulff 2009, pp. 157–169, 189–192, 258–261, 313–346; Lerner 2017, pp. 74–82, 91–92. Many other scholars were also attracted by the symbolist circle around George, for a variety of reasons: on archaeologist Richard Delbrueck, e.g., cf. Palladino 2017.

117• Lerner 2017, pp. 114–115.

118• Diehl 1901, 1904, 1906–1908; on Diehl's "Theodora" and its context, see Ronchey 2003.

119• Foletti 2013, esp. pp. 188–191, with further bibliography.

were correct. The iconography of Byzantine emperors was indeed stable from the reign of Justinian II (685–695, 705–711) onwards. What Grabar posited, historical sources and images confirm: it was the attributes of the imperial office that were the crucial elements in this kind of imagery. In other words, if we are talking about Byzantine emperors, the clothes made the man. Recent scholarship has only served to reinforce Grabar's conclusion in this regard.[120]

The quality and historical accuracy of Grabar's analysis mean that *L'empereur dans l'art byzantin* is still valuable for present-day art historians. And yet, let us admit that it is easy to see where Mathews' suspicions might come from. Is it really possible that Grabar, in the Europe of the mid-1930s – with charismatic dictators arising all around Europe, and with books like *Kaiser Friedrich der Zweite* being published – could remain totally objective when writing about Byzantine emperors and their office?[121]

Kantorowicz's research almost unavoidably brings to mind the way Adolf Hitler was portrayed by his supporters. In the famous *Bannerträger* by Hubert Lanzinger, painted between 1934 and 1936, Hitler is shown as a mounted knight in armor, holding a swastika banner in his right hand **{31}**. Intentionally or not, this picture recalled the *Bamberg Horseman*, a statue which Kantorowicz (and others) thought was of Frederick II himself.[122] In the same years, Mussolini was often portrayed as a Roman emperor. In both cases, these images were part of a cult of personality around the ruler they depicted.[123] Grabar's interwar European environment, then, consisted not only of scholarly texts, but also of pictures of would-be emperors, reproduced obsessively in the mass media and displayed in public spaces.

It is interesting to look at how French "rulers" – the presidents of the Republic – were portrayed in the same era. They were always depicted with the same three objects: an evening suit, a red sash across the chest, and to their left, a cruciform plaque – the *Grand Croix de la Légion d'Honneur* (of which the president is grand master). The faces are different, but when these pictures are set side

120• See, e.g., the collective volume Tougher 2019.

121• Some of the ideas developed here are also presented in Foletti 2021.

122• On Lanzinger's painting, see Krause 2018; Kantorowicz 1927, p. 77. See also Schweizer 2007, pp. 91–105; Ruehl 2015, pp. 166–223.

123• Gundle 2013.

31} Hubert Lanzinger, *Der Bannerträger*,
c. 1934–1936

by side, one gets a strong impression of their sameness **{32a–c}**.[124] Are these presidential portraits intended as pictures of the function more than of the individuals who hold it? This French attitude to the president contrasts with the visual representations of many sovereigns throughout history and is totally different from the way other European nations were portraying their dictators at the time. The French seem to have been affirming that, in a democracy, the people are sovereign, rather than any one individual.

Once we have taken into account the situation in Grabar's own country of residence, it is harder to lump *L'empereur dans l'art byzantine* together with books like *Kaiser Friedrich der Zweite.* This does not mean that Grabar was forcing an argument that the Byzantine Empire was similar to the French Republic. But whereas Mathews thinks that Grabar's book was inspired by nostalgia for the Romanovs, we believe, on the contrary, that his view of Byzantine imperial imagery was determined, subconsciously, perhaps, by his more immediate French surroundings.

If this is indeed the case, then we have a perfect example of the hybrid thinking that could result when Russian émigrés were acculturated to the French way of thinking. As we discussed earlier, the very idea of Byzantine studies was, in the beginning at least, linked with the political ambitions of the Romanov emperors. Given the milieu in which Grabar grew up, it was natural for him to take an interest in precisely this field. But with Grabar's emigration and integration into French society, his perspective changed. His Byzantium no longer had to be the precursor of anything, nor did he have to show that the Romanovs were direct successors of the Roman emperors. By the 1930s, Grabar's research into one of the most autocratic empires in history could be productively carried out in democratic surroundings.

124• On the question of the dress of French presidents in general, see Fleurdoge 2015.

32 a) Gaston Doumergue (1924–1931)
b) Paul Doumer (1931–1932)
c) Albert Lebrun (1932–1940)

3/

BYZANTIUM IN CRISIS

The story we have been narrating until now is a story of Russian émigré scholarship under the influence of new, democratic surroundings in Central and Western Europe. The history of France and Czechoslovakia would be dramatically altered by totalitarian regimes during the Second World War and its aftermath. The present chapter will be a consideration, in three parts, of how scholarship and art history can survive and react to such situations. First, we will look at the writings and destiny of Grabar in wartime, especially during the German occupation of France. We will then analyse the life of the Kondakov Institute during the same period. The final part of the chapter will deal with the fate of the Kondakov Institute after the war, when it enjoyed a few short years of respite before being dismantled by yet another totalitarian regime.

GRABAR AND THE WAR

The political situation in France in the late 1930s is well known. After participating, in 1938, in the "ritual sacrifice" of Czechoslovakia to the Nazis, the French still held out hope that war could be avoided.[1] The following months, however, showed that the German intention to provoke a military conflict could not be countered. France therefore started to prepare for war, with the general mobilization declared on September 2, 1939 as a direct consequence of the German invasion of Poland {33}. The day after, France declared

1 • Record 2007; Kvaček 2018.

33} General mobilization of 1939

war on Germany.[2] As we have mentioned already, Grabar was drafted into the army, but due to his advanced age, poor eyesight, and specific linguistic skills, he was not sent to the frontline but appointed second-class reserve interpreter to the navy in Toulon {34}:

> “*During the first year of the war (1 September 1939 – 1 September 1940), I served as interpreter and encoder to officers in the navy (by the way, I never once had to translate a text in any of the three languages which were my domain), where I spent countless days and nights deciphering dispatches which rarely had any military importance.*”[3]

2• For the perception of this conflict by the French intelligentsia and a summary of historical information see Charpentier 2008.

3• “*Pendant la première année de la guerre (1er septembre 1939–1er septembre 1940), je fus mobilisé comme officier-interprète et chiffreur à la marine (à ce propos, je n'ai pas eu une seule fois à traduire un texte quelconque, dans les trois langues qui étaient de mon domaine), où j'ai passé d'innombrables heures diurnes et nocturnes consacrées au déchiffrage de dépêches qui rarement avaient une importance militaire quelconque.*”, “Esquisse biographique”, p. 27.

Grabar found the de-coding work he was assigned to do highly repetitive and useless:

“*I was bored, and so my thoughts continually drifted back to what I was researching. It was then and there that I decided I was going to prepare the large book entitled ‘Martyrium’, which would appear in 1946.*”[4]

From Grabar's boredom sprang what would be one of his largest and most important publications, to which we will return later. The history of the phoney war and the subsequent invasion of France is well known. After the invasion on May 10, 1940, everything was over by June 22 of the same year.[5] France, represented by General Pétain, capitulated, and was divided into two zones – the North, under the direct control of Nazi Germany, and the so-called “free zone” in the south, with Vichy as capital and Maréchal Pétain as president.[6] The South was also subject to Nazi authority, however, and collaborated with the Reich in many ways, including the deportation of Jews.[7]

After the French surrender, Grabar was demobilized with a nomination for official recognition of his merits.[8] He left the South, returned to Paris, and started life under the Nazi occupation. Unfortunately, none of Grabar's personal letters from this period have survived. In his memoirs, however, he did write a few lines about conditions under German rule:

“*It was during wartime, 1939–45, that we had to live through some bad moments, for example when Anglo-Saxon* [i.e. British and American] *planes came to bomb the neighbourhood. Their bombs were aimed at the Renault factories, whose carpentry workshops were very close to us, and we knew that the Germans made wooden parts for their planes there. One of these bombs tore down part of the house facing ours, but luckily it only slightly injured one woman (who was, ironically, an Englishwoman). But these air raids meant that with each alert, we would descend with our children and a suitcase filled with ‘household treasures’ into the cellar. Our house was never hit and it was*

4• *“Je m'ennuyais, et je revenais par la pensée à mes sujets de réflexion professionnelle. C'est là et alors que j'allais préparer le grand livre, qui sous le titre ‘Martyrium’, allait paraître en 1946.”*, “Esquisse biographique”, p. 27.

5• Launay 1972.

6• Azéma/Bédarida 2000.

7• Klarsfled 1983; Burrin 1995.

8• ACF/FAG/BC, “document militaire”.

quite 'instructive' to see how, after the end of an alert in which anything had been destroyed, the inhabitants of the cellars rushed out to gather wood (the remains of doors or windows, for example) and take it for use as firewood.

Throughout the war, since I was classified as 'Aryan' according to the terminology of the time, I could continue my teaching at the École des Hautes Etudes."[9]

We can see, then, that his life must have been similar to that of many others: apart from the inherent danger of bombing raids – which were increasingly frequent as the war dragged on – he faced practical problems every day. There was no fuel for heating, as he indicated in his memoirs, and Nazi racist propaganda had also radically transformed the city.[10] Grabar was lucky enough to be considered "Aryan", and thus kept his job, but he must have known others who were not so lucky.[11] We have little information about his daily life under the occupation, but Grabar's family was surely affected by the typical problems: food was rationed (although one might occasionally buy something on the black market), and travel through Paris was complicated and risky.

On the other hand, if we know little about Grabar's life in these years, this must mean that he and his family suffered no more than those around them. He does not seem to have had any particular problems with the Nazi authorities, unlike some members of the Kondakov Institute in Prague, as we will see below. In this climate, he pursued his research and taught, and the size and depth of *Martyrium,* his two-volume work that would be published in 1946, reflects how much time Grabar must have had on his hands.

9• *"C'est du temps de la guerre 1939–45 que nous avons eu à passer de mauvais moments, lorsque les avions anglo-saxons venaient bombarder le quartier. Leurs bombes étaient destinées aux usines Renaud, dont les ateliers de menuiserie étaient très proches de nous, et nous savions que les allemands y confectionnaient les parties de leurs avions qui étaient en bois. Une de ces bombes arracha une partie de la maison qui nous faisait face, mais la chance a voulu qu'elle ne fit qu'une blessée légère (qui était d'ailleurs une anglaise). Mais ces raids d'avions faisaient que, à chaque alerte, nous descendions avec nos enfants, et une valise remplie de 'trésors domestiques', dans la cave. Mais notre maison n'a pas reçu de bombes et il était assez 'instructif' à voir comment, après la fin d'une alerte, qui correspondait à des démolitions de détails, les habitants des caves se précipitaient sur les morceaux de bois (restes de portes, de fenêtres) pour les emporter et s'en servir comme du bois de chauffage.*

Pendant toute la guerre, étant 'aryen' selon la terminologie de l'époque, j'ai continué mon enseignement à l'École des Hautes Études.", "Esquisse biographique", p. 26.

10• On the situation in France, see, e.g., Laub 2010.

11• In order to continue to his work, Grabar surely had to have received a so-called *certificat d'aryanité*.

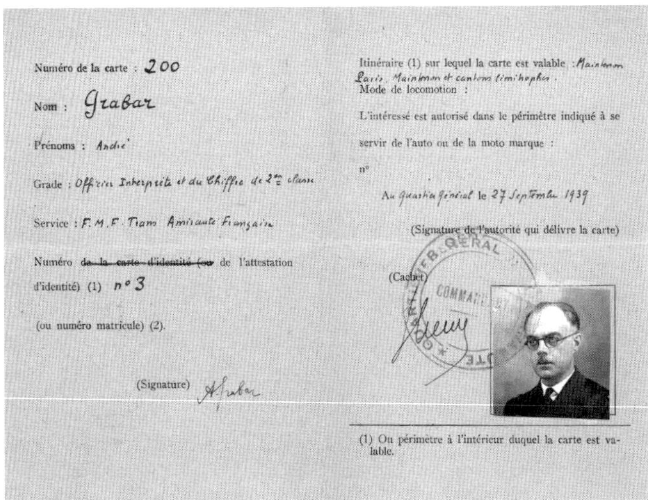
Numéro de la carte : 200

Nom : Grabar

Prénoms : André

Grade : Officier Interprète et du Chiffre de 2me classe

Service : F.M.F. Tiam Amirauté Française

Numéro ~~de la carte d'identité (ou~~ de l'attestation d'identité) (1) n° 3

(ou numéro matricule) (2).

(Signature) A. Grabar

Itinéraire (1) sur lequel la carte est valable : Maintenon Paris, Maintenon et cantons limitrophes.
Mode de locomotion :

L'intéressé est autorisé dans le périmètre indiqué à se servir de l'auto ou de la moto marque :

n°

Au Quartier Général le 27 Septembre 1939

(Signature de l'autorité qui délivre la carte)

(Cachet)

(1) Ou périmètre à l'intérieur duquel la carte est valable.

34} **Admiralty circulation card of André Grabar, 1939**

In a city partially paralyzed by the war, scholarship must have been a refuge from the depressing reality Grabar saw around him every day. Kondakov, in his memoirs, described how he responded the same way during his last months in Russia.[12] For an intellectual, creative activity gives meaning to life, and scholarship gives order and sense to daily reality, something we can understand much better while under an international quarantine.

In wartime, Grabar could still teach, but his audience had different interests now, and this, too, shaped the trajectory of his thought.

> “[I taught] *in front of a very small circle of listeners, and since they were much more interested in Western works, especially French, than in Byzantine works, I made an effort in this direction. I therefore occupied myself with the end of Antiquity and the very early Middle Ages in France, Britain, Spain, and Italy. It enriched me very much.*”[13]

These two sentences hint at a major change in Grabar's work. Before the war, he had worked almost exclusively on Eastern art. If and

12• Foletti 2017a, pp. 62–63.

13• “[*J'enseignais*] *devant un très petit cercle d'auditeurs, et comme celui-ci s'intéressait beaucoup plus aux œuvres occidentales, surtout françaises, qu'aux œuvres byzantines, j'ai fait un effort de ce côté, et me suis occupé de la fin de l'Antiquité et du très haut Moyen Âge, en France, en Grande-Bretagne, en Espagne, en Italie. Cela m'a beaucoup enrichi.*”, “Esquisse biographique”, p. 26.

COLLÈGE DE FRANCE
FONDATION SCHLUMBERGER POUR LES ÉTUDES BYZANTINES

MARTYRIUM

RECHERCHES SUR LE CULTE DES RELIQUES
ET L'ART CHRÉTIEN ANTIQUE

PAR

ANDRÉ GRABAR

DIRECTEUR D'ÉTUDES A L'ÉCOLE DES HAUTES ÉTUDES

1er VOLUME

ARCHITECTURE

COLLÈGE DE FRANCE
1, Place Marcelin-Berthelot, 1

1946

1. Salonique. St-Georges. Un martyr anonyme. - 2. Ravenne. Chapelle Archiépiscopale. Abside. La Vierge.

35 a} Frontispiece of André Grabar, *Martyrium. Recherches sur le culte des reliques et l'art chrétien antique*, 2 vols, Paris 1946
b} Pl. XXIX of André Grabar, *Martyrium. Recherches sur le culte des reliques et l'art chrétien antique*, 2 vols, Paris 1946

when he dealt with the Latin West, he did so in order to understand works located in the East, or perhaps "imported" from the East to the West.[14] Now, suddenly, he opened his thought to the entire Mediterranean. This may be why, immediately after the war, he became one of the leading art historians in the world.

But why was Grabar's small audience so much keener on French art now? This was not what Grabar had been brought to Paris for, after all. We do not know whether different kinds of students were now attending Grabar's lectures, or whether the change reflects a broader change in mood within French society. Scholars such as Michela Passini or François-René Martin have shown that, at least as far as the Middle Ages are concerned, interwar French scholarship was profoundly nationalistic.[15] This was the case all over Europe at the time. We have already mentioned the German nationalism of Kantorowicz, but many others worked along nationalistic lines.[16] In the late thirties, Grabar's audience, at least, was still interested in hearing and reading about "Byzantium", but under the humiliating occupation, the situation changed.[17] The reaction of the majority of the French intelligentsia and media, after the first

14• E.g., in Grabar 1924, 1931a.

15• Passini 2012, sp. pp. 145–228; Martin 2012.

16• For art history, see, e.g., Michaud 2015.

17• Launay 1972.

shock, was to look to the past for proof of the nation's glory.[18] Grabar needed to keep his audience interested, at least to some degree, and this pushed his scholarly interests in a new direction. The parallel with the aged Kondakov arriving in Czechoslovakia is clear. Nor was this the first time Grabar had enlarged the scope of his work in response to his surroundings. In Bulgaria, he had studied "Bulgarian art"; once in France, his perspective on Byzantium was radically transformed. In Strasbourg he had already touched on some Western topics, albeit tangentially, but in wartime Paris, with the French nation reduced to nothing more than its history, Grabar made France and the Latin West the new focus of his research.

As noted above, during the war Grabar concentrated on writing his fundamental monograph *Martyrium* **{35a–b}**. The idea, which came to him while he was with the navy, was to write a Christian "sequel" to *L'empereur*. The new book embraced both "East" and "West", which was only natural given the new focus of Grabar's work. It analyses the material manifestations of the cult of martyrs and their relics, i.e. the architecture of martyria and the birth of a visual vocabulary for representing the martyrs. In his memoirs, Grabar makes this comment on *Martyrium*:

"*After the book on the Byzantine emperor and his place in the Christian iconographic tradition, I switched, with 'Martyrium', to the problems of how the arts encouraged people to believe in the holiness of places and objects which had been in contact with holy figures and saints* [...] *My reflections on this vast subject, which I consider essential to understanding the cult of the masses, are based on the testimony of artworks in all media, everywhere, and in all periods.*"[19]

Despite the wide chronological and geographical framework proposed by Grabar, *Martyrium* focuses mainly on Late Antiquity.

18• For a general account, see Burrin 1995. For a good example of this type of reaction in the pages of the Catholic journal *La Croix*, see Crane 2004. An interesting case study, centered on one French region, of the diverse reactions to the defeat can be found in Panicacci 2007.

19• *"Après l'ouvrage sur l'empereur byzantin et sa place dans la tradition iconographique chrétienne (thème monarchique et étatique), je passai ainsi, avec le 'Martyrium' aux problèmes des apports aux arts des croyances à la sainteté des lieux et des objets ayant été en contact avec les personnages divins et saints* [...] *Mes réflexions sur ce vaste sujet, que je considère comme essentiel dans le culte des masses, s'appuient sur le témoignage d'innombrables traces sur des œuvres d'art de toutes techniques, partout et à toutes les époques."*, "Esquisse biographique", p. 34.

Grabar had previously touched on this period in *L'empereur*, but until now it had been marginal to his research. Grabar's *Martyrium* was published at a time of renewed interest in Late Antiquity, and readers' response to the book seems to have been very much conditioned by their varying notions of this epoch.

The reception of the book was decidedly mixed among Catholic scholars, something which Grabar attributed to the link he posited between the Antique cult of heroes and the Christian cult of martyrs.[20] Grabar saw continuity where Catholic scholars saw rupture. We believe that this contrast was made more evident by the renewal of the cult of martyrs after the Second World War. For Catholics, the blood of the martyrs – some of them as recent as Maximilian Kolbe (1894–1941) – was to be seen as a completely new beginning, a radical renewal not only for the Church but for all of society. This idea can be clearly perceived in the preaching and letters of Pope Pius XII (1939–1958).[21] Describing the sacrifices of Catholics in Germany, he writes:

> "*The generous victims in Germany, who, for twelve years from 1933 on, sacrificed their own property, their freedom, their own lives to Christ and to the Church, raise their hands to God in an expiatory prayer.*"[22]

These sacrifices by Catholics under totalitarian regimes reminded Catholics of the martyrs of the Early Church under the Roman emperors. In this context, Grabar's book would never be welcome. The "continuity" that he highlights between "pagan" and Christian cultures – a continuity which, Grabar himself notes, had never posed a problem before – was hard to accept in the post-war world, where Catholics were hoping for radical renewal after a historical turning point.[23]

During and after the war, secular French scholars were also very interested in Late Antiquity, but for them, rather than being the era of the Christian martyrs, it was a time of paradigmatic change

20• "Esquisse biographique", p. 34.

21• See, e.g., Pius XII 1945, 1947.

22• *"Le vittime generose, che durante dodici anni, dal 1933, in Germania hanno fatto a Cristo e alla sua Chiesa il sacrificio dei propri beni, della propria libertà, della propria vita, innalzano a Dio le loro mani in oblazione espiatoria."*, *Idem* 1945.

23• "Esquisse biographique", p. 34.

in European history in general.[24] Did the catastrophe of war encourage scholars to look more closely at such periods in history? It is well-known that in those same years, a group of German émigrés to the United States – Richard Krautheimer (1897–1994), Kurt Weitzmann (1904–1993), and the above-mentioned Erwin Panofsky – were extremely interested in "revivals" and "renaissances" during the Middle Ages. It has already been plausibly shown how Panofsky projected the present onto the past in his seminal article "Renaissances and Renascences".[25] According to this interpretation of Panofsky's work, he saw in these repeated renaissances a sort of prefiguration of Europe's future. Once German barbarism ended, civilization would be renewed. Similar mechanisms can also be observed in the writings of Krautheimer on medieval Rome and of Weitzmann on the Byzantine court in the tenth century.[26] These scholars shared not only the notion of rebirth, but also the idea of humanism re-emerging after the "Dark Ages".[27]

In mid-twentieth-century France, scholars began to perceive Late Antiquity as the beginning of a new culture which led naturally into the world of early medieval France. The crisis of Late Antiquity – within the chronological frames proposed by Grabar – was caused, or at least exacerbated by, the arrival of the Goths and Lombards, which made things complicated because these two groups were considered, in the nineteenth century and the first half of the twentieth, part of the "German race".[28] Claudio Azzara has explained how this "racial identity" made Italian historians despise the Lombards. In the years leading up to the unification of Italy in 1861, these barbarians were equated with Italian's nineteenth-century enemies, the "Germanic" Austro-Hungarians.[29] A second wave of anti-Lombard historiography was linked, according to Azzara, with the Second World War.[30] The intellectual notion of some kind of ideal *romanitas*, genetically different from the Germanic invaders lay at the base of these views. These ideas now seem ridiculous,

24• Mazza 2008.

25• Panofsky 1944; see also Landauer 1994.

26• Krautheimer 1942; Weitzmann 1948.

27• On the notion of "renaissances" in cultural history, see the classic Ferguson 1948; Masse 2010.

28• None of the populations were, however, actually "Germans", see Goffart 2006, pp. 187–229.

29• Azzara 2011, p. 81.

30• *Ibidem*.

since we know that modern "Italians" are, genetically speaking, descendants of the Romans, Goths, Lombards, Normans, etc.

Questions of identity were considerably more complex for French historians. In very general terms, French historians emphasised their Gallo-Roman heritage in the same way Italian historians emphasised their Roman heritage. For both groups of historians, the German invader was opposed to the local "post-Roman" community. But the barbarian invaders had also established the Kingdom of the Franks, considered by many the precursor of France itself.

The problem was that the Germans also claimed Charlemagne.[31] To them, he was the one who had re-founded the Christian Roman Empire, and was thus the direct predecessor of German rulers, including Hitler. The Teutonic conception of Charlemagne incorporated a kind of dichotomy between the "German barbarian empire" – for the propagandists of the Third Reich, their "barbarian" German origins were as much a part of their identity as the Germanic imperial tradition – and the "Gallo-Roman Latin tradition".[32] This explains the name of the brigade of the *Waffen-SS* made up of French collaborators – "Charlemagne", with the Frankish emperor now put forward as a symbol uniting Germans and Frenchmen.[33]

With the Germans attempting to co-opt Charlemagne and his empire, Grabar and his colleagues' decision to focus on a still earlier period – on Late Antique and early medieval southern European (i.e. Roman) culture – seems natural enough. This is not to say that Grabar's work was nothing more than a response to external events. At the same time, however, we are now much more aware of how even subtle changes in what society at large is thinking about can influence even the most serious and objective of scholars.[34] The war, in any case, marks a turning point in Grabar's research. He turned from Byzantium to the West, and to how those cultures interacted.

It is thus quite interesting to read Grabar's own words about Byzantine studies in France during the war:

> "*Byzantine studies, during the war, shared the fate of all intellectual activities in France. Research was impeded or momentarily stopped by the mobilization*

31• On this thorny question, see, e.g., Tellenbach 1982; Schieffer 2006.

32• See, e.g., von See 1994; for the field of art history, see Michaud 2015, with further bibliography.

33• Brose 2015, pp. 835–837.

34• Kultermann 1990 [1966].

of scholars, by military operations, evacuations, the closing of libraries, the splitting up of archives, and by various political or economic obstacles, if not by hunger itself. And even more than research as such, the printing of books and journals was constantly impeded during this period (due to lack of paper, of electricity, of manpower, of transport). ❞[35]

In this short overview, printed just after liberation, Grabar speaks of the war only as far as it imposed economic and practical obstacles to research, which it certainly did. What he does not mention, however, is society's changing mood and how it may have encouraged him to take his research in a new direction. Grabar's new focus is clear enough in the *Cahiers archéologiques*, a major project launched immediately after the war (but which Grabar had already been preparing during the war, as we know from a letter he sent to Henri Grégoire).[36] The second part of its title, *Fin de l'Antiquité et Moyen Âge*, has new meaning in the light of what we have just discussed **{36}**. Like *Martyrium*, the *Cahiers* are devoted to an era rather than a place, and the fact that Grabar and other contributors perceived the entire Mediterranean as one cultural area was already evident in the first issues. The *Cahiers archéologiques* would become a true spiritual successor to *Seminarium Kondakovianum*, but with more coverage of the West. This geographical realignment was assured by Grabar's decision to bring Jean Hubert (1902–1994), a prominent specialist in the early Middle Ages in the West, onto the editorial staff of the journal.[37]

Grabar's article "Plotin et les origines de l'esthétique médiévale", published in the very first issue of the *Cahiers archéologiques,* was still further evidence of how the scholar's focus had shifted.[38] The article is an attempt to explain the shift in artistic styles – from illusionistic to bidimensional images – that occurred at the beginning of the

35• *"Les études byzantines, pendant la guerre, ont partagé le sort de toutes les activités intellectuelles en France. La recherche a été entravée ou momentanément arrêtée par la mobilisation de plusieurs érudits, par les opérations militaires, les évacuations, la fermeture des bibliothèques, la dispersion des fichiers, par divers obstacles d'ordre politique et économique, voire par la sous-alimentation. Et plus encore que la recherche proprement dite, l'impression des livres et des revues a été constamment entravée, pendant la période envisagée (absence de papier, de courant électrique, de main d'œuvre, de transport).",* Grabar 1944–1945, p. 431.

36• This letter is reproduced by Henri Grégoire in the journal *Byzantion* as an editorial addition to the article written by Grabar, see Grabar 1944–1945.

37• Erlande-Brandenburg 1995.

38• Grabar 1945.

CAHIERS ARCHÉOLOGIQUES

FIN DE L'ANTIQUITÉ ET MOYEN AGE

PUBLIÉS PAR

ANDRÉ GRABAR

I

Contributions de :
A. Piganiol - A. Grabar - L. Massignon
W. Seston - F. Benoit - L. Bréhier
J. Hubert - A. Frolov - May Vieillard

VANOEST
ÉDITIONS D'ART ET D'HISTOIRE
PARIS, 3 et 5, rue du Petit-Pont - Ve

MCMXLV

36} **Frontispiece of *Cahiers archéologiques. Fin de l'Antiquité et Moyen Âge*, I (1945)**

medieval period.[39] According to Grabar, this shift took place over the entire Mediterranean. Discussing Plotinus also gave Grabar an occasion to reflect on the humanistic values linked closely with the beginning of a new phase of European culture in Late Antiquity; this notion of decay and rebirth brings his work closer to that of Panofsky, Weitzmann, and Krautheimer.[40] It is thus tempting to see Grabar's article, too, as a sort of celebration of new hope after the end of the war. As Plotinus was the beginning of a new culture, so would the *Cahiers archéologiques* be the beginning of a glorious new era in medieval studies. Significantly, while the article deals with a decisive moment of the visual culture of the medieval world, it leaves the Christian manifestations of this change to the side. Grabar takes a pagan philosopher as his guide, an idea which suited the mentality of the new French Republic infinitely better than it would have suited the mentality of Imperial Russia.

While Grabar's experience of the Nazi occupation does not seem to have been particularly traumatic, its impact on his scholarship is hard to dispute. His methodology remained unaffected, and he maintained the fundamental objectivity of his approach, but the topics he was interested in and the questions he asked were very much different.

39• Grabar 2018; Palladino 2018.

40• Foletti/Rosenbergová 2020.

THE *INSTITUTUM KONDAKOVIANUM* AND THE GERMAN OCCUPATION

We noted, in our first chapter, the plight of the Kondakov Institute in the late 1930s, and the decision to divide the members of the Institute between Czechoslovakia and Belgrade.[41] After the split of the Institute into two parts and the catastrophic air raid which took the lives of Rasovskij and his wife Rasovskaja-Okuněva, all remaining property of the Institute was returned to Prague. The wartime years that followed were, not surprisingly, dramatic ones for the Institute and its scholars.

This section of our book, about the Kondakov Institute in wartime, is based on correspondence and contracts in the Institute's archives in Prague, as well as a very important text which was recently discovered in the archives of Columbia University in New York. Among the personal documents left by Georgij Vernadskij is an entire box of containing items relating to the Kondakov Institute, including an eighty-page manuscript that Nikolaj Andrejev presented to Vernadskij.[42] To this manuscript Andrejev added a commentary explaining that the manuscript was intended as an explanation of what had happened at the Institute under the German occupation of Czechoslovakia. It is clear that even in the 1960s, when he wrote the manuscript, the subject was still a painful and polemical one for him and for others. After Andrejev's death, his official memoirs would be published, with a large part of them dedicated to his time in Prague.[43] In this later version, however, there are fewer details, so we will be using the unpublished text from Columbia University to reconstruct both the events and the climate of those years as precisely as possible.

The limits of Andrejev's unpublished manuscript should also be acknowledged. It was written in the 1960s, some twenty years after the events in question, and the text is far from impartial. One of its purposes was obviously to justify Andrejev's own actions as leader of the Institute during the war. We have thus attempted to verify

41 • See *supra*, pp. 63–66.

42 • Nikolay Andreyev, Material supplied by Dr. N. E. Andreyev, Formerly Student, Fellow and Acting Director of the Kondakov Institute in Prague, CUL/BA/VC, box 158 (further "Andreyev Memoirs").

43 • Andreyev 2009.

and complement Andrejev's statements, whenever possible, with documentation in the Institute's archives in Prague.[44] Beyond the facts of the matter, we will also try to understand how some of these scholars behaved and felt as they attempted to continue their work under two totalitarian regimes.

SCHOLARLY RESEARCH UNDER THE PROTECTORATE

With the split of the Institute, it was decided that the Prague branch would effectively cease to be a real research institute, and that all scholarly activities would be moved to Belgrade. In keeping with this decision, the last issue of the *Annales de l'Institut Kondakov* was actually published in Belgrade in 1940. No other issue would ever appear, although we know that two further issues were prepared for eventual publication after the war.[45] The articles for one of them were gathered during the last years of the war, the idea being to publish just as soon as the conflict ended; there was never any suggestion that it should be published before then. This was the explicit policy of the Institute, formulated by Andrejev and accepted by the executive committee of the Institute:

> "*1) **Not to print any books** (actually because it was feared that Germans would then shove in something on Nazi lines, the overt justification being the impossibility of obtaining paper for works not connected with the war* [...]*).*"[46]

In other words, the desire to not have their work used by the Germans in any way was just as strong an obstacle to publication as any practical problems with printing supplies. We struggle to imagine a scholarly institute deciding to go into "inner exile",[47] even when three of its most prominent members, Toll', Ostrogorskij, and Rasovskij, had left the country. It would have been easy enough to assemble materials contributed by those who remained in Prague, such as Myslivec, Dvorník, and Andrejev himself, or by colleagues in Germany. Nonetheless, the Institute stuck by its decision. According to Andrejev, the priorities in wartime were: to enlarge the library's collection, to

44• On the question of autobiography, see, once again, Tassi 2007.

45• See *supra*, pp. 63–66.

46• "Andreyev Memoirs", pp. 47–48.

47• About the notion of "inner exile" or "inner emigration", see, e. g., Bock 1998.

enlarge as much as possible the institution's collection of art objects (especially Russian panel paintings), and to prepare the above-mentioned *Annales* for printing after the war.[48] The goal was not just to be less visible, but to prepare for a better future. This is the same attitude as Grabar attributed to Byzantinists in occupied France. It was a sort of intellectual hibernation, only in the case of the Institute in Prague the decision was conscious and shared.

A look through Andrejev's notes and the archives of the Institute turns up few exceptions to this policy. A few lectures were organised during the occupation, but they were only semi-public, effectively open only to the Institute's local members.[49] Whereas Grabar adapted his research to the needs of his wartime audience, in Prague there was silent continuity. There would be no publications, but the library and collections would be enlarged in the same way as before the war.

FINANCES

The beginning of the war brought, as one would expect, many problems. We have already spoken about the fact that from 1938, many of the honorary members quit paying their contributions to the Institute because of various circumstances relating to the war and occupation.[50] At the same time, state subsidies for the Institute were dramatically reduced. To top it all off, the Princess Jašvil, one of the key figures in raising funds, died in 1939.[51] As a consequence, the Institute found itself in danger of financial collapse, but the situation would soon improve.

Andrejev tells us that in the time between the Munich Agreement and the formation of the Protectorate, the Institute was able to sell most of its remaining stock of books for a very good price. Andrejev was contacted by a man who, it seems, feared that the Czechoslovak crown would soon lose its value. He therefore bought as many copies of *Seminarium* as he could, hoping to be able to sell them later on. This transaction momentarily kept the Institute afloat.[52]

48• "Andreyev Memoirs", pp. 47–48.

49• Zaoral 2013, p. 552.

50• See *supra*, pp. 68–70.

51• "Andreyev Memoirs", p. 18; Iberl 2011.

52• "Andreyev Memoirs", pp. 15–16.

During the first part of the war, Andrejev himself was unable to live off his salary from the Institute and had no savings. He thus found additional work at the Free Russian University of Prague (*Rušká lidová/svobodná univerzita v Praze*). This organization had existed since the early days of the First Republic but had lost much of its independence under the Protectorate; its rector was replaced and the institution was put under the control of Berlin's Russian community. Nevertheless, the Free Russian University never became explicitly pro-Nazi.[53]

The key figure for the financial survival of the Institute was, as we mentioned earlier, Prince Karel Schwarzenberg. Born in 1911, he was introduced to the work of the *Seminarium* by the Princess Jašvil on April 3, 1934, at the age of 23. He soon began to participate in its activities and promised his financial support.[54] On April 20, he officially became an honorary member. Starting in 1935, he gave the Institute 500 crowns each year, and donated books and art objects as well. In 1935 he donated a reproduction of Andrej Rublev's *Trinity* and a portrait of the Tsar Alexej I Michajlovič. In 1937, he donated books concerning heraldry.[55] In early 1938, at a time when the Institute was under increasing financial pressure, the following letter was sent to Schwarzenberg:

> "*Dear Prince, please accept, on behalf of the Kondakov Institute, our sincerest thanks for your help in one of the most difficult moments of its existence. Your gift of 7,000 crowns ensures that we will be able to cover next year's rent. Thank you once again for your generous gift.*"[56]

Schwarzenberg's importance to the Institute could not be clearer; without his support, there was no guarantee that the rent could be paid. The next year, Schwarzenberg increased his membership contribution to 10,000 crowns, and donated further artworks and books. By mid-1939, the tone of the correspondence between

53• Mach 2012, pp. 81–93.

54• Zaoral 2013.

55• All the letters are in the box UDU-AV/KI-16 Schwarzenberg, K.

56• *"Cher Prince, veuillez accepter de la part de l'Institut Kondakov les remerciements les plus sincères pour votre aide dans l'un des moments les plus difficiles de son existence. Votre don de 7000 couronnes nous permet d'être rassurés quant aux frais de loyer pour l'année prochaine. Encore merci pour votre don généreux."*, UDU-AV/KI-16 Schwarzenberg, K., letter from the secretary of the IK, dated to the 21st April 1938.

Schwarzenberg and the Institute had become much more personal and friendly, with Andrejev inquiring about the health of Schwarzenberg's mother.

Schwarzenberg was very creative in finding ways to support the Institute. In September 1939, he bought books published by the Institute for a total of 20,000 crowns.[57] The peak of his generosity would be reached in August 1940. Germany had invaded and defeated France, and was waging an all-out aerial assault on Great Britain. In the midst of that, Schwarzenberg gave the Institute a membership fee of 65,000 crowns. According to a letter from Andrejev dated September 7, Schwarzenberg had explicitly asked that this donation be used to enlarge the collections of the Institute, support its daily operation, enlarge its premises, and produce further publications.[58] Andrejev remarked that this gift would ensure the Institute's full and active existence for years to come.

The Institute had found a true patron in the midst of a war, one who was also actively engaged in the life of the organisation. Schwarzenberg himself made light of the donation, claiming that it was the best use that could be made of accidental profit from his land holdings. Andrejev, in his memoirs, remembered it like this:

> “*Here are 50,000 crowns. Will you accept them as advance payment of my life-membership fee? Please do not thank me. We have just sold some timber very profitably to the mills who wish to build up reserves. I am so deeply indebted to the Institute, to the princess and her daughter that I am only too happy to help the Institute when it is really in need of assistance.*”[59]

Andrejev recalls Schwarzenberg's generosity and nobility but gets the amount wrong. Andrejev may have mis-remembered the exact sum twenty years later, or perhaps Schwarzenberg had first mentioned 50,000 crowns and then increased the amount when

57• UDU-AV/KI-16 Schwarzenberg, K.

58• “*Vaše Jasnošti, Potvrzuji příjem Vašeho jednorázového členškého příšpěvku v obnose* K. *65.000* [...] *Tato čáštka dle Vašeho přání bude určena na zařízení a zvětšení míštnošti Inštitutu za účelem umíštění jeho šbírek a na vydávání jeho prací.*” [Your Highness, I acknowledge receipt of your one-time membership fee of 65,000 crowns (...) According to your wishes, this amount will be allocated to the equipment and enlargement of the Institute's rooms to accommodate its collections and to publish its works.], see UDU-AV/KI-16 Schwarzenberg, K., letter of September 7, 1940.

59• “Andreyev Memoirs”, p. 26

sending the money. Andrejev's letter implies that an oral agreement had preceded it.

As we mentioned in the first chapter of this book, the other major source of income for the Institute during the war was the sale of coloured prints of Russian "icons" in Germany.[60] Printed by Václav Neubert's firm, these images were surprisingly popular in the Reich:

"*The financial situation was showing constant improvement. Orders for colored icon prints; coming chiefly from the Catholic regions of Germany, were now past for thousands of copies. In the middle of 1944, a Mr. Kletsanda, formerly a General in the Czech army and now Chairman of same firm, placed an order for one hundred thousand prints and was negotiating a rebate for a further order of 200,000. All this made it possible for the Institute to carry out the above-mentioned program. Salaries were raised in 1943 to levels then current into the Protectorate.*"[61]

Even Andrejev struggled to understand why Germans wanted to buy so many prints of Russian devotional paintings.[62] We have seen how "Russian icons" became more and more familiar to Western European audiences after the First World War, and have discussed the books about them that were published in those years across the continent.[63] But those publications were targeted at very educated buyers, and according to François Bœspflug, this type of image did not enter the popular culture of Western European Catholics until after the Second Vatican Council of 1962–1965.[64] So why were hundreds of thousands of Russian images sold all over Nazi Germany as the Reich's armies did battle with Russia itself?

The only thing, we think, that can explain this popularity is the style of the images themselves. After many examples of "icons" were restored at the beginning of the twentieth century, the very bidimensional and hieratic aesthetics of medieval Russian panel painting became very popular in avant-garde circles both in Russia and

60• See *supra*, p. 70 and Jančárková/Gagen 2019.

61• "Andreyev Memoirs", p. 48.

62• *Ibidem*, p. 49.

63• Kondakov 1927b; Muratoff 1931; on the reception of "icons" in various countries, see, i.e., Kyzlasova 2010; Marks 2012; Foletti 2016a; Salmond 2017. See also Taroutina 2018.

64• Bœspflug 2007.

in the West.[65] To intellectuals, these images were impressive examples of "primitive" painting, and we discussed their aesthetic appeal when we talked about the lecture delivered by Prince Schwarzenberg in the 1930s.[66]

One thing that is often forgotten in discussions of Eastern devotional panel paintings is the fact that some of the most popular Western devotional images, whether medieval or Early Modern, had very similar formal features. Good examples are the famous panel painting from Częstochowa and the icon of Old Brno {37}, but the instances are manifold.[67] Interestingly enough, the Jesuits promoted these images, with their pre-modern style, in the seventeenth and eighteenth centuries. They distributed copies of the image of the so-called *Salus Populi Romani*, one of the most important medieval Roman panel paintings, throughout Europe and beyond.[68] We believe, then, that this "medieval" style, synthetic and extremely effective, was well known in the Catholic parts of Germany and other Central European countries. Such "primitive" images were venerated at important pilgrimage sites in the Early Modern period, and these sites – e.g. the Michaelskirche in Vienna, the Freisinger image, Częstochowa, and many in Bohemia and Moravia – attracted pilgrims well into the twentieth century.[69] We think, then, that the popularity of the Russian devotional paintings was due to features that they shared with other pre-modern devotional paintings, and had nothing at all to do with their being from Russia.

We suspect that bidimensional and non-mimetic images remained immensely popular even as the most refined Early Modern images were being produced. We have mentioned André Grabar's thought on the neo-Platonic perspective and the origins of medieval aesthetics. Grabar was sympathetic to the bidimensional style because of his Russian origins, but the same aesthetic appears to have survived in popular culture in the West for centuries after it disappeared from learned circles. The images produced and widely distributed by the Kondakov Institute are proof that this aesthetic was alive at least until the Second World War. Perhaps it is no

65• Leardi 2010; Martin 2012; Foletti 2016a.

66• See *supra*, pp. 72–74.

67• On the "icon" of Old Brno, see Frantová/Pecinová 2013.

68• Wolf 1990; Jakubec 2013; Michel 2017.

69• See, e.g., Schellewald 2019.

37} Icon of Old Brno, second half of the 13th century (?), Church of the Assumption of the Virgin Mary, Brno

coincidence that is was a German scholar, Hans Belting, who shed new light on the tradition of devotional panel paintings precisely as the Iron Curtain was collapsing. He investigated this tradition in both East and West and proposed a new paradigm for understanding how these images worked, a phenomenon which he later termed as their "iconic presence".[70]

A SCHOLARLY INSTITUTION CAUGHT BETWEEN OCCUPIERS AND RESISTANCE

Thanks to Schwarzenberg and the paradoxical popularity of the Institute's prints of Russian "icons", the institution arrived at the end of the war with a full bank account, a much larger library, and a vast collection of medieval and Early Modern art objects. The survival of the Institute, however, depended on much more than money. The occupation was a tragic time which only got worse after the assassination of Reinhard Heydrich in June 1942.[71] This is not the place to review this event nor the subsequent atrocities at Lidice and Ležáky;[72] suffice it to say that life in Prague, especially after 1942, was far from simple. Food was rationed, a curfew was imposed, and supposed enemies of the regime were executed, their names posted around the city on an almost daily basis.[73]

The Institute's political situation was, to say the least, complicated. Before Hitler attacked the Soviet Union in 1941, Nazi Germany was officially allied with Stalin.[74] It seemed entirely possible that Hitler would come after White Russian émigrés, and the Kondakov Institute would be destroyed in the process. This never happened, but the beginning of the war was still difficult and dangerous for the Institute. After the Belgrade branch was established, a conflict erupted between Rasovskij in Belgrade and Andrejev in Prague. Ostensibly, as we can see in Andrejev's memoirs and letters preserved in Prague, the conflict was about the transfer of books and other belongings from Prague to Belgrade.[75] When Rasovskij arrived in Belgrade, he

70• Belting 1990, 2016.

71• Bryant 2009, pp. 179–207.

72• Macková/Ulrych 2004.

73• Bryant 2009.

74• Moorhouse 2014.

75• "Andreyev Memoirs"; Hrochová 1995, p. 33; Beißwenger 2005 [2001], pp. 59–61.

wanted the Institute's whole library to follow him, but this was next to impossible. As Andrejev explained, the Protectorate "had forbidden the removal from the country of all valuable cultural objects, so that the remaining books would have to be dispatched through diplomatic channels, i.e. the Yugoslav Embassy in Prague".[76] In this Andrejev was simply stating the facts.

Once the war started, even these channels were closed, and the tone of Rasovskij's letters to Prague became more and more menacing. The Belgrade branch also expected to receive the proceeds of the international sale of the Institute's publications, but these funds were not forwarded, and Zaoral believes that this may be the root of the problems between Rasovskij and Andrejev.[77]

In his memoirs, Andrejev offers a simple explanation for not sending these funds: from early 1939, some of the Institute's commercial agents ceased paying for the publications they sold. Andrejev mentions the agent in Leipzig, Otto Harrassowitz, who had not paid the Institute for a long time even as he continued to order their books.[78] For the people left in Prague, the loss of the Institute's collections was a heavy blow which greatly reduced their prestige. Andrejev tells of a visit from Nikolaj Okuněv, who had come to verify exactly what had already been sent to Belgrade. Okuněv – who incidentally was the father of Rasovskij's wife, Irena Rasovskaja-Okuněva – was shocked enough to recommend that Andrejev ask for the protection of the Slavonic Institute of Prague. Okuněv also reminded Andrejev that the Kondakov Institute had always been financially supported by the Czechoslovak government, and suggested that transferring its property out of the country would be construed as a "criminal offense".[79] Okuněv's suggestion meant that the Prague branch of the Institute was now under pressure from the Belgrade branch on one side, and the Slavonic Institute in Prague on the other. Andrejev shored up his position by creating an advisory board composed of Myslivec, Schwarzenberg, Savickij, the Princess Jašvil, and General Černavin.[80] This committee supported

76• "Andreyev Memoirs", p. 12.

77• Zaoral 2013,

78• "Andreyev Memoirs", p. 15.

79• *Ibidem*, pp. 17–18.

80• See *supra*, pp. 65–66.

Andrejev in his attempts to keep the Prague branch and its activities intact.

After Bohemia and Moravia were annexed to the Third Reich in March 1939, the situation in Prague became almost intolerably tense.[81] According to Andrejev:

> "*Utter uncertainty enveloped everyone in Czechoslovakia; people were seized by fear and hatred for the victorious Nazis. In these circumstances, the flood of letters, chiefly from Dr. Rasovsky, demanding the mailing of books, was simply ludicrous.*"[82]

This conflict between the Belgrade and Prague branches of the Institute culminated when Ostrogorskij wrote a letter to Professor Herwig Hamperl (1899–1976), vice-rector of the German University.[83]

> "*Unexpectedly, at one p.m. an urgent message came by hand from the Rectorate of the German University addressed to Dr. Andreyev that Professor Hamperl would expect him the following morning at 10 o'clock and that he would be required to comment on a letter received by Professor Hamperl from Prof. G. A. Ostrogorsky, which was attached. The purport of the letter was as follows: Ostrogorsky, writing in his capacity as Chairman of the Board of the Kondakov Institute, said that it had come to his knowledge that Dr. Andreyev, the youngest member of the Institute left in Prague after the departure of the Institute for Belgrade, in order to liquidate various pending matters, is now taking the liberty of misinforming the German authorities by creating the impression of fictitious scientific work done in Prague, makes unauthorized statements on behalf of the Institute, where he has no scientific or administrative standing, and appropriates property and funds belonging to the Kondakov Institute.*"[84]

This letter could have had lethal consequences for both Andrejev and the Institute. Had it fallen into the hands of the Gestapo, Andrejev would have been arrested and quite possibly executed, since the occupiers were severely punishing all crimes, especially ones that

81• Glettler/Lipták/Mísková 2004.

82• "Andreyev Memoirs", p. 18.

83• On the German University, see Míšková 2003; regarding Hamperl, see his autobiography, Hamperl 1972, pp. 192–193.

84• "Andreyev Memoirs", pp. 37–38.

impacted the economy of the Protectorate.[85] Andrejev, of course, accused Rasovskij of being behind this letter, but we have no proof of Rasovskij's involvement.[86] Andrejev also tells us how the Institute's advisory board, gathered that very evening, reacted to the letter. They wrote a memo to Hamperl explaining the situation, informing him of all Andrejev had done after Toll's departure, and describing the conflict between the two branches of the Institute. Karel Schwarzenberg himself translated the memo into German, again proving himself invaluable to the Institute. Perhaps out of respect for Schwarzenberg, Hamperl's judgement of the Institute's situation was sympathetic:

"*Thank your God that this vile letter was addressed to me, otherwise you would already be in prison. I believe your interpretation of the facts, for all the data we have on you absolutely contradicts Ostrogorsky's assertations. Besides, we know Schwarzenberg and Savitsky. I am surprised that such a well-known scientist as Ostrogorsky should appear so foolish and dishonest. I must report all this to my superiors. Of course you need not answer Ostrogorsky's letter; he probably imagines that you will never see it. I shall duly inform you of my superiors' decision.*[87] [...]

For your Council's information, I have written to Professor Ostrogorsky that the data in his possession is not correct. We checked the Institute's and Dr. Andreyev's activities and found nothing contrary to the resolutions of the Institute's Board or the laws of the Protectorate which are the safeguard of the Institute in Prague."[88]

The conflict between the two branches ended only with the death of Rasovskij and his wife in the German assault on Belgrade in April of 1941. The independence of the Institute remained in danger, however, since Hamperl was convinced that it should be part of the German University in Prague:

"*We are studying the matter. The best course would perhaps be to give your Institute new premises – in the buildings of the German University.*"[89]

85• Tauchen 2015.

86• "Andreyev Memoirs", pp. 38–39.

87• *Ibidem*, p. 39.

88• *Ibidem*, p. 40.

89• *Ibidem*.

Andrejev was aware of the dangers of such an arrangement, both for his person and the Institute, since it would mark them as collaborators. He did his best to resist the suggestion, and in the end, Hamperl gave up, ostensibly for purely practical reasons:

"*However, it would probably be too much trouble and would be expensive to remove and re-arrange everything, besides which if this were to happen I believe Prince Schwarzenberg might be vexed, having been a protector of your Institute, to come himself under the protection of our University. We are therefore leaving things as they are. You are Institutsleiter, but you will henceforth be responsible to Professor Weingart, Byzantologist of our University, whom you recently elected honorary member of your Institute. You will report to him, but in special cases you may as before have recourse to me.*"[90]

Under this arrangement, the Institute was safe, since it was formally under German authority, but it remained in its own premises and kept its own advisory board. Andrejev remembered Weingart as a tolerant and supportive colleague:

"*Professor Weingart, whom Dr. Andreyev had already seen in connection with his election to honorary membership, was a serious elderly scholar, entirely immersed in problems of his science. He had already visited the Institute. Now he asked Dr. Andreyev to come and see him at his flat in connection with his having been appointed 'Commissar of the Institute'.* [...] *Professor Weingart* [upon meeting Andrejev told him] *'I hold your work in high esteem and have not the slightest wish to interfere with it. Please go on working and inform me once a year of the progress achieved. Let me advise you to manage the financial affairs of the Institute without asking our organizations for anything'. In fact, Weingart never interfered with the Institute, but on the other hand never did anything for it, fully occupied by his own work on the history of Byzantine art. He never again visited the Institute where he was 'Reichskommissar'.*"[91]

Andrejev's memory cannot be correct here, since the only Byzantinist named Weingart active in Prague between the wars was Miloš Weingart (1890–1939), who died on January 12, 1939. This was before the events narrated by Andrejev, all of which must have

90• "Andreyev Memoirs", p. 40.

91• *Ibidem*, p. 41.

happened between March 1939, when the Protectorate was created, and April 1941, when the Belgrade branch was destroyed. The only possible explanation is that Andrejev was confusing Weingart with someone else. A look at the staff of the German University in Prague in these years turns up Eduard Winter (1896–1982), whose surname also begins in W and who was interested enough in Byzantium to publish, in 1942, a book entitled *Byzanz und Rom im Kampf um die Ukraine, 955–1939*.[92] Winter, moreover, was intimately involved with the Nazi regime, being a member of the "Reinhard Heydrich Foundation" and later collaborating with a Referent of the RSHA (a kind of "Ministry of Police Affairs") in Czechoslovakia and Ukraine.[93] His wartime transfer to Ukraine would also explain the lack of direct supervision of the Institute. Be that as it may, this arrangement permitted the Institute a large degree of independence for the duration of the war.

We should remind that the project of the "Reinhard Heydrich Foundation" was to incorporate all Slavonic institutes in Bohemia under one unique German administration. This was, however, entirely successful for the Kondakov Institute.[94] Nonetheless, various parties were suspicious of the Institute's "neutrality". At some point during the war, Andrejev received a visit from a German art historian from Munich, Dr. Johann J. Morper (1899–1980):

> "*The Institute received an unexpected visit from a German in uniform* [...] *who in high-sounding terms started praising Kondakov and his work and made a* [...] *speech in front of his portrait, expressing his delight at finding himself in 'this temple of scholarship'.* [...] *He said that though he had been conscripted as a private, he had been transferred to the Cultural Department of the Protectorate and that he was to 'write a special report on the Institute, which was a jewel not only of the Protectorate but of the Third Reich' and so on.*"[95]

Morper had corresponded with *Seminarium* between the wars and voiced his appreciation of its work.[96] Because of the prestige of the

92• Winter 1942.

93• See Němec 2008; Fillafer 2016.

94• Němec 2011, p. 93.

95• "Andreyev Memoirs", pp. 20–21.

96• UDU-AV/KI-14.

Institute in his eyes, he wanted it to be incorporated into existing German academic structures, which was something Andrejev wanted to avoid at all costs. This sensitive situation was resolved by Prince Schwarzenberg, who explained the benefits of having such an international scholarly institution in Prague.[97] Schwarzenberg appears to have convinced Morper that keeping this prestigious international research centre independent would demonstrate that the Nazi regime had a tolerant attitude towards culture and scholarship.

Schwarzenberg was able to protect the Institute at an official level, but the threats came in other guises as well. We know that the Institute was infiltrated at least twice, once by the Germans and once by the Resistance. A certain visitor named Dedio pretended to be a young German interested in Russian culture, then, once satisfied that the Institute was not involved in any anti-German activities, revealed himself to be an SS officer. On another occasion a young Czech lady presented herself as a visitor from Vienna, but her mission was to look for signs of collaboration with the Nazi authorities. She found none.[98] Andrejev had to walk a fine line, neither openly rejecting overtures from the Germans, nor working too closely with them. Any misstep could have led to his death and that of the Institute. *Volens nolens*, he adopted the attitude described in the early seventeenth century by Torquato Accetto in his book *Della dissimulazione onesta* – "On Honest Dissimulation".[99] This approach was adopted by many under Nazi occupation, and not only in Czechoslovakia.[100] The ambivalence of the situation can be seen in a photograph of the interior of the Institute; next to portraits of Kondakov and Beljaev hung – probably for the entire duration of the war – portraits of Hitler and Emil Hácha (1872–1945), the Czech president during the Protectorate {38}.

The Institute, despite these challenges, survived the war. In the very last months of the conflict, some of the library was moved out of Prague to where it would be safe from air raids, but soon thereafter the entire collection and library were put in new premises on Haštalská Street, rented with the generous support of Karel Schwarzenberg.

97• "Andreyev Memoirs", p. 23.

98• Foletti 2019, pp. 82–83.

99• Accetto 2012 [1641].

100• Palladino 2017.

НИКОЛАЙ МИХ.
БѢЛЯЕВЪ
1899—1930
П-Я

38} Kondakov Institute interior, Haštalská Street, Prague, 1940s

THE *INSTITUTUM KONDAKOVIANUM* AND COMMUNISM

Prague had to wait until May 1945 to be freed from the German occupation. The first forces to confront the Wehrmacht and the SS were those of General Andrej Vlasov (1901–1946), a very ambivalent figure who had served in both the Soviet and German armies.[101] A bit later, the city was liberated for good by the Red Army itself. As we now know, liberation was not the Soviet leadership's only plan for the Czech lands.[102] According to the Yalta agreement, they were to be integrated into the Soviet sphere of influence, and the Red Army, especially the SMERSH, immediately began to arrest, deport, and execute potential opponents of Bolshevik rule.[103] While Prague was still celebrating its liberation, the Soviets were taking control of the country. This would have an immediate and dramatic impact on the Kondakov Institute.

With the arrival of the Red Army, some items from the Institute's collections were immediately transferred to the Soviet Union. Among these, it seems, was the Institute's one panel painting attributed (at that time) to Andrej Rublev, possibly the most important Russian painter of the fifteenth century.[104] The exact number of items taken by the Red Army is impossible to determine, at least on the basis of the archives we have been able to consult. Nor does it appear that a list of such items was ever compiled, either in Prague or in the Soviet Union (at least according to those who have investigated the Kondakov Institute in Russian archives). These material losses were only the beginning, however. On May 23, 1945, just a few days after the Russians entered Prague, Andrejev was arrested and sent to a Soviet prison camp in eastern Germany. He was freed two years later thanks to the personal intervention of Hana Benešová (1885–1974), the wife of Czechoslovak President Beneš, with the help of Prince Schwarzenberg.[105] Nevertheless, Andrejev was denied permission to return to Czechoslovakia, and left for England before continuing on to the United States.

101 • Hoffmann 2003.

102 • Šebek 2019.

103 • For a general overview see, e.g., Sviták 1990.

104 • "Andreyev Memoirs", pp. 52, 57.

105 • For the full story, see Andreyev 2009, pp. 183–235.

In the meantime, the remaining members of the Kondakov Institute attempted to resume their pre-war activities. Karel Schwarzenberg was appointed Acting Director, and work was begun on a new volume of the journal *Seminarium Kondakovianum*. After the Communist putsch of February 1948, however, Prince Schwarzenberg was forced to resign from all his functions and flee the country. Věra Hrochová believes that Zdeněk Nejedlý (1878–1962), the head of the Czechoslovak Academy of Sciences, decided in 1948 to incorporate the Institute into his academy.[106] According to Roman Zaoral, the decision was made later.[107] In any case, on August 17, 1951, in accordance with a decision made by the Soviet government, the Kondakov Institute joined the Czechoslovak Academy of Sciences. There it essentially disappeared, which was what some former members thought should happen. Ostrogorskij, for instance, had opined in the late 1940s that without the Russian émigrés who had founded the Institute, its continued existence made little sense.[108] Thus, after twenty-six years informal and formal existence, the Institute's legacy and property became part of the Department of Art History at the Czechoslovak Academy of Sciences.

106• Hrochová 1995, p. 34.

107• Zaoral 2013.

108• Archives RAN, f.1609, op.2, d.349, l.10–11, letter of Ostrogorskij to Florovskij, 25.12.1947: "The activity of the Institute ended [...] in my understanding with the death of D.A. Rassovsky [...] A scholarly institution lives through the persons who lead it. Those who can lead this institution, maintain the level of its research and above all its special character, have been absent since the departure of N.P. Toll', the death of D.A. Rassovsky [...] and the even earlier death of N.M. Beliaev." See Beißwenger 2005 [2001], p. 65.

CONCLUSION

Now that we have followed the parallel (and not entirely independent) stories of the Kondakov Institute and of André Grabar, it is clear that much remains to be done. This book must now end, but we hope that it will be taken as a call to further investigate how the first wave of Russian emigration affected the arts, the humanities, and the sciences outside of Russia itself. We have only looked at the field of Byzantine studies, but we hope that this has been useful. As Giovanni Gasbarri pointed out in 2015, "Byzantium" has never been systematically examined from an epistemological standpoint; we hope that our book has been at least a small step in the right direction.[1]

At this point in our research, however, we think that at least a few conclusions can be drawn. First, our notions of "Byzantium" owe much to Russians who emigrated to the West in the aftermath of the Russian Revolution, and their perception of that civilization was much affected by their experience of life outside the motherland. "Byzantium", which for centuries had been considered the direct predecessor of the Russian Empire, and something which legitimized its successor's expansionist ambitions and its spiritual authority, was suddenly wrenched out of that framework. As a consequence of that mass exodus of scholars and art objects, and way in which those scholars were dispersed around the world, the "Empire of Constantinople" would now be a transnational phenomenon.

1 • Gasbarri 2015, pp. 12–13.

Second, the reaction of Grabar and of the Kondakov Institute's scholars to the political upheavals of the 1930s helped define Byzantine studies as well. The ominous rise of Nazi Germany may have felt more menacing in Czechoslovakia than in France, which sat behind the supposedly formidable *Maginot Line*. In the end, neither allies nor military preparation saved either country from brutal occupation. If one looks at the archives of the Kondakov Institute from these years, or reads the memoirs of Andrejev or Grabar, one is left with the impression that these scholars already assumed a democratic background to their scholarly work. Then, when occupation came and destroyed that background, their public work essentially ceased. Of the scholars we have followed, none but Rasovskij and Rasovskaja-Okuněva was the victim of direct (while accidental) violence, and yet, the war had a profound impact on their destinies.

The war had some effects on these scholars which appear decisive. Under Andrejev, the Kondakov Institute had far more contact with the Czech cultural elite, so that when the war ended, one could have imagined a bright future for the institution, finally integrated into Czechoslovakia. Grabar, in occupied Paris, discovered a new passion for Western medieval art, and soon helped to formulate the idea of a shared Mediterranean heritage for East and West. Out of the darkness came new ideas and hope.

At least for the Konkakov Institute, those hopes were false: the integration of Czechoslovakia into the Communist world did not permit the survival of a Russian émigré institution. It would be easy to blame the end of this institution on the USSR and nobody else, but that would be an oversimplification. The Czechoslovak reaction to German violence during the war turned into an aggressive nationalism once the country had been liberated. The phenomenon was not an isolated one. Just as Czechoslovakia expelled its ethnic German population, so would Turkey expel the Jews from Edirne, and so on in various countries around Europe. What would be, in those times, the Kondakov Institute's chances of survival if its members were not studying Czech or Slovak art? This question will remain unanswered. Yet, the history of art history in Czechoslovakia in the following decades indicates a deep autoreferential introspection.

We must return, now, to the title of this book: "Byzantium or Democracy?" Such a question is everything but rhetorical. By formulating it, we wished to underline the immense impact of political history on scholarship. In the thirty years we have examined in this book, from Kondakov's arrival in Prague in 1922 to the definitive suppression of the Institute bearing his name in 1952, "Byzantium" remained a very fluid concept. Invented in Early Modern Europe, it continued, and continues, to change along with the surroundings of those who study it.

ABBREVIATIONS

- **ACF/FAG/BC** = Archives du Collège de France, Paris, Fonds André Grabar, boîte complémentaire
- **CUL/BA/VC** = Columbia University Libraries, New York, Manuscripts collections, Bakhmeteff Archive, Vernadsky Collection
- **PNP/FNK** = Památník národního písemnictví, Prague, Fond Nikodim Pavlovič Kondakov
- **RAN** = Rossijskoj Akademii Nauk, Moscow
- **UDU-AV/KI** = Archiv Ústavu dějin umění Akademie věd ČR, Prague, Fond Kondakovova Institutu
- **"ANDREYEV MEMOIRS"** = Nikolay Andreyev, Material supplied by Dr. N. E. Andreyev, Formerly Student, Fellow and Acting Director of the Kondakov Institute in Prague, CUL/BA/VC, box 158
- **"ESQUISSE BIOGRAPHIQUE"** = ACF/FAG/BC, "Esquisse biographique"

BIBLIOGRAPHY

- **AA.VV. 1924:** *Nikodim Pavlovič Kondakov. 1844–1924. K vosmidesjatiletju so dnja roždenija* [Nikodim Pavlovič Kondakov. 1844–1924. On the Occasion of His Eightieth Birthday], Prague 1924.
- **ACCETTO 2012 [1641]:** Torquato Accetto, *Della dissimulazione onesta*, Milan 2012 [1641].
- **AGOSTINO 1991:** Marc Agostino, *Le pape Pie XI et l'opinion (1922–1939)*, Rome 1991.
- **AINALOV 1961 [1900]:** Dimitri V. Ainalov, *The Hellenistic Origins of Byzantine Art*, Cyril Mango ed., Elisabeth and Serge Sobolevitch transl., New Brunswick 1961 [1900].
- **AJNALOV 1900:** Dmitrij V. Ajnalov, *Ellinističeskie osnovy vizantijskogo iskusstva* [The Hellenistic Origins of Byzantine Art], Saint Petersburg 1900.
- **AJNALOV 1928:** Dmitrij V. Ajnalov, "Novyj ikonografičeskij obraz Christa" [New Iconographical Image of Christ], *Seminarium Kondakovianum*, II (1928), pp. 19–24.
- **AKSENOVA 1993:** Jelena P. Aksenova, "Institut im. N.P. Kondakova: popytki reanimacii (po materialam archiva A.V. Florovskogo)" [The Institute Named after N. P. Kondakov: Attempts at Resuscitation (Based on Materials from the Archive of A. V. Florovskij)], *Slavjanovedenie*, 4 (1993), pp. 63–74.
- **ALFÖLDI 1934:** Andreas Alföldi, "Die Ausgestaltung des monarchischen Zeremoniells am römischen Kaiserhofe", *Mitteilungen des Deutschen Archäologischen Instituts. Römische Abteilung*, 49 (1934), pp. 1–118.
- **ANDALORO 2006:** Maria Andaloro, "L'irruzione delle 'nuove immagini'", in *L'orizzonte tardoantico e le nuove immagini 312–468*, vol. 1: *La pittura medievale a Roma 312–1431*, Maria Andaloro ed., Rome 2006, pp. 15–31.
- **ANDERLE 1987:** Josef Anderle, "Karel Schwarzenberg: Czech Nobleman and Historian (1911–1986)", *Kosmas: Journal of Czechoslovak and Central European Studies*, 6/1 (1987), pp. 103–106.

- **ANDERSON 1937:** William Anderson, "Nordische Bildkunst des ersten Jahrhunderts", *Annales de l'Institut Kondakov*, 9 (1937), pp. 23–38.
- **ANDREEVA 1929:** Marija A. Andreeva, "Drevnij persten' iz' Varny" [An Old Sigillary Ring from Varna], *Byzantinoslavica*, I (1929), pp. 151–158.
- **ANDREYEV 2009:** Nikolay Andreyev, *A Moth on the Fence: Memoirs of Russia, Estonia, Czechoslovakia, and Western Europe*, Catherine Andreyev ed., Patrick Miles transl., Surbiton 2009.
- **ANDREYEV/SAVICKÝ 2004:** Catherine Andreyev, Ivan Savický, *Russia Abroad. Prague and the Russian Diaspora, 1918–1938*, New Haven / London 2004.
- **AVTONOMOVA 2004:** Natal'ja Avtonomova, "Verso un mondo senza oggetti", in *Da Giotto a Malevič. La reciproca meraviglia*, catalogue of the exhibition, (Rome, Scuderie del Quirinale, 2 October 2004 – 9 January 2005), Stefania Maninchedda ed., Milan 2004, pp. 300–307.
- **AZÉMA/BÉDARIDA 2000:** *La France des années noires*, vol. I: *De la défaite à Vichy*, Jean-Pierre Azéma, François Bédarida eds, Paris 2000.
- **AZZARA 2011:** Claudio Azzara, "I longobardi in Italia e i longobardi nella storia d'Italia", in *I Longobardi del Sud*, Giuseppe Roma ed., Rome 2011, pp. 79–83.
- **BACCI 2020:** Michele Bacci, "Sacred Spaces vs. Holy Sites: On the Limits and Advantages of a Hierotopic Approach", in *Icons of Space. Studies in Hierotopy and Iconography*, Jelena Bogdanović ed., London 2020 (in print).
- **BARTLOVÁ 2016:** Milena Bartlová, *Unsere "nationale" Kunst*, Ostfildern 2016.
- **BASCIANI 2010:** Alberto Basciani, "Un archeologo al servizio della monarchia bulgara. La parabola di Bogdan Filov (1940–44)", in *Intellettuali versus democrazia. I regimi autoritari nell'Europa sud-orientale (1933–1953)*, Francesco Guida ed., Rome 2010, pp. 111–157.
- **BEIßWENGER 2005 [2001]:** Martin Beißwenger, *Das Seminarium Kondakovianum in Prag (1925–1950)*, M.A. thesis, (Humboldt-Universität, Berlin), 2005 [2001].
- **BELJAEV 1927:** Nikolaj M. Beljaev, "Blagoveščenie. Novyj pamjatnik grečeskoj ikonopisi" [Blagoveščenie. A New Monument to Greek Iconography], *Seminarium Kondakovianum*, I (1927), pp. 215–224.
- **BELJAEV 1929:** Nikolaj M. Beljaev, "Očerki po vizantiiskoj archeologii, I. Fibula v Vizantii; II. Chersonesskaja moščechranitel'nica" [Essays on Byzantine Archaeology, I. Fibulae in Byzantium; II. The Cherson Reliquary], *Seminarium Kondakovianum*, III (1929), pp. 49–114.
- **BELJAEV 1930:** Nikolaj M. Beljaev, "Obraz Bož'ej Materi Pelagonitisy" [The Image of the Mother of God Pelagonitissa], *Byzantinoslavica*, II (1930), pp. 386–394.

- **BELJAEV 1932:** Nikolaj M. Beljaev, *Ikona Božiej Materi Umilenija iz sobranija Soldatenkovych* [The Icon of Our Lady "Umilenie" from the Soldatenkov Collection], Prague 1932.
- **BELJAEV 1996:** S. A. Beljaev, "Iz istorii stanovlenija Seminarija imeni akademika N.P. Kondakova" [About the History of the Establishment of the Seminar Named after N. P. Kondakov], in *Russkaja emigracija v Evrope (20-e – 30-e gody XX veka)*, Moscow 1996, pp. 3–34.
- **BELJAEV 2000:** S. A. Beljaev, "Seminarij imeni N. P. Kondakova – neot'emtemaja čast' russkoj nacional'noj kul'tury" [The Seminar with the Name N. P. Kondakov – an Indissociable Part of Russian National Culture], *Drevnjaja Rus'*, 1 (2000), pp. 95–105.
- **BELTING 1990:** Hans Belting, *Bild und Kult. Eine Geschichte des Bildes vor dem Zeitalter der Kunst*, Munich 1990.
- **BELTING 2016:** Hans Belting, "Iconic Presence. Images in Religious Traditions", *Material Religion*, XII/2 (2016), pp. 235–237.
- **BERGER 2003:** Albrecht Berger, "Les projets byzantins de Louis II de Bavière", in *Byzance en Europe*, Marie-France Auzépy ed., Saint-Denis 2003, pp. 75–85.
- **BESANÇON 1974:** Alain Besançon, *Être russe au XIXe siècle*, Paris 1974.
- **BIDLO 1917:** Jaroslav Bidlo, *Kultura byzantská: její vznik a význam* [Byzantine Culture: Its Origin and Meaning], Prague 1917.
- **BIDLO *et al.* 1929:** Jaroslav Bidlo *et al.*, "Úvodní slovo" [Foreword], *Byzantinoslavica*, I (1929), pp. I–II.
- **BOBRINSKOY 1995:** Olga Bobrinskoy, "La Première République tchécoslovaque et l'émigration russe (1920–1938): la spécificité d'une politique d'asile", *Revue d'études comparatives Est-Ouest*, 26 (1995), pp. 153–175.
- **BOCK 1998:** Hans M. Bock, "Tentation totalitaire, 'émigration intérieure' et exil des intellectuels sous le IIIe Reich", in *Pour une histoire comparée des intellectuels*, Michel Trebitsch, Marie-Christine Granjon eds, Paris 1998, pp. 96–110.
- **BŒSPFLUG 2007:** François Bœspflug, "La redécouverte de l'icône chez les catholiques. Le cas français", in Spieser 2007, pp. 31–54.
- **BOGDANOVIČ 1913:** Evgenij Bogdanovič, *Trechstoletie deržavnomu domu Romanovych* [300th Anniversary of Rule of the House of Romanov], Saint Petersburg 1913.
- **BORN 1932:** Wolfgang Born, "Das Tiergeflecht in der nordrussischen Buchmalerei", *Seminarium Kondakovianum*, V (1932), pp. 63–96.
- **BORN/JANATKOVÁ/LABUDA 2004:** *Die Kunsthistoriographien in Ostmitteleuropa und der nationale Diskurs*, Robert Born, Alena Janatková, Adam Labuda eds, Berlin 2004.

- **BOUREAU 1990:** Alain Boureau, *Histoires d'un historien, Kantorowicz*, Paris 1990.
- **BRANDES 2008:** Detlef Brandes, *Die Sudetendeutschen im Krisenjahr 1938*, Oldenbourg/Munich 2008.
- **BRISAC/LENIAUD 1987:** Catherine Brisac, Jean-Michel Leniaud, "Adolphe-Napoléon Didron ou les média au service de l'art chrétien", *Revue de l'art*, 77 (1987), pp. 33–42.
- **BROGLIO 2000:** Francesco Margiotta Broglio, "Pio XI", in *Enciclopedia dei Papi*, Massimo Bray ed., vol. III, Rome 2000, pp. 617–632.
- **BROSE 2015:** Alain Brose, "Charlemagne dans l'idéologie national-socialiste", *Revue belge de philologie et d'histoire*, 93/3–4 (2015), pp. 811–842.
- **BRUBAKER 2012:** Leslie Brubaker, *Inventing Byzantine Iconoclasm*, London 2012.
- **BRUEGEL 1973:** Johann W. Bruegel, *Czechoslovakia before Munich: The German Minority Problem and the British Appeasement Policy*, New York 1973.
- **BRYANT 2009:** Chad C. Bryant, *Prague in Black: Nazi Rule and Czech Nationalism*, Cambridge, MA 2009.
- **BURGMANN 2001:** Ludwig Burgmann, "Byzantinoslavica, Prag 1929–1999", *Rechtshistorisches Journal*, 20 (2001), pp. 28–32.
- **BURRIN 1995:** Philippe Burrin, *La France à l'heure allemande, 1940–1944*, Paris 1995.
- **BYSTROV 1993:** Vladimír Bystrov, "Zrada dlouhá přes půl století" [A Half Century Long Betrayal], in Veber 1993, pp. 95–110.
- **CASTELNUOVO 1999:** Enrico Castelnuovo, "'Primitifs' e 'Fin de siècle'", in *Storia dell'arte e politica culturale intorno al 1900. La Fondazione dell'Istituto Germanico di Storia dell'Arte di Firenze*, Max Seidel ed., Venice 1999, pp. 47–54.
- **CASTELNUOVO 2004:** Enrico Castelnuovo, "L'infatuazione per i primitivi intorno al 1900", in *Arti e storia nel Medioevo*, vol 4: *Il Medioevo al passato e al presente*, Enrico Castelnuovo, Giuseppe Sergi eds, Turin 2004, pp. 785–809.
- **CHAPOUTOT 2017:** Johann Chapoutot, *La Révolution culturelle nazie*, Paris 2017.
- **CHARPENTIER 2008:** Pierre-Frédéric Charpentier, *La drôle de guerre des intellectuels français: 1939–1940*, Panazol 2008.
- **CHATELET 1989:** Albert Chatelet, "De l'Institut d'histoire de l'art moderne à l'institut d'histoire de l'Art, 1919–1988", *Formes*, 7 (1989), n.p.
- **CHINYAEVA 1993:** Elena Chinyaeva, "Ruská emigrace v Československu: vývoj Ruské pomocné akce" [Russian Emigration in Czechoslovakia: the Development of the Russian Help Action], *Slovanský přehled*, 79 (1993), pp. 14–24.

- **CHINYAEVA 1994:** Elena Chinyaeva, "Russian Émigrés and Czechoslovak Society: Uneasy Relations", in Veber 1994, pp. 46–64.
- **CHINYAEVA 2001:** Elena Chinyaeva, *Russians Outside Russia. The Émigré Community in Czechoslovakia 1918–1938*, Munich 2001.
- **CHRISTE 2005:** Yves Christe, "André Grabar et l'Occident", *Comptes rendus des séances de l'Académie des Inscriptions et Belles-Lettres*, CXLIX/3 (2005), pp. 1117–1123.
- **CORNWALL 1992:** Mark Cornwall, "Dr. Edvard Beneš and Czechoslovakia's German Minority, 1918–1943", in *The Czech and Slovak Experience*, John Morison ed., Houndmills/Basingstoke 1992, pp. 178–182.
- **COURCELLE 1946:** Pierre Courcelle, "Review of: *Cahiers archéologiques. Fin de l'Antiquité et Moyen-Âge*, t. 1; publiés par A. Grabar, 1945", *Revue des Études Anciennes*, XLVIII/3–4 (1946), pp. 298–300.
- **CRANE 2004:** Richard F. Crane, "La Croix and the Swastika: The Ambiguities of Catholic Responses to the Fall of France", *The Catholic Historical Review*, 90/1 (2004), pp. 45–66.
- **CUMONT 1932:** Franz Cumont, "L'Adoration des Mages et l'art triomphal de Rome", in *Atti della Pontificia Accademia di Archeologia, Serie IIa, Memorie II*, Rome 1932, pp. 82–105.
- **DAGRON 1992:** Gilbert Dagron, "Préface: André Grabar (1896–1990)", in Grabar 1992, pp. 5–10.
- **DAGRON 2005:** Gilbert Dagron, "André Grabar et les images", *Comptes rendus des séances de l'Académie des Inscriptions et Belles-Lettres*, CXLIX/3 (2005), pp. 1125–1128.
- **CORCY 2005:** Stéphanie Corcy, *La vie culturelle sous l'Occupation*, Paris 2005.
- **DECTER 1989:** Jacqueline Decter, *Nicholas Roerich. The Life and Art of a Russian Master*, Rochester 1989.
- **DEJMEK/KOVÁČ 2018:** Jindřich Dejmek, Dušan Kováč, "Kořeny moderní československé státnosti před první světovou válkou" [The Roots of Modern Czechoslovak Statehood before the First World War], in *Československo. Dějiny státu*, Jindřich Dejmek *et al.* eds, Prague 2018, pp. 51–97.
- **DELBRUECK 1929:** Richard Delbrueck, *Die Consulardiptychen und verwandte Denkmäler*, Berlin [i.a.] 1929.
- **DELIGNE (n.d.):** *Souvenirs de Nicolaï Stepanovitch Grabar*, Fanchon Deligne transl., (n.d.).
- **DIDRON 1845:** *Manuel d'iconographie chrétienne, grecque et latine*, Adolphe-Napoléon Didron ed., Paul Durand transl., Paris 1845.
- **DIEHL 1900:** Charles Diehl, "Les Études byzantines en France", *Byzantinische Zeitschrift*, 9/1 (1900), pp. 1–13.

- **DIEHL 1901:** Charles Diehl, *Justinien et la civilisation Byzantine au VIe siècle*, Paris 1901.
- **DIEHL 1904:** Charles Diehl, *Théodora impératrice de Byzance*, Paris 1904.
- **DIEHL 1906-1908:** Charles Diehl, *Figures byzantines*, Paris 1906–1908.
- **DIEHL 1920:** Charles Diehl, *Byzance. Grandeur et décadence*, Paris 1920.
- **DIEHL 1925:** Charles Diehl, "Compte-rendu: *Byzantion. Revue international des Études byzantine*, 1924", *Journal des savants*, 2 (1925), pp. 90–91.
- **DIEHL 1931:** Charles Diehl, "La légende de l'empereur Théophile", *Seminarium Kondakovianum*, IV (1931), pp. 33–37.
- **DMITRIEVA 2018:** Marina Dmitrieva, "Towards a Transnational History of Russian Culture: The N. P. Kondakov Institute in Prague", in *Transcending the Borders of Countries, Languages, and Disciplines in Russian Émigré Culture*, Christoph Flamm *et al.* eds, Cambridge 2018, pp. 173–198.
- **DRBAL 2008:** Vlastimil Drbal, "Der Archäologe N. P. Toll und seine Teilnahme an den Ausgrabungen in Dura-Europos (Syrien)", *Byzantinoslavica*, 1–2 (2008), pp. 53–70.
- **DRESSLER 2009:** *Eurasie: espace mythique ou réalité en construction?*, Wanda Dressler ed., Brussels 2009.
- **DU CANGE 1657:** Charles du Fresne, Sieur Du Cange, *Histoire de l'Empire de Constantinople sous les empereurs français*, 2 vols, Paris 1657.
- **DUFRENNE 1990:** Suzy Dufrenne, "André Grabar (1896–1990)", *Cahiers de civilisation médiévale*, 35/137 (1992), pp. 101–107.
- **DVORNÍK 1926:** František Dvorník, *Les Slaves, Byzance et Rome au XIe siècle*, Paris 1926.
- **DVORNÍK 1929:** František Dvorník, "Quelques données sur les Slaves extraites du tome 4 Novembris des 'Acta Sanctorum'", *Byzantinoslavica*, 1 (1929), pp. 35–47.
- **DVORNÍK 1933:** František Dvorník, *Les légendes de Constantin et de Méthode vues de Byzance*, (= Byzantinoslavica Supplementa, 1), Prague 1933.
- **DVORNÍK 1938:** František Dvorník, "L'affaire de Photios dans la littérature latine du Moyen-Âge", *Annales de l'Institut Kondakov*, 10 (1938), pp. 69–93.
- **ELSNER 2002:** Jaś Elsner, "The Birth of Late Antiquity: Riegl and Strzygowski in 1901", *Art History*, 25/3 (2002), pp. 358–379.
- **ELSNER 2020:** Jaś Elsner, "The Viennese Invention of Late Antiquity: Between Politics and Religion in the Forms of Late Roman Art", in *Empires of Faith in Late Antiquity. Histories of Art and Religion from India to Ireland*, Jaś Elsner ed., Cambridge 2020, pp. 110–127.
- **ELSNER/LORENZ 2012:** Jaś Elsner, Katharina Lorenz, "The Genesis of Iconology", *Critical Inquiry*, 38/3 (2012), pp. 483–512.

- **ERLANDE-BRANDENBURG 1995:** Alain Erlande-Brandenburg, "Jean Hubert (1902–1994) [note biographique]", *Bibliothèque de l'École des chartes*, 153/2 (1995), pp. 583–585.
- **ÉTUDES BYZANTINES 1935:** "Les études byzantines à Strasbourg", *Byzantion*, 10/1 (1935), pp. 377–379.
- **FEDOSEYEV 1976:** Ivan A. Fedoseyev, "Vernadsky, Vladimir Ivanovich", in *Dictionary of Scientific Biography*, Charles C. Gillispie ed., vol. XIII, New York 1976, pp. 616–620.
- **FERGUSON 1948:** Wallace K. Ferguson, *The Renaissance in Historical Thought: Five Centuries of Interpretation*, Boston 1948.
- **FILLAFER 2016:** Franz L. Fillafer, "Das Elend der Kategorien. Aufklärung und Josephinismus in der zentraleuropäischen Historiographie 1918–1945", in *Josephinismus zwischen den Regimen: Eduard Winter, Fritz Valjavec und die zentraleuropäischen Historiographien im 20. Jahrhundert*, Franz L. Fillafer, Thomas Wallnig eds, Vienna [i.a.] 2016, pp. 51–101.
- **FLEURDOGE 2015:** Denis Fleurdoge, "Les parures liturgiques du pouvoir. Usages pratiques et codifications symboliques du vêtement par le Président de la République", in *Le vêtement saisi par le droit*, Alain Pousson ed., Toulouse 2015, pp. 41–66.
- **FLORENSKY 2002:** Pavel Florensky, *Beyond Vision. Essays on the Perception of Art*, Nicoletta Misler ed., London 2002.
- **FLOROVSKIJ 1928:** Antonij V. Florovskij, "Russkie istoriki-emigranty v Prage" [Russian historians-emigrants in Prague], *Russkie v Prage, 1918–1928 gg.*, Sergej P. Postnikov ed., Prague 1928, pp. 262–268.
- **FOLETTI 2008:** Ivan Foletti, "The Last Kondakov. Rediscovery of a Manuscript", *Orientalia Christiana Periodica*, 74/II (2008), pp. 495–502.
- **FOLETTI 2009:** Ivan Foletti, "Kondakov a ruská ikona. Kondakovova analýza soudobého ikonopisectiví a její vliv na ruskou společnost začátku XX. století" [Kondakov and the Russian Icon. Kondakov's Analysis of Contemporary Icon-Painting and Its Effects on Russian Society at the Start of the Twentieth Century], in *2. ročník konference studentů doktorských programů dějin umění v České republice. Masarykova univerzita*, Luba Hédlová, Robert Mečkovský, Jitka Matulková eds, Brno 2009, pp. 6–13.
- **FOLETTI 2010:** *La Russie et l'Occident. Relations intellectuelles et artistiques au temps des révolutions russes*, conference proceedings (Université de Lausanne, 20–21 March 2009), Ivan Foletti ed., Rome 2010.
- **FOLETTI 2012:** Ivan Foletti, "André/Andrej Nikolajevič Grabar", in Heid/Dennert 2012, vol. I, pp. 601–602.
- **FOLETTI 2013:** Ivan Foletti, "Tra classicismi e avanguardie: la ricezione dell'estetica bizantina in Francia e in Russia a cavallo tra Otto

e Novecento", in *Phantazontes: visioni dell'arte bizantina*, Valentina Cantone, Silvia Pedone eds, Padua 2013, pp. 175–255.

- **FOLETTI 2014:** Ivan Foletti, "Nikodim Kondakov et Prague. Comment l'émigration change l'histoire (de l'art)", *Opuscula historiae artium*, 62/2 (2014), pp. 2–11.
- **FOLETTI 2016a:** Ivan Foletti, "The Russian View of a 'Peripheral' Region. Nikodim P. Kondakov and the Southern Caucasus", in *The Medieval South Caucasus: Artistic Cultures of Albania, Armenia and Georgia*, (= Convivium Supplementum 2016), Ivan Foletti, Erik Thunø, Adrien Palladino eds, Brno/Turnhout 2016, pp. 2–17.
- **FOLETTI 2016b:** Ivan Foletti, "L'icona, una costruzione storiografica?: dalla Russia all'Occidente, la creazione di un mito", *Annali di critica d'arte*, 12 (2016), pp. 175–194.
- **FOLETTI 2017a:** Ivan Foletti, *From Byzantium to Holy Russia. Nikodim Kondakov (1844–1925) and the Invention of the Icon*, Rome 2017.
- **FOLETTI 2017b:** Ivan Foletti, "Des femmes à l'autel? Jamais! Les diaconesses (veuves et prêtresses) et l'iconographie de la Théotokos", in *Féminité et masculinité altérées : transgression et inversion des genres au Moyen Âge*, Eva Pibiri, Fanny Abbott eds, Tavarnuzze 2017, pp. 51–92.
- **FOLETTI 2018a:** Ivan Foletti, "Nikodim Kondakov, Russia and Czechoslovakia: Byzantine Studies, the Link Between East and West", in Foletti/Lovino/Tvrzníková 2018, pp. 18–37.
- **FOLETTI 2018b:** Ivan Foletti, "L'exposition des icônes de 1913 à Saint-Pétersbourg: la découverte des origines chrétiennes russes", in *Re-thinking, Re-making, Re-living Christian Origins*, Ivan Foletti *et al.* eds, Rome 2018, pp. 323–330.
- **FOLETTI 2019:** Ivan Foletti, "Russian Inputs in Czechoslovakia: When Art History Meets History. The *Institutum Kondakovianum* During the Nazi Occupation", in *Inventing Medieval Czechoslovakia 1918–1968. Between Slavs, Germans, and Totalitarian Regimes*, Ivan Foletti, Adrien Palladino eds, Brno/Rome 2019, pp. 63–92.
- **FOLETTI 2020a:** Karolina Foletti, "Presenting Russia to the West. Helene Iswolsky – Russian Catholic Émigré Intellectual", in Foletti/Palladino 2020.
- **FOLETTI 2020b:** Ivan Foletti, "After Kondakov: the Heritage of Russian Emigration in the Czech Lands", in Foletti/Palladino 2020.
- **FOLETTI 2021:** Ivan Foletti, "How to Write Images about the Medieval World: André Grabar and His Byzantium. The Case of *L'empereur dans l'art byzantin* (1936)", *Word & Image*, 37 (2021), (submitted).
- **FOLETTI/FOLETTI 2019:** Karolina Foletti, Ivan Foletti, "Moskva nebo Řím? Rusko-byzantská architektura a translatio imperii?" [Moscow or

Rome? Russian-Byzantine Architecture and the Translatio Imperii?], in *Moskva – Třetí Řím. Od ideje k symbolu*, Pavel Boček ed., Prague 2019, pp. 185–199.

- **FOLETTI/LOVINO 2018:** *Orient oder Rom? Prehistory, History and Reception of a Historiographical Myth (1880–1930)*, Ivan Foletti, Francesco Lovino eds, Brno/Rome 2018.
- **FOLETTI/LOVINO/TVRZNÍKOVÁ 2018:** *From Kondakov to Hans Belting Library. Emigration and Byzantium – Bridges Between Worlds*, Ivan Foletti, Francesco Lovino, Veronika Tvrzníková eds, Brno/Rome 2018.
- **FOLETTI/PALLADINO 2019:** Ivan Foletti, Adrien Palladino, "Medieval Art and Czechoslovakia. Between Nationalist Discourse and Transcultural Reality, an Introduction", in *Inventing Medieval Czechoslovakia 1918–1968. Between Slavs, Germans, and Totalitarian Regimes*, Ivan Foletti, Adrien Palladino eds, Brno/Rome 2019, pp. 11–20.
- **FOLETTI/PALLADINO 2020:** *Transformed by Emigration. Welcoming Russian Intellectuals, Scientists, and Artists (1917–1945)*, (= Convivium Supplementum 2020, I), Ivan Foletti, Adrien Palladino eds, Brno/Turnhout 2020.
- **FOLETTI/ROSENBERGOVÁ 2020:** Ivan Foletti, Sabina Rosenbergová, "Rome Between Lights and Shadows: Re-considering 'Renaissances' and 'Decadences' in Early Medieval Rome", in *Convivium Supplementum 2020, II*, Chiara Bordino, Chiara Croci, Vedran Sulovsky eds, (forthcoming).
- **FOSHKO 2009:** Katherine Foshko, "The Paul Doumer Assassination and the Russian Diaspora in Interwar France", *French History*, 23/3 (2009), pp. 383–404.
- **FRANTOVÁ/PECINOVÁ 2013:** Zuzana Frantová, Kristýna Pecinová, "The Icon of Old Brno: A Reconsideration", *Opuscula historiae artium*, 62 (2013), pp. 62–75.
- **GAIDENKO 2008:** Piama P. Gaidenko, "Philosophie russe et pensée européenne: le cas de Vladimir S. Soloviev", *Diogène*, 222 (2008), pp. 32–47.
- **GALLO/PROVOST 2018:** *Nancy-Paris 1871–1939. Des bibliothèques au service de l'enseignement universitaire de l'histoire de l'art et de l'archéologie*, Daniela Gallo, Samuel Provost eds, Paris 2018.
- **GASBARRI 2015:** Giovanni Gasbarri, *Riscoprire Bisanzio. Lo studio dell'arte bizantina a Roma e in Italia tra Ottocento e Novecento*, Rome 2015.
- **GILLGREN/SNICKARE 2012:** Peter Gillgren, Mårten Snickare, "Introduction: By the Tomb of St Genesius", *Performativity and Performance in Baroque Rome*, Peter Gillgren ed., Farnham 2012, pp. 1–14.
- **GLETTLER/LIPTÁK/MÍSKOVÁ 2004:** *Geteilt, besetzt, beherrscht: Die Tschechoslowakei 1938–1945: Reichsgau Sudetenland, Protektorat Böhmen und Mähren, Slowakei*, Monika Glettler, Lubomír Lipták, Alena Mísková eds, Essen 2004.

- **GOFFART 2006:** Walter Goffart, *Barbarian Tides. The Migration Age and the Later Roman Empire*, Philadelphia 2006.
- **GRABAR 1918:** Andrej Grabar, “Freski Apostol’skogo pridela Kievo-Sofijskogo sobora” [The Frescoes of the Apostles Chapel of the Cathedral of Saint Sophia in Kiev], *Zapiski Otdeleniâ russkoj i slavânskoj arheologii Russkogo arheologičeskogo obŝestva*, 12 (1918), pp. 98–106.
- **GRABAR 1921-1922:** Andrej Grabar, “Bolgarskie cerkvi-grobnicy” [Byzantine Sepulcher-Churches], *Izvestija na Bălgarskija archeologičeski institut*, 1 (1921–1922), pp. 103–135.
- **GRABAR 1921:** Andrej Grabar, “Stenopisat na crkvata ‘Sv. Cetirideset macenici’ v Veliko Tarnovo” [The Mural Paintings of the Church of ‘the Forty Martyrs’ in Tirnovo], *Godišnik*, 2 (1921), pp. 90–112.
- **GRABAR 1924:** André Grabar, *Bojanskata cŭrkva. Architektura – živopis / L’église de Boïana. Architecture – peinture,* foreword of Bogdan Filov, Sofia 1924.
- **GRABAR 1928a:** André Grabar, *La peinture religieuse en Bulgarie*, preface of Gabriel Millet, 2 vols, Paris 1928.
- **GRABAR 1928b:** André Grabar, *Recherches sur les influences orientales dans l’art balkanique*, Paris 1928.
- **GRABAR 1931a:** André Grabar, *La Sainte Face de Laon. Le mandylion dans l’art orthodoxe*, Prague 1931.
- **GRABAR 1931b:** André Grabar, “Nikolaj Michajlovič Běljaev”, *Byzantion*, 6/1 (1931), pp. 517–518.
- **GRABAR 1935:** André Grabar, “Les fresques des escaliers à Sainte-Sophie de Kiev et l’iconographie impériale byzantine”, *Seminarium Kondakovianum*, VII (1935), pp. 103–118.
- **GRABAR 1936:** André Grabar, *L’empereur dans l’art byzantin: recherches sur l’art officiel de l’Empire d’Orient*, Paris 1936.
- **GRABAR 1938:** André Grabar, “Paul Perdrizet et les études byzantines (1870–1938)”, *Byzantion*, 13 (1938), pp. 777–779.
- **GRABAR 1940:** André Grabar, “L’expansion de la peinture russe aux XVIe et XVIIe siècles”, *Annales de l’Institut Kondakov*, 11 (1940), pp. 65–93.
- **GRABAR 1941:** André Grabar, “Le thème religieux des fresques de la synagogue de Doura (245–256 après J.-C.)”, *Revue de l’histoire des religions*, 123 (1941), pp. 143–192.
- **GRABAR 1942:** André Grabar, “Les découvertes aniconiques du Baouït”, *Bulletin de la société nationale des Antiquaires de France*, (1942), pp. 180–181.
- **GRABAR 1943:** André Grabar, *Les Miniatures du Grégoire de Nazianze de l’Ambrosienne (Ambrosianus 49–50), Album*, Paris 1943.
- **GRABAR 1944-1945:** André Grabar, “La byzantinologie française pendant la guerre: 1940–1945”, *Byzantion*, 17 (1944–1945), pp. 431–438.

- **GRABAR 1944:** André Grabar, "Images de la Théophanie et de la Majesté du Christ dans les absides antiques et romanes", *Bulletin de la société nationale des Antiquaires de France*, (1943–1944), p. 40.
- **GRABAR 1945:** André Grabar, "Plotin et les origines de l'esthétique médiévale", *Cahiers archéologiques*, 1 (1945), pp. 15–34.
- **GRABAR 1946:** André Grabar, *Martyrium. Recherches sur le culte des reliques et l'art chrétien antique*, 2 vols, Paris 1946.
- **GRABAR 1968a:** André Grabar, *L'art de la fin de l'Antiquité et du Moyen Âge*, 3 vols, Paris 1968.
- **GRABAR 1968b:** André Grabar, "Martyrium ou 'vingt ans après'", *Cahiers archéologiques*, XVIII (1968), pp. 239–244.
- **GRABAR 1990:** André Grabar, "Les mosaïques de Kiev. André Grabar", in *La bibliothèque imaginaire du Collège de France*, Paris 1990, pp. 115–116.
- **GRABAR 1992:** André Grabar, *Les origines de l'esthétique médiévale*, preface of Gilbert Dagron, Paris 1992.
- **GRABAR 2018:** André Grabar, *Plotinus and the Origins of Medieval Aesthetics,* Adrien Palladino trans., ed., and intr., Brno/Rome 2018.
- **GRÜNEWALD 1982:** Eckhart Grünewald, *Ernst Kantorowicz und Stefan George. Beiträge zur Biographie des Historikers bis zum Jahre 1938 und seinem Jugendwerk "Kaiser Friedrich der Zweite",* Wiesbaden 1982.
- **GUKER 1992:** Jeanne Guker, "Ivan Bounine, prix Nobel 1933", in *Les prix Nobel de littérature*, Régis Boyer ed., Paris 1992, pp. 393–401.
- **GUNDLE 2013:** Stephen Gundle, "Mass Culture and the Cult of Personality", in *The Cult of the Duce: Mussolini and the Italians*, Stephen Gundle, Christopher Duggan, Giuliana Pieri eds, Manchester 2013, pp. 72–90.
- **HALPERIN 1982:** Charles J. Halperin, "George Vernadsky, Eurasianism, the Mongols, and Russia", *Slavic Review*, 41 (1982), pp. 477–493.
- **HALPERIN 1985:** Charles J. Halperin, "Russia and the Steppe: George Vernadsky and Eurasianism", *Forschungen zur osteuropäischen Geschichte*, 36 (1985), pp. 55–194.
- **HAMPERL 1972:** Herwig Hamperl, *Werdegang und Lebensweg eines Pathologen*, Stuttgart 1972.
- **HANZAL 2002:** Josef Hanzal, *Josef Pekař: život a dílo* [Josef Pekař: Life and Work], Prague 2002.
- **HARDIMAN 2017:** Louise Hardiman, "'The Loving Labourer through Space and Time': Aleksandra Pogosskaia, Theosophy, and Russian Arts and Crafts, c. 1900–1917", in *Modernism and the Spiritual in Russian Art. New Perspectives*, Louise Hardiman, Nicola Kozicharov eds, Cambridge 2017, pp. 69–90.
- **HASELSTEINER 2000:** *The Prague Slav Congress 1848: Slavic Identities*, Horst Haselsteiner ed., Stuttgart/Hannover 2000.

- **HAVLÍKOVÁ 2004:** Lubomíra Havlíková, "Lubor Niederle (1865–1944)", *Akademický bulletin*, 6 (2004), pp. 24–25.
- **HAZERA 2018:** Jean-Claude Hazera, *Comment meurent les démocraties: Mussolini, Hitler, Roosevelt, Franco, Pétain...*, Paris 2018.
- **HEID/DENNERT 2012:** *Personenlexikon zur Christlichen Archäologie. Forscher und Persönlichkeiten vom 16. bis zum 21. Jahrhundert*, Stefan Heid, Martin Dennert eds, 2 vols, Regensburg 2012.
- **HEIMANN 2009:** Mary Heimann, *Czechoslovakia: The State That Failed*, New Haven / London 2009.
- **HELLER 1997:** Michel Heller, *Histoire de la Russie et de son Empire*, Paris 1997.
- **HERLIHY 1977:** Patricia Herlihy, "The Ethnic Composition of the City of Odessa in the Nineteenth Century", *Harvard Ukrainian Studies*, 1/1 (1977), pp. 53–78.
- **HERLIHY 1986:** Patricia Herlihy, *Odessa. A History, 1794–1914*, Cambridge, MA 1986.
- **HEWRYK 1982:** Titus D. Hewryk, *The Lost Architecture of Kiev*, New York 1982.
- **HLAVÁČKOVÁ 1995**: *Ze sbírek bývalého Kondakovova institutu. Ikony, koptské textilie* [From the Collections of the Former Kondakov Institute. Icons, Coptic Textiles], Hana J. Hlaváčková ed., Prague 1995.
- **HLÔŠKOVÁ/ZELENKOVÁ 2008:** *Slavista Jiří Polívka v kontexte literatúry a folklóru* [Slavist Jiří Polívka in the Context of Literature and Folklore], Hana Hlôšková, Anna Zelenková eds, 2 vols, Bratislava/Brno 2008.
- **HOFFMANN 2003:** Joachim Hoffmann, *Die Tragödie der "Russischen Befreiungsarmee" 1944/45. Wlassow gegen Stalin*, Munich 2003.
- **HOPKINS 1979:** Clark Hopkins, *The Discovery of Dura-Europos*, Bernard Goldman ed., New Haven / London 1979.
- **HOURIHANE 2012:** *From Minor to Major: The Minor Arts in Medieval Art History*, Colum Hourihane ed., Princeton 2012.
- **HOUŠKA 2007:** Vítězslav Houška, *T. G. Masaryk: myslitel a státník* [T. G. Masaryk: Thinker and Statesman], Karviná/Paris 2007.
- **HROCHOVÁ 1972:** Věra Hrochová, "Les études byzantines en Tchécoslovaquie", *Balkan Studies*, 13 (1972), pp. 301–311.
- **HROCHOVÁ 1989:** Věra Hrochová, "Das Institut N. P. Kondakov und Ivan Dujčev", *Studia Slavico-Byzantina et Mediaevalia Europensia*, 1 (1989), pp. 90–102.
- **HROCHOVÁ 1991:** Věra Hrochová, "L'institut N.P. Kondakov", in *XVIII. Meždunarodnyj kongress vizantinistov. Rezjume soobščenij*, vol. 1, Moscow 1991, p. 448.
- **HROCHOVÁ 1995:** Věra Hrochová, "Činnost Institutu N. P. Kondakova v Praze a jeho mezinárodní význam" [The Activities of the N. P. Kondakov Institute in Prague and Its International Significance], in Veber 1995, pp. 32–41.

- **IBERL 2011:** Kateřina Iberl, "Natalie Grigorjevna Jašvilová: sloup Seminaria Kondakoviana" [Natalie Grigorjevna Jašvilová: Pillar of the Seminarium Kondakovianum], *Parrésia*, 5 (2011), pp. 323–333.
- **JAKOBSON 1932:** Roman Jakobson, "Book Review of: André Vaillant, *Les chants épiques des Slaves du Sud*, Paris 1932", *Byzantinoslavica*, IV (1932), pp. 194–202.
- **JAKOBSON 1944:** Roman Jakobson, Henri Grégoire, "D. A. Rasovskij", *Annuaire de l'Institut de Philologie et d'Histoire Orientales et Slaves*, 7 (1939–1944), pp. 535–537.
- **JAKUBČO 2020:** Martin Jakubčo, *Dmitri Vlasevič Ainalov*, Ph.D. thesis, (Masaryk University, Brno), 2020.
- **JAKUBEC 2013:** Ondřej Jakubec, "Obraz 'Salus populi romani' u brněnských jezuitů a obraznost potridentského katolicismu na předbělohorské Moravě" [The 'Salus Populi Romani' Image at the Brno Jesuits and the Imagination of Post-Tridentine Catholicism in Pre-White Mountain Battle Moravia], in *Jezuité a Brno. Sociální a kulturní interakce koleje a města (1578–1773)*, Hana Jordánková, Vladimír Maňas eds, Brno 2013, pp. 77–98.
- **JANČÁRKOVÁ 2005:** Julie Jančárková, "Praga – Belgrad – Praga. AINPK v Belgrade" [Prague – Belgrade – Prague. The AINPK in Belgrade], *Prilozi za knizevnost, jezik, istoriju i folklor (Bělehrad)*, 70/1–4 (2005), pp. 269–280.
- **JANČÁRKOVÁ 2012:** Julie Jančárková, "G. A. Ostrogorskij i Archeologičeskij institut im. N. P. Kondakova v Prage" [G. A. Ostrogorskij and the Kondakov Institute in Prague], *Byzantinoslavica*, LXX/1–2 (2012), pp. 53–75.
- **JANČÁRKOVÁ 2017:** Julie Jančárková, "Archeologičeskij Institut Im. N. P. Kondakova v Prage v Gody Vtoroj Mirovoj Vojny. K Voprosu o Formirovanii Kollekcij" [The Kondakov Archaeological Institute in Prague During the Second World War. The Question of the Formation of the Collections], *Trudy Gosudarstvennogo Ermitaža*, LXXXIX (2017), (= *Vizantija v kontexte mirovoj kultury. Konferencija, posvjaščennaja pamjati A. V. Bank [1906–1984]*), pp. 499–506.
- **JANČÁRKOVÁ 2019:** Julie Jančárková, "Nikolaj Okuněv i samaja bol'šaja vystavka russkogo iskusstva v Čechoslovakii" [Nikolaj Okuněv and the Largest Exhibition of Russian Art in Czechoslovakia], *Slavjanskij al'manach*, 1–2 (2019), pp. 271–281.
- **JANČÁRKOVÁ/GAGEN 2017:** Julie Jančárková, Sergej Gagen, "K voprosu o stanovlenii vizantinovedenija v Čechoslovakii, Review of: Jaroslav Bidlo, Milada Paulová, *Střet generací? Paměti a vzájemná korespondence zakladatelů české byzantologie a slovanských studií*, Daniela Brádlerová, Jan Hálek eds, Prague 2014" [About the Problem of the Rising of Investigations

of Byzantium in Czechoslovakia, Review of: Jaroslav Bidlo, Milada Paulová, *Clash of Generations? Memories and Mutual Correspondence of the Founders of Czech Byzantology and Slavonic Studies*, Daniela Brádlerová, Jan Hálek eds, Prague 2014], Christianskij Vostok. *Serija posvjaščennaja izučeniju christianskoj kul'tury narodov Azii i Afriki. Novaja serija*, VIII/14 (2017), pp. 527–536.

- **JANČÁRKOVÁ/GAGEN 2019:** Julie Jančárková, Sergej Gagen, "Pravoslavnoje iskusstvo kak massovyj tovar na territorii Tretjego Rejcha i okkupirovannych territorijach vo vremja Vtoroj mirovoj vojny (Po materialam archiva Archeologičeskogo instituta imeni N. P. Kondakova v Prage)" [Orthodox Art as a Mass Commodity on the Territory of the Third Reich and the Occupied Territories During World War II (Based on Materials from the Archives of the N.P. Kondakov Archaeological Institute in Prague)], *Wiener Slavistisches Jahrbuch*, VII/1 (2019), pp. 256–269.
- **JOHNSON 2007:** Sam Johnson, "'Communism in Russia Only Exists on Paper': Czechoslovakia and the Russian Refugee Crisis, 1919–1924", *Contemporary European History*, 16/3 (2007), pp. 371–394.
- **JOHNSTON 1988:** Robert H. Johnston, *New Mecca, New Babylon: Paris and the Russian Exiles, 1920–1945*, Kingston/Montreal 1988.
- **KADLEC 1946:** Jaroslav Kadlec, *Byzantské křesťanství u slovanských národů* [Byzantine Christianity in the Slavic Nations], Prague 1946.
- **KALITINSKIJ 1928:** Alexander P. Kalitinskij, "K voprosu o nekotorych formach dvuplastinčatych fibul iz Rossii" [On the Question of the Form of Two-Part Fibulae from Russia], *Seminarium Kondakovianum*, II (1928), pp. 277–280.
- **KALITINSKIJ 1929:** Alexander P. Kalitinskij, "Otčet o rabotach Seminarija imeni Kondakova (Seminarium Kondakovianum) v Prage za četvertyj god ego suščestvovanija" [Report on the Works of the Seminar Named after Kondakov (Seminarium Kondakovianum) in Prague in the Fourth Year of Its Existence], *Seminarium Kondakovianum*, III (1929), pp. 328–330.
- **KALITINSKIJ 1930:** Alexander P. Kalitinskij, "La question des fibules byzantines en Russie", in *L'art byzantin chez les Slaves. Les Balkans. Recueil dédié à la mémoire de Théodore Ouspensky*, Paris 1930, pp. 378–386.
- **KANTOROWICZ 1927:** Ernst Kantorowicz, *Kaiser Friedrich der Zweite*, Berlin 1927.
- **KANTOROWICZ 1931:** Ernst Kantorowicz, *Kaiser Friedrich der Zweite. Ergänzungsband: Quellennachweise und Exkurse*, Berlin 1931.
- **KAZAKOVA 2014:** Olga Kazakova, "Les pavillons russes aux Expositions Universelles du XIXe siècle: expression de l'identité qui n'a jamais existé", *Diacronie*, 18/2 (2014), [online: https://journals.openedition.org/diacronie/1411, accessed 19.07.2019].

- **KENEZ 1974:** Peter Kenez, *Civil War in South Russia, 1918*, Los Angeles / London 1974.
- **KERNER 1921:** Robert J. Kerner, "Two Architects of New Europe: Masaryk and Beneš", *The Journal of International Relations*, 12/1 (1921), pp. 27–43.
- **KHRUSHKOVA 2012a:** Ljudmila G. Khrushkova, "Nikodim Pavlovič Kondakov", in Heid/Dennert 2012, vol. 2, pp. 751–754.
- **KHRUSHKOVA 2012b:** Ljudmila G. Khrushkova, "Dmitrij Vlas'evič Ajnalov", in Heid/Dennert 2012, vol. 1, pp. 53–54.
- **KHRUSHKOVA 2012c:** Ljudmila G. Khrushkova, "Jakov Ivanovič Smirnov", in Heid/Dennert 2012, vol. 2, pp. 1172–1173.
- **KIMERLING WIRTSCHAFTER 2006:** Elise Kimerling Wirtschafter, "The Groups Between: Raznochintsy, Intelligentsia, Professionals", *The Cambridge History of Russia*, vol. 2: *Imperial Russia, 1689–1917*, Dominic Lieven ed., Cambridge 2006, pp. 245–263.
- **KITZINGER 1990/1992:** Ernst Kitzinger, "Gedenkworte für André Grabar", in *Reden und Gedenkworte. Orden Pour le Mérite für Wissenschaften und Künste*, 23 (1990/1992), pp. 59–62.
- **KLARSFELD 1983:** Serge Klarsfeld, *Vichy-Auschwit: le rôle de Vichy dans la solution finale de la question juive en France*, 2 vols, t. 1: *1942*, t. 2: *1943–1944*, Paris 1983.
- **KOHL 1844:** Johann G. Kohl, *Russia. St. Petersburg, Moscow, Kharkoff, Riga, Odessa, the German Provinces on the Baltic. The Steppes, the Crimea and the Interior of the Empire*, London 1844.
- **KONDAKOV 1876:** Nikodim P. Kondakov, *Istoria vizantijskago iskusstva i ikonografii po miniaturach grečeskich rukopisej* [History of Byzantine Art and Iconography, in the Miniatures in Greek Manuscripts], Odessa 1876.
- **KONDAKOV 1881:** Nikodim P. Kondakov, *Mozaiki mečeti Karchie-Džamisi – μονή της χώρας – v Konstantinopole* [The Mosaics of the Kariye Camii Mosque – *μονή της χώρας* – in Constantinople], Odessa 1881.
- **KONDAKOV 1882:** Nikodim P. Kondakov, *Putešestvie na Sinaj v 1881 godu. Iz putevych vpečatlenij. Drevnosti Sinajskago Monastyrja* [Voyage to the Sinai in 1881. Travel Notes. Antiquities from the Sinai Monastery], Odessa 1882.
- **KONDAKOV 1890:** Nikodim P. Kondakov, *Opis' pamjatnikov drevnosti v nektorich chramach Gruzii* [Description of Ancient Monuments in Some Temples in Georgia], Saint Petersburg 1890.
- **KONDAKOV 1891:** Nikodim P. Kondakov, *Imperatorskij Ermitaž. Ukazatel otdelenija Srednich Vekov i epochi Vozroždenija* [Imperial Hermitage. Catalogue of the Medieval and Renaissance Sections], Saint Petersburg 1891.
- **KONDAKOV 1896:** Nikodim P. Kondakov, "N.P. Kondakov", in *Biografičeskij slovar' professorov i prepodavatelej imperatorskogo S.-Peterburgskogo universiteta*

za istekšuju tret'ju četvert' veka ego suščestvovanija 1869–1894, vol. I, Saint Petersburg 1896, pp. 337–340.

- **KONDAKOV 1901:** Nikodim P. Kondakov, *O situaci russkoj narodnoj živopisi* [Regarding the Situation of Russian Folk Painting], Saint Petersburg 1901.
- **KONDAKOV 1902:** Nikodim P. Kondakov, *Pamjatniki Christianskogo Iskusstva na Afone* [The Monuments of Christian Art on Athos], Saint Petersburg 1902.
- **KONDAKOV 1904:** Nikodim P. Kondakov, *Archeologičeskoje putešestvie po Sirii i Palestine* [Archaeological Voyage to Syria and Palestine], Saint Petersburg 1904.
- **KONDAKOV 1905:** Nikodim P. Kondakov, *Ikonografija Gospoda Boga i Spasa našego Iisusa Christa: istoričeskij i ikonografičeskij očerk* [Iconography of Our Lord and Saviour Jesus Christ: Historical and Iconographic Essay], Saint Petersburg 1905.
- **KONDAKOV 1906:** Nikodim P. Kondakov, *Izobraženija russkoj kniažeskoj semi v miniatiurach XI veka* [The Representation of the Russian Princely Family in the Miniatures of the Eleventh Century], Saint Petersburg 1906.
- **KONDAKOV 1909:** Nikodim P. Kondakov, *Makedonia. Archeologičeskoe putešestvie* [Macedonia. Archaeological Voyage], Saint Petersburg 1909.
- **KONDAKOV 1914:** Nikodim P. Kondakov, *Ikonografija Bogomateri* [Iconography of the Mother of God], vol. I, Saint Petersburg 1914.
- **KONDAKOV 1915:** Nikodim P. Kondakov, *Ikonografija Bogomateri* [Iconography of the Mother of God], vol. II, Saint Petersburg 1915.
- **KONDAKOV 1919:** Nikodim P. Kondakov, "Živye novosti s Zapada" [Live News from the West], *Južnoe Slovo*, 20 September 1919.
- **KONDAKOV 1924:** Nikodim P. Kondakov, "Les costumes orientaux à la Cour Byzantine", *Byzantion*, I (1924), pp. 7–49.
- **KONDAKOV 1927a:** Nikodim P. Kondakov, *Vospominanija i dumy* [Recollections and Thoughts], Prague 1927.
- **KONDAKOV 1927b:** Nikodim P. Kondakov, *The Russian Icon*, Oxford 1927.
- **KONDAKOV 1928–1933:** Nikodim P. Kondakov, *Russkaja Ikona* [The Russian Icon], 4 vols, Prague 1928–1933.
- **KONDAKOV 1929:** Nikodim P. Kondakov, *Příspěvky k dějinám středověkého umění a kultury / Očerky i zametki po istorii srednevekovago iskusstva i kultury* [Essays and Thoughts on Medieval Culture and Art], Prague 1929.
- **KONDAKOV 1931:** Nikodim P. Kondakov, "Conférence sur la civilisation antique", *Seminarium Kondakovianum*, IV (1931), pp. 4–32.
- **KONDAKOV 2011:** Nikodim P. Kondakov, *Iconographie de la Mère de Dieu, vol. III*, Ivan Foletti transl. and ed., Rome 2011.

- **KONDAKOV 2014:** Nikodim Kondakov, *Iconografia della Madre di Dio*, Ivan Foletti transl. and ed., Rome 2014.
- **KONDAKOV/TOLSTOJ 1889-1899:** Nikodim P. Kondakov, Ivan I. Tolstoj, *Russkija drevnosti v pamjatnikach iskusstva* [Russian Antiquities and Art Treasures], 6 vols, Saint Petersburg 1889–1899.
- **KORLIAKOV 2012:** Andreï Korliakov, "Le grand exode russe, 1917–1939. Tous les chemins mènent en France", in *Figures de l'émigré russe en France au XIXe et XXe siècle. Fiction et réalité*, Charlotte Krauss, Tatiana Victoroff eds, Leiden 2012, pp. 29–54.
- **KOVALEVA/ŠIPUNOVA 2014:** Marina D. Kovaleva, Marija V. Šipunova, "Komitet popečitel'stva o russoj ikonopisi (1901–1918): istorija i dejatel'nost'" [Committee Guardianship of Russian Iconography (1901–1918): History and Activities], *Vestnik RGGU*, 17/139 (2014), pp. 70–80.
- **KRAUSE 2018:** Stefan Krause,"'Modernism is now verboten': Hubert Lanzingers 'Bannerträger' – Ikonografie und Geschichte eines Gemäldes", in *Zwischen Ideologie, Anpassung und Verfolgung. Kunst und Nationalsozialismus in Tirol*, catalogue of the exhibition, (Tiroler Landesmuseum Ferdinandeum, 14.12.2018–07.04.2019), Wolfgang Meighörner ed., Innsbruck 2018, pp. 20–29.
- **KRAUTHEIMER 1942:** Richard Krautheimer, "The Carolingian Revival of Early Christian Architecture", *The Art Bulletin*, 24/1 (1942), pp. 1–27.
- **KRAUTHEIMER 1953:** Richard Krautheimer, "Review of: Grabar 1946", *The Art Bulletin*, 35/1 (1953), pp. 57–61.
- **KULTERMANN 1990 [1966]:** Udo Kultermann, *Geschichte der Kunstgeschichte: der Weg einer Wissenschaft*, Munich 1990 [1966].
- **KVAČEK 2018:** Robert Kvaček, *Poslední den: Mnichov – Praha, 1938* [The Last Day: Munich – Prague, 1938], Prague 2018.
- **KYZLASOVA 1999:** Irina L. Kyzlasova, "Novoe o rannem etape naučnoj dejatel'nosti A. N. Grabara (1919–1924 gg.)" [New about the Early Stages of the Scientific Activity of A. N. Grabar (1919–1924)], in Smirnova 1999a, pp. 82–86.
- **KYZLASOVA 2000:** Irina L. Kyzlasova, *Istoria otečestvennoj nauki ob iskusstve Vizantii i drevnej Rusi 1920–1930 gody. Po materialam archivov* [The History of Patriotic Studies Dedicated to the Art of Byzantium and of Ancient Russia, 1920–1930. Based on Archival Material], Moscow 2000.
- **KYZLASOVA 2010:** Irina L. Kyzlasova, "L'exposition d'icônes russes en Europe et aux USA de 1929 à 1932, en tant que début de la gloire mondiale de la peintre russe ancienne", in Foletti 2010, pp. 181–196.
- **LABARTE 1864-1866:** Jules Labarte, *Histoire des arts industriels au Moyen Âge et à l'époque de la Renaissance*, 6 vols, Paris 1864–1866.

- **LABRUSSE 2007:** Rémi Labrusse, "Byzance et l'art moderne. La référence Byzantine dans les cercles artistiques d'avant-garde au début du XXe siècle", in Spieser 2007, pp. 55–89.
- **LABRUSSE 2018:** Rémi Labrusse, "Modernité byzantine: l'Exposition international d'art byzantine de 1931 à Paris", in *Le double voyage: Paris-Athènes (1919–1939)*, Lucile Arnoux-Farnoux, Polina Kosmadaki eds, Athens 2018, pp. 221–242.
- **LANDAUER 1981:** Carl Landauer, "Das Nachleben Aby Warburgs", *Kritische Berichte*, 9 (1981), pp. 61–71.
- **LANDAUER 1994:** Carl Landauer, "Erwin Panofsky and the Renascence of the Renaissance", *Renaissance Quarterly*, 47/2 (1994), pp. 255–281.
- **LAPO 2001:** Andrei V. Lapo, "Vladimir I. Vernadsky (1863–1945), Founder of the Biosphere Concept", *International Microbiology*, 4 (2001), pp. 47–49.
- **LARSON/FLACH 2013:** *Darwin and Theories of Aesthetics and Cultural History*, Barbara Larson, Sabine Flach eds, Farnham [i.a.] 2013.
- **LAUB 2010:** Thomas J. Laub, *After the Fall: German Policy in Occupied France, 1940–1944*, New York 2010.
- **LAUNAY 1972:** Michel Launay, *L'Armistice de 1940*, Paris 1972.
- **LEARDI 2002:** Geraldine Leardi, "Una mostra d'arte bizantina a Grottaferrata: l'evento, i protagonisti e il contesto culturale romano di primo Novecento", *Studi Romani*, 50 (2002), pp. 311–333.
- **LEARDI 2010:** Geraldine Leardi, "'Tout est dans la mesure'. Matisse davanti alle icone russe nel 1911", in Foletti 2010, pp. 11–30.
- **LERNER 2017:** Robert E. Lerner, *Ernst Kantorowicz: A Life*, Princeton/Oxford 2017.
- **LIDOV 2006:** Alexej Lidov, "Hierotopy. The Creation of Sacred Spaces as a Form of Creativity and Subject of Cultural History", in *Hierotopy. Creation of Sacred Spaces in Byzantium and Medieval Russia*, Alexej Lidov ed., Moscow 2006, pp. 32–58.
- **LIDOVA 2020:** Maria Lidova, "The Rise of Byzantine Art and Archaeology in Late Imperial Russia", in *Empires of Faith in Late Antiquity. Histories of Art and Religion from India to Ireland*, Jaś Elsner ed., Cambridge 2020, pp. 128–160.
- **LINGUA 1999:** *Icona e avanguardie. Percorsi dell'immagine in Russia*, Graziano Lingua ed., Turin 1999.
- **LOVINO 2016a:** Francesco Lovino, "Leafing Through 'Seminarium Kondakovianum', I.: Studies on Byzantine Illumination", *Convivium*, III/1 (2016), pp. 206–213.
- **LOVINO 2016b:** Francesco Lovino, "Southern Caucasus in Perspective: the Scholarly Debate Through the Pages of "Seminarium Kondakovianum"

and "Skythika" (1927–1938)", in *The Medieval South Caucasus: Artistic Cultures of Albania, Armenia and Georgia*, (= Convivium Supplementum 2016), Ivan Foletti, Erik Thunø, Adrien Palladino eds, Brno/Turnhout 2016, pp. 36–51.

- **LOVINO 2017:** Francesco Lovino, "Communism vs. Seminarium Kondakovianum", *Convivium*, IV/1 (2017), pp. 142–157.
- **LOVINO 2018:** Francesco Lovino, "Seminarium Kondakovianum / Byzantinoslavica: A Comparison", in Foletti/Lovino/Tvrzníková 2018, pp. 38–55.
- **LOVINO 2019:** Francesco Lovino, "Constructing the Past through the Present: The Eurasian View of Byzantium in the Pages of *Seminarium Kondakovianum*", in *Trends and Turning Points. Constructing the Late Antique and Byzantine World*, Matthew Kinloch, Alex MacFarlane eds, Leiden/Boston 2019, pp. 14–28.
- **LOVINO 2020:** Francesco Lovino, "Byzantium on Display. Scholars, Collectors and Dealers at the Exposition Internationale d'Art Byzantin", *Journal of the History of Collections*, 32/2 (2020).
- **LUKEŠ 1996:** Igor Lukes, *Czechoslovakia Between Stalin and Hitler: The Diplomacy of Edvard Beneš in the 1930s*, New York / Oxford 1996.
- **LUSTIGOVÁ 2007:** Martina Lustigová, *Karel Kramář. První československý premiér* [Karel Kramář. The First Czechoslovak Prime Minister], Prague 2007.
- **MACH 2012:** Jaromír Mach, *Ruští intelektuálové v emigraci a jejich institucionální základna v Praze (na modelu Ruské svobodné univerzity a přidružených institucí, 1923–1945)* [Russian Intellectuals in Exile and Their Institutional Base in Prague (on the Model of the Russian Free University and Associated Institutions, 1923–1945], Ph.D. thesis, (Masaryk University, Brno), 2012.
- **MACHONIN 1995:** Sergej Machonin, *Příběh se závorkami* [A Story with Parentheses], Prague 1995.
- **MACKENZIE 1948 [1947]:** Compton Mackenzie, *Dr. Beneš*, Josef Lowenbach transl., Prague 1948 [1947].
- **MACKOVÁ/ULRYCH 2004:** *Kinderschicksale aus Lidice: Erinnerungen, Zeugnisse, Dokumente. Anhand von Erzählungen und Erinnerungen Lidicer Frauen und Kinder*, Jolana Macková, Ivan Ulrych eds, Nymburk 2004.
- **MAGUIRE 1991:** Henry Maguire, "André Grabar. 1896–1990", *Dumbarton Oaks Papers*, 45 (1991), pp. xii–xv.
- **MALÍŘ 2016:** Jiří Malíř, "Cyrilometodějská tradice na Moravě koncem 19. a počátkem 20. století ve službách politiky" [The Cyrillo-Methodian Tradition in Moravia in the Late 19th and Early 20th Century in the Service of Politics], in *Středověký kaleidoskop pro muže s hůlkou: věnováno Františku Šmahelovi k životnímu jubileu*, Eva Doležalová, Petr Sommer eds, Prague 2016, pp. 394–412.

- **MAREŠ 2000:** František V. Mareš, *Cyrilometodějská tradice a slavistika* [The Cyrillo-Methodian Tradition and Slavonic Studies], Prague 2000.
- **MARÈS 2015:** Antoine Marès, *Edvard Beneš: Un drame entre Hitler et Staline*, Paris 2015.
- **MARINESCU 1925:** Constantin Marinescu, *Compte-rendu du premier Congrès international des études byzantines: Bucarest, 1924*, Bucharest 1925.
- **MARITCHIK-SIOLI 2019:** Youlia Maritchik-Sioli, "'Tout poète est par essence un émigré': Marina Tsvetaeva et l'exil", *ILCEA*, 34 (2019) = *Femmes et migrations aux XIXe et XXe siècles: regards et representations*, [online: https://journals.openedition.org/ilcea/5881, accessed 09.06.2020].
- **MARKS 2012:** Richard Marks, "Russian Icons Through British Eyes c. 1830–1930", in *A People Passing Rude: British Responses to Russian Culture*, Anthony Cross ed., Cambridge 2012, pp. 69–88.
- **MARTIN 2008:** François-René Martin, "L'administration du génie national. L'exposition des primitifs français de 1904", in *Medioevo/Medioevi: Un secolo di esposizioni d'arte medievale*, Enrico Castelnuovo, Alessio Monciatti, eds, Pisa 2008, pp. 93–108.
- **MARTIN 2012:** François-René Martin, "Le moine-peintre et le primitif. L'invention des 'Primitifs' russes dans une perspective internationale", *Cahiers du monde russe*, 53/2–3 (2012), pp. 476–477.
- **MASARYK 1971 [1913]:** Tomáš Garrigue Masaryk, *La Russia e l'Europa. Studi sulle correnti spirituali in Russia*, Etore Lo Gatto ed., 2 vols, Bologna 1971 [1913].
- **MASARYK 1992 [1922]:** Tomáš Garrigue Masaryk, "Pomoc Rusku Evropou a Amerikou" [Aid to Russia, across Europe and America], in *Otevřit Rusko Evropě. Dvě stati k ruské otázce v roce 1922*, Věra Olivová ed., Prague 1992, pp. 7–21.
- **MASARYK 2016 [1918/1920]:** Tomáš Garrigue Masaryk, *Nová Evropa: stanovisko slovanské* [New Europe: The Slavonic Viewpoint], Prague 2016 [1918/1920].
- **MASARYKOVÁ 1931:** Alice Masaryková, "Souvenirs sur les conférences de N. P. Kondakov", *Seminarium Kondakovianum*, IV (1931), pp. 1–3.
- **MASSE 2010:** *La Renaissance? Des Renaissances? (VIIIe–XVIe siècles)*, Marie-Sophie Masse ed., Paris 2010.
- **MATHEWS 1993:** Thomas F. Mathews, *The Clash of Gods: A Reinterpretation of Early Christian Art*, Princeton 1993.
- **MAUFROY 2010:** Sandrine Maufroy, "Les premiers congrès internationaux des études byzantines: entre nationalisme scientifique et construction internationale d'une discipline", *Revue germanique internationale*, 12 (2010), pp. 229–240.

- **MAZZA 2008:** Mario Mazza, "*Spätantike*: genesi e trasformazioni di un tema storiografico (da Burckhardt a Mickwitz e Marrou via Riegl)", in *Alois Riegl (1858–1905) un secolo dopo*, Proceedings of the international conference (Rome, 30 November – 2 December 2005), Rome 2008, pp. 65–114.
- **MCHITARJAN 2006:** Irina Mchitarjan, *Das "russische Schulwesen" im europäischen Exil. Zum bildungspolitischen Umgang mit den pädagogischen Initiativen der russischen Emigranten in Deutschland, der Tschechoslowakei und Polen (1918–1939)*, Bad Heilbrunn 2006.
- **MCHITARJAN 2009:** Irina Mchitarjan, "Prague as the Centre of Russian Educational Emigration: Czechoslovakia's Educational Policy for Russian Emigrants (1918–1938)", *Paedagogica Historica*, XLV/3 (2009), pp. 369–402.
- **MED 2004:** Jaroslav Med, *Spisovatelé ve stínu* [Writers in the Shadow], Prague 2004.
- **MEDVEDEV 1995:** *Archivy russkich vizantinistov v Sankt-Peterburge* [The Archives of Russian Byzantinists], Igor P. Medvedev ed., Saint Petersburg 1995.
- **MEDVEDEV 1997:** Igor P. Medvedev, "K istorii osnovanija 'Vizantijskogo vremennika'. Neizvestnyje dokumenty i fakty" [On the History of the "Vizantijskij Vremennik". Unknown Documents and Facts], in *Rossija i Christianskij Vostok*, vol. 1, Moscow 1997, pp. 226–244.
- **MEDVEDKOVA 2016:** Olga Medvedkova, "André Grabar et la filiation entre l'art antique, l'art byzantin et russe ancien dans l'historiographie russe", *Revue des études slaves*, LXXXVII/1 (2016), pp. 95–102.
- **MĚŠŤAN 1994:** Antonín Měšťan, "Vorwort", *Germanoslavica. Zeitschrift für germano-slavische Studien*, 1 (VI) (1994), pp. 1–2.
- **MEYER 2009:** Caspar Meyer, "Rostovtzeff and the Classical Origins of Eurasianism", *Anabases. Traditions et réceptions de l'Antiquité*, 9 (2009), pp. 157–197.
- **MICHAUD 2015:** Éric Michaud, *Les Invasions barbares. Une généalogie de l'histoire de l'art*, Paris 2015.
- **MICHEL 2017:** Christian Michel, "La présentation d'images médiévales romaines à la période moderne. Quelques pistes de réflexion", in *Survivals, revivals, rinascenze. Studi in onore di Serena Romano*, Nicolas Bock, Ivan Foletti, Michele Tomasi eds, Rome 2017, pp. 207–216.
- **MILLER 2008:** Alexey Miller, "Natsiia, Narod, Narodnost' in Russia in the 19th Century: Some Introductory Remarks to the History of Concepts", *Jahrbücher für Geschichte Osteuropas*, 56/3 (2008), pp. 379–390.
- **MILLET 1926:** Gabriel Millet, "Les noms des auriges dans les acclamations de l'hippodrome (étude critique sur le Livre des Cérémonies)",

Recueil d'études dédiées à la mémoire de N. P. Kondakov. Archéologie, histoire de l'art, études byzantines, Prague 1926, pp. 279–295.

- **MÍŠKOVÁ 2003:** Alena Míšková, "Die deutsche Universität Prag im Vergleich mit anderen deutschen Universitäten in der Kriegszeit", in *Universitäten in nationaler Konkurrenz: zur Geschichte der Prager Universitäten im 19. und 20. Jahrhundert*, Hans Lemberg ed., Munich 2003, pp. 167–175.
- **MONDZAIN 1996:** Marie-José Mondzain, *Image, icône, économie. Les sources byzantines de l'imaginaire contemporain*, Paris 1996.
- **MONTESQUIEU 1838 [1734]:** Charles-Louis de Secondat, Baron de la Brède et de Montesquieu, *Considérations sur les causes de la grandeur des Romains et de leur décadence*, Paris 1838 [1734].
- **MOORHOUSE 2014:** Roger Moorhouse, *The Devils' Alliance: Hitler's Pact with Stalin, 1939–1941*, London 2014.
- **MORÁVKOVÁ 2016:** Naděžda Morávková, *Plzeňan Kamil Krofta* [Pilsenan Kamil Krofta], Pilsen 2016.
- **MOŠIN 1935:** Vladimir A. Mošin, "N. Kondakov et son Institut", *Byzantion*, 10 (1935), pp. 782–786.
- **MOTTE 1999:** André Motte, "En relisant *Lux perpetua*. Franz Cumont et les savants de son temps", *Mélanges de l'École française de Rome. Italie et Méditerranée*, 111/2 (1999), pp. 507–524.
- **MOXEY 2001:** Keith Moxey, *The Practice of Persuasion: Paradox and Power in Art History*, Ithaca, NY 2001.
- **MURATOFF 1931:** Paul Muratoff, *Trente-cinq primitifs russes*, catalogue of the collection Jacques Zolotnitzky, preface of Henri Focillon, Paris 1931.
- **MURATOV 1913a:** Pavel Muratov (?), "Vozrast Rossii" [The Age of Russia], *Sofija*, 1 (1914), pp. 1–3.
- **MURATOV 1913b:** Pavel Muratov, "Predislovie" [Foreword], in *Vystavka* 1913, pp. 3–4.
- **MURATOV 1914:** Pavel Muratov, "'Russkaja živopis' do serediny XVII veka'" [Russian Painting up to the Mid-Seventeenth Century], in *Istoria russkogo iskusstva*, Igor Grabar ed., vol. IV, Moscow 1914, pp. 5–406.
- **MURATOV 1925:** Pavel Muratov, *La pittura russa antica*, Prague/Rome 1925.
- **MURATOV/MURATOVA 2011:** Aleksandr Muratov, Dita Muratova, "Diplomaty Josef i Vaclav Girsa" [The Diplomats Josef and Vaclav Girsa], *Russkoje Slovo*, 4 (2011), pp. 16–20; 5 (2011), pp. 18–21; 6 (2011), pp. 16–19.
- **MURATOVA 2004:** Xenia Muratova, "La riscoperta delle icone russe e il 'revival' bizantino", in *Arti e storia del Medioevo*, vol. IV: *Il Medioevo al passato e al presente*, Enrico Castelnuovo, Giuseppe Sergi eds, Turin 2004, pp. 589–606.

- **MURATOVA 2008:** Xenia Muratova, "Per la storia dell'arte medievale in Russia. Gli inizi: collezionisti, amatori, scrittori, eruditi, editori, primi storici d'arte", in *Medioevo: arte e storia*, Atti del Convegno internazionale di studi (Parma, 18–22 settembre 2007), Arturo C. Quintavalle, Parma 2008, pp. 120–130.
- **MURATOVA 2010:** Xenia Muratova, "Pavel Muratov historien d'art en Occident", in Foletti 2010, pp. 65–95.
- **MUROMCEVA 2002 [1930]:** Vera N. Muromceva-Bunina, "N. P. Kondakov (K pjatiletiju so dnja smerti)" [N. P. Kondakov (Five Years after His Death)], in Nikodim P. Kondakov, *Vospominanija i dumy*, Irina L. Kyzlasova ed., Moscow 2002 [1930], pp. 348–358.
- **MUZJ 2005 [1995]:** Maria Giovanna Muzj, *Un maître pour l'art chrétien: André Grabar. Iconographie et théophanie*, Charles-André Bernard transl., Paris 2005 [1995].
- **MYSLIVEC 1932a:** Josef Myslivec, "Ikonografie Akatistu Panny Marie" [The Iconography of the Akathistos of the Virgin Mary], *Seminarium Kondakovianum*, V (1932), pp. 97–129.
- **MYSLIVEC 1932b:** Josef Myslivec, "K ikonografii russkych svjatych" [On the Iconography of Russian Saints], *Byzantinoslavica*, IV (1932), pp. 418–430.
- **MYSLIVEC 1946:** Josef Myslivec, "Dimitrij A. Rasovskij", *Byzantinoslavica*, VIII (1939–1946), pp. 329–331.
- **MYSLIVEC 1947:** Josef Myslivec, "Archeologický Ústav N. P. Kondakova v letech 1938–1946" [The Archaeological Institute of N. P. Kondakov in the Years 1938–1946], *Ročenka slovanského ústavu v Praze*, 12 (1947), p. 221.
- ***NA RUBEŽE DVUCH KUL'TUR* 2012:** *Na rubeže dvuch kul'tur: Russkaja emigracija v mežvojennoj Čechoslovakii* [At the Turn of Two Cultures: Russian Emigration in Interwar Czechoslovakia], Moscow 2008.
- **NĚMEC 2008:** Jiří Němec, "Eduard Winter (1896–1982). 'Eine der bedeutendsten Persönlichkeiten der österreichischen Geistesgeschichte unseres Jahrhunderts ist in Österreich nahezu unbekannt'", in *Österreichische Historiker 1900–1945. Lebensläufe und Karrieren in Österreich, Deutschland und Tschechoslowakei in wissenschaftlichen Porträts*, Karel Hruza ed., Vienna/Cologne/Weimar 2008, pp. 619–676.
- **NĚMEC 2011:** Jiří Němec, "Pražská věda mezi Alfredem Rosenbergem a Reinhardem Heydrichem. K prehistorii Říšské nadace Reinharda Heydricha pro vědecká bádání v Praze" [Prague Research Between Alfred Rosenberg and Reinhard Heydrich. About the Prehistory of the Reich's Reinhard Heydrich's Foundation for Scientific Research in Prague], *Studia Historica Brunensia*, 58/2 (2011), pp. 85–105.

- **NĚMEC 2017:** Jiří Němec, "Kamil Krofta and Czechoslovak Identity among Czechs, Slovaks and Germans and Others", in *Transregional Versus National Perspectives on Contemporary Central European History. Studies on the Building of Nation-States and Their Cooperation in the 20th and 21st Century*, Michal Vít, Magdalena M. Baran eds, Stuttgart/Hannover 2017, pp. 161–173.
- **NĚMEC 2018:** Jiří Němec, "Potopení demokratického ostrova" [The Sinking of a Democratic Island], in *Osmičky. Osudová výročí českých a československých dějin končící na jednu číslici*, Libor Jan *et al.* eds, Brno 2018, pp. 205–237.
- **NIEDERLE 1902:** Lubor Niederle, *Slovanské starožitnosti* [Slavonic Antiquities], 2 vols, Prague 1902.
- **O'MEARA 2019:** Patrick O'Meara, *The Russian Nobility in the Age of Alexander I*, London [i.a.] 2019.
- **OFFORD 2015:** *French and Russian in Imperial Russia*, Derek Offord *et al.* eds, Edinburg 2015.
- **OKUNĚV 1929:** Nikolaj Okuněv, "Altarnaja pregrada XII veka v Nerezi" [The 12th-Century Rood Screen in Nerezi], *Seminarium Kondakovianum*, III (1929), pp. 5–23.
- **OKUNĚV 1931:** Nikolaj Okuněv, "Nikolaj Michajlovič Beljaev", *Ročenka Slovanského ústavu*, (1931), pp. 204–213.
- **OKUNĚV 1936:** Nikolaj Okuněv, "Aril'e. Pamjatnik serbskago iskusstva XIII v." [Arilje. A Monument of Serbian Art of the 13th Century], *Seminarium Kondakovianum*, VIII (1936), pp. 221–255.
- **OLIN 2000a:** Margaret Olin, "'Early Christian Synagogues' and 'Jewish Art Historians'. The Discovery of the Synagogue of Dura-Europos", *Marburger Jahrbuch für Kunstwissenschaft*, 27 (2000), pp. 7–28.
- **OLIN 2000b:** Margaret Olin, "Art History and Ideology: Alois Riegl and Josef Strzygowski", in *Cultural Visions: Essays in the History of Culture*, Penny Schine Gold, Benjamin C. Bax eds, Amsterdam 2000, pp. 151–170.
- **OLIVOVÁ 1972:** Věra Olivová, *The Doomed Democracy, Czechoslovakia in a Disputed Europe, 1914–1938*, London 1972.
- **OSTROGORSKIJ 1927:** Georgij Ostrogorskij, "Soedinenie voprosa o sv. ikonach s christologičeskoj dogmatikoj v sočinijach pravoslavnych apologetov perioda ikonoborčestva" [Discussion about the Question of Holy Icons with Christological-Dogmatic into the Texts of the Orthodox Apologists During the Period of Iconoclasm], *Seminarium Kondakovianum*, I (1927), pp. 35–48.
- **OSTROGORSKIJ 1931:** Georgij Ostrogorskij, "Nikolaj Michajlovič Beljaev", *Seminarium Kondakovianum*, IV (1931), pp. 253–260.
- **OSTROGORSKY 1933:** Georg Ostrogorsky, "Rom und Byzanz im Kampfe um die Bilderverehrung", *Seminarium Kondakovianum*, VI (1933), pp. 73–88.

- **OSTROGORSKY 1936:** Georg Ostrogorsky, "Das Kondakov-Institut in Prag (1925–1935)", *Byzantinische Zeitschrift*, 36 (1936), pp. 276–277.
- **PALLADINO 2017:** Adrien Palladino, "*Della dissimulazione onesta*. Richard Delbrueck, an 'Image' of Late Antiquity at the Dawn of National Socialism", *Convivium*, IV/1 (2017), pp. 52–69.
- **PALLADINO 2018:** Adrien Palladino, "André Grabar, Plotinus, and the Potency of Late Antique Images", in Grabar 2018, pp. 12–54.
- **PALLADINO 2019:** Adrien Palladino, "The Wolfgang Born – Kondakov Institute Correspondence. Art History, Freedom, and the Rising Fear in the 1930s", *Convivium*, VI/2 (2019), pp. 128–135.
- **PALLADINO 2020:** Adrien Palladino, "Transforming Medieval Art from Saint Petersburg to Paris: André Nikolajevič Grabar's Fate and Scholarship Between 1917 and 1945", in Foletti/Palladino 2020.
- **PANICACCI 2007:** Jean-Louis Panicacci, "Le traumatisme de la défaite de juin 1940", *Cahiers de la Méditerranée*, 74 (2007), pp. 275–303.
- **PANOFSKY 1932:** Erwin Panofsky, "Zum Problem der Beschreibung und Inhaltsdeutung von Werken der bildenden Kunst", *Logos*, 21 (1932), pp. 103–119.
- **PANOFSKY 1944:** Erwin Panofsky, "Renaissance and Renascences", *The Kenyon Review*, 6/2 (1944), pp. 201–236.
- **PASSINI 2010:** Michela Passini, "Pour une histoire transnationale des expositions d'art ancien. Les Primitifs exposés à Bruges, Sienne, Paris et Düsseldorf (1902–1904)", *Intermédialités*, 15 (2010), pp. 15–32.
- **PASSINI 2012:** Michela Passini, *La fabrique de l'art national: le nationalisme et les origines de l'histoire de l'art en France et en Allemagne, 1870–1933*, Paris 2012.
- **PASSINI 2017:** Michela Passini, *L'œil et l'archive: une histoire de l'histoire de l'art*, Paris 2017.
- **PASTON 2003:** Eleonora V. Paston, *Abramcevo: iskusstvo i žizn'* [Abramcevo: Art and Life], Moscow 2003.
- **PEELING 2014:** Siobhan Peeling, "Emigration (Russian Empire)", in *1914–1918-online. International Encyclopedia of the First World War*, Ute Daniel *et al.* eds, Berlin 2014, [online: www.1914-1918-online.net, accessed 12.08.2020].
- **PEKAŘ 1922:** Josef Pekař, *Dějiny československé* [Czechoslovak History], Prague 1922.
- **PEKAŘ 1929:** Josef Pekař, *Smysl českých dějin* [The Meaning of Czech History], Prague 1929.
- **PENTCHEVA 2010:** Bissera Pentcheva, *The Sensual Icon: Space, Ritual, and the Senses in Byzantium*, University Park, PA 2010.

- **PERDRIZET 1922:** Paul Perdrizet, Negotium perambulans in tenebris, *Études de démonologie gréco-orientale*, Strasbourg 1922.
- **PERDRIZET 1932:** Paul Perdrizet, "De la véronique et de sainte Véronique", *Seminarium Kondakovianum*, V (1932), pp. 1–15.
- **PETTINAROLI 2015:** Laura Pettinaroli, *La politique russe du Saint-Siège (1905–1939)*, Rome 2015.
- **PINTO/LAFRANCONI 2006:** *Gli storici dell'arte e la peste*, Sandra Pinto, Matteo Lafranconi eds, Milan 2006.
- **PIUS XII 1945:** Pius XII, "Nell'accogliere", 2 June 1945, [online: https://www.vatican.va/content/pius-xii/it/speeches/1945/documents/hf_p-xii_spe_19450602_accogliere.html, accessed 16.04.2020].
- **PIUS XII 1947:** Pius XII, "Chirografo di Sua Santità a Harry S. Truman, president degli Stati Uniti d'America", 26 August 1947, [online: http://w2.vatican.va/content/pius-xii/en/letters/documents/hf_p-xii_lett_19470826_have-just.html, accessed 16.04.2020].
- **PODRO 1982:** Michael Podro, *The Critical Historians of Art*, New Haven 1982.
- **POILPRÉ 2005:** Anne-Orange Poilpré, "Bilan d'une décennie de réactions à l'ouvrage de Thomas F. Mathews, *Clash of Gods*, Princeton, 1993", *Antiquité tardive*, 13 (2005), pp. 377–385.
- **PROVOST 2016:** Samuel Provost, "Paul Perdrizet de l'université aux établissements Gallé, le parcours original d'un chercheur éclectique", *Annales de l'Est, Association d'historiens de l'Est*, 2 (2015), pp. 299–317.
- **RAEFF 1990:** Marc Raeff, *Russia Abroad. A Cultural History of the Russian Emigration, 1919–1939*, Oxford 1990.
- **RASOVSKIJ 1927a:** Dimitrij A. Rasovskij, "Drevne-russkoe svetskoe mirovozzrenie" [The Old Russian Secular Worldview], *Zapiski Russkogo istoričeskogo obščestva v Prage*, 1 (1927), pp. 23–24.
- **RASOVSKIJ 1927b:** Dimitrij A. Rasovskij, "O roli černych klobukov v istorii drevnej Rusi" [The Role of Black Hats in the History of Ancient Russia], *Seminarium Kondakovianum*, I (1927), pp.93–109.
- **RASOVSKIJ 1933:** Dimitrij A. Rasovskij,"Pečenegi, Torki i Berendei na Rusi i v Ugrii" [Pechenegs, Turks and Berendei in Russia and Hungary], *Seminarium Kondakovianum*, VI (1933), pp. 1–66.
- **RASOVSKIJ 1935:** Dimitrij A. Rasovskij, "Les Comans et Byzance", in *Actes du IV*[e] *Congres des études byzantines*, vol.1, Sofia 1935, pp. 346–354.
- **RATCHINSKI 2003:** André Ratchinski, "G. V. Vernadski (1887–1973) et le mouvement eurasien", in *Les historiens de l'émigration russe*, Danièle Beaune-Gray ed., Paris 2003, pp. 43–48.
- ***RATTI* 1996:** *Achille Ratti, pape Pie XI*, Actes du colloque (Rome, 15–18 mars 1989), Rome 1996.

- **RAULFF 2009:** Ulrich Raulff, *Kreis ohne Meister. Stefan Georges Nachleben*, Munich 2009.
- **RECORD 2007:** Jeffrey Record, *The Specter of Munich: Reconsidering the Lessons of Appeasing Hitler*, Washington, D.C. 2007.
- **REDIN 1897:** Jegor K. Redin, "Professor Nikodim Pavlovič Kondakov. K tridcatiletnej godovščine ego učenopedagogičeskoj dejatel'nosti" [Professor Nikodim Pavlovič Kondakov. On the Occasion of the Thirtieth Anniversary of His Scientific and Pedagogical Activities], *Zapiski Russkogo Archeologičeskogo Obščestva*, IX (1897), pp. 1–32.
- **REID 2001:** Susan E. Reid, "Socialist Realism in the Stalinist Terror: The *Industry of Socialism* Art Exhibition 1935–41", *The Russian Review*, 60/2 (2001), pp. 153–184.
- ***REPORT* 1932:** *Report of the Kondakov Institute*, Prague 1932.
- ***REPORT* 1933:** *Report of the Kondakov Institute*, Prague 1933.
- ***REPORT* 1934:** *Report of the Kondakov Institute*, Prague 1934.
- ***REPORT* 1935:** *Report of the Kondakov Institute*, Prague 1935.
- ***REPORT* 1936:** *Report of the Kondakov Institute*, Prague 1936.
- ***REPORT* 1937:** *Report of the Kondakov Institute*, Prague 1937.
- **RHINELANDER 1974:** Lawrence Hamilton Rhinelander, "Exiled Russian Scholars in Prague: The Kondakov Seminar and Institute", *Canadian Slavonic Papers*, 16/3 (1974), pp. 331–352.
- **RIEGL 1901:** Alois Riegl, *Die spätrömische Kunst-Industrie nach den Funden in Österreich-Ungarn im Zusammenhange mit der Gesamtentwicklung der Bildenden Künste bei den Mittelmeervölkern*, Vienna 1901.
- **ROERICH 1930:** Jurij N. Roerich, *The Animal Style among the Nomad Tribes of Northern Tibet*, Prague 1930.
- **ROHÁČEK 1995:** Jiří Roháček, "N. P. Kondakov a jeho pražské dědictví" [N. P. Kondakov and His Prague Heritage], *Dějiny a současnost*, 2 (1995), pp. 34–38.
- **ROHÁČEK 2014:** Jiří Roháček, "The Archive of the Institute of N. P. Kondakov", *Convivium*, I/1 (2014), pp. 219–221.
- **ROLLAND 1946:** Paul Rolland, "Review of: *Cahiers archéologiques, fin de l'Antiquité et Moyen-Âge*, t. 1; publiés par A. Grabar, 1945", *Revue belge d'archéologie et d'histoire de l'art*, 16 (1946), pp. 91–92.
- **RONCHEY 2003:** Sylvia Ronchey, "La *femme fatale*, source d'une byzantinologie austère", in *Byzance en Europe*, Marie-France Auzépy ed., Saint-Denis 2003, pp. 153–175.
- **ROSOV 1995:** Vladimir A. Rosov, "Institut Urusvati i Institut N.P. Kondakova: istorija vzaimootnošenij, 1930–1932" [The Urusvati Institute and the N. P. Kondakov Institute: History of Relationships, 1930–1932],

in *Meždunarodnaja konferencija "Russkaja, ukrainskaja i belorusskaja ėmigracija v Čechoslovakii meždu dvumja mirovymi vojnami"*, vol. 2, Prague 1995, pp. 643–652.

- **ROSSIJSKIJE UČENYJE-GUMANITARII 2008:** *Rossijskije učenyje-gumanitarii v meževojennoj Čechoslovakii* [The Russian Scholars in Interwar Czechoslovakia], Moscow 2008.
- **ROSTOVTZEFF 1929:** Michail I. Rostovtzeff, *Le centre de l'Asie, la Russie, la Chine et le style animal*, (bilingual French-Russian), Prague 1929.
- **ROUBANKOV 2009:** Kirill S. Roubankov, "Prazdnovanie 300-letija doma Romanovich (1913 g.) v vospominanijach členov dinastii i ich približennych" [The Festivities of the 300th Anniversary of Rule of the House of Romanov (1913) in the Memoires of the Members of the Dynasty and Their Relatives], *Chronos*,1 (2009), [online: http://www.hrono.ru/proekty/romanov/2rc44.php, accessed 17.07.2019].
- **ROUILLARD 2010:** Linda M. Rouillard, "Grabar, André (July 26, 1896, Kiev – October 5, 1990, Paris), Archaeologist and Art Historian of Classical Antiquity, Byzantium, and the Middle Ages", in *Handbook of Medieval Studies. Terms, Methods, Trends*, Albrecht Classen ed., vol. III, Berlin / New York 2010, pp. 2320–2323.
- **ŘOUTIL 2013:** Michal Řoutil, "Kníže Karel VI. Schwarzenberg a jeho učitel ikonomalby Pimen Maximovič Sofronov (na materiálu archivu Archeologického institutu N. P. Kondakova v Praze)" [Karel VI Schwarzenberg and His Teacher of Icon Painting Pimen Maksimovich Sofronov (Based on the Archival Sources of the Archeological Institute of N. P. Kondakov, Prague)], *Parrésia*, 7 (2013), pp. 261–282.
- **RUEHL 2015:** Martin A. Ruehl, *The Italian Renaissance in the German Historical Imagination, 1860–1930*, Cambridge 2015.
- **RUSAKOV 1975:** Yuriy A. Rusakov, "Matisse in Russia in the Autumn of 1911", *The Burlington Magazine*, 117/866 (1975), pp. 284–291.
- **RUSSO 2005:** Eugenio Russo, "Per leggere 'The Clash of Gods. A Reinterpretation of Early Christian Art' di Thomas F. Mathews", in *Scontro di Dei. Una reinterpretazione dell'arte paleocristiana*, Alessandro Dell'Aira transl., Eugenio Russo ed., Milan 2005, pp. IX–L.
- **SABRUK 1971:** Sava Sabruk, "L'institut Kondakov", *Bulletin d'information et de coordination* [Association Internationale des Études Byzantines], 5 (1971), pp. 40–41.
- **SALMOND 1996:** Wendy R. Salmond, *Arts and Crafts in Late Imperial Russia: Reviving the Kustar Art Industries*, Cambridge 1996.
- **SALMOND 2010:** Wendy R. Salmond, "How America Discovered Russian Icons: The Soviet Loan Exhibition of 1930–32", in *Alter Icons: The Russian*

Icon and Modernity, Jefferson J. A. Gatrall, Douglas Greenfield eds, Philadelphia 2010, pp. 128–143.

- **SALMOND 2017:** Wendy R. Salmond, "Ellis H. Minns and Nikodim Kondakov's The Russian Icon (1927)", in *Modernism and the Spiritual in Russian Art. New Perspectives*, Louise Hardiman, Nicola Kozicharov eds, Cambridge 2017, pp. 165–193.
- **SAMUELS 1979:** Ernest Samuels, *Bernard Berenson: The Making of a Connoisseur*, Cambridge/London 1979.
- **SANSTERRE 2008:** Jean-Marie Sansterre, "Deux témoignages sur la Sainte Face de Laon au XIIIe siècle?", *Revue belge de philologie et d'histoire*, 86/2 (2008), pp. 273–285.
- **SAUL 2013:** Norman E. Saul, *The Life and Times of Charles R. Crane, 1858–1939: American Businessman, Philanthropist, and a Founder of Russian Studies in America*, Lanham 2013.
- **SAVELLI 2014:** Dany Savelli, "L'exaltation des Roerich au Petit Tibet, ou à la naissance du New Age", *Études mongoles et sibériennes, centrasiatiques et tibétaines*, 45 (2014), [online: https://journals.openedition.org/emscat/2423, accessed 09.06.2020].
- **SAVICKIJ 1927:** Petr N. Savickij, "Geopolitičeskie zametki po russkoi istorii" [Geopolitical Notes in Russian History] in Georgij V. Vernadskij, *Načertanie russkoj istorii*, vol. 1, Prague 1927, pp. 234–236.
- **ŠČEKOTOV 1914:** Ivan Ščekotov, "'Ikonopis' kak iskusstvo. Po povodu sobranika ikon I. S. Ostrouchova i S. P. Rjabušinskago" [Icon-Painting as Art. On the Basis of the Collection of Icons of I. S. Ostrouchov and S. P. Rjabušinskij], *Russkaja Ikona*, II (1914), pp. 115–142.
- **SCHALLER 2002:** Helmut Schaller, *Der Nationalsozialismus und die slawische Welt*, Regensburg 2002.
- **SCHELLEWALD 2008:** Barbara Schellewald, "'Le byzantinisme est le rêve qui a bercé l'art européen dans son enfance'. Byzanz-Rezeption und die Wiederentdeckung des Mosaiks im 19. Jahrhundert", *Mitteilungen des Kunsthistorischen Institutes in Florenz*, 52/1 (2008), pp. 123–148.
- **SCHELLEWALD 2019:** Barbara Schellewald, "Die Freisinger Marienikone im Wandel – Ästhetischer Duktus, inhaltliche Akzentuierung und das Phänomen der Übermalung", in *Das Freisinger Lukasbild. Eine byzantinische Ikone und ihre tausendjährige Geschichte*, Antje Bosselmann-Ruickbie, Carmen Roll, Catharina Blänsdorf, Heike Stege eds, Paderborn 2019, pp. 33–61.
- **SCHIEFFER 2006:** Rudolf Schieffer, "Konzepte des Kaisertums", in *Heilig – Römisch – Deutsch. Das Reich im mitterlalterlichen Europa*, Bernd Schneidmüller, Stefan Weinfurter eds, Dresden 2006, pp. 44–56.

- **SCHRAMM 1924:** Percy E. Schramm, "Das Herrscherbild in der Kunst des frühen Mittelalters", in *Vorträge der Bibliothek Warburg*, vol. 2: *Vorträge 1922/23*, Fritz Saxl ed., Berlin/Leipzig 1924, pp. 145–224.
- **SCHWEIZER 2007:** Stefan Schweizer, *"Unserer Weltanschauung sichtbaren Ausdruck geben". Nationalsozialistische Geschichtsbilder in historischen Festzügen zum "Tag der Deutschen Kunst"*, Göttingen 2007.
- **ŠEBEK 2019:** Jaroslav Šebek, "Ve svobodě se rodily zárodky budoucí nesvobody. Utváření politického systému po roce 1945 v kontextu společenských změn" [In the Freedom Were Born the Roots of Future Servitude. Constitution of the Political System after 1945 in the Context of the Social Transformations], in *Vítězství a osvobození 1945*, Jan Němeček, Petr Prokš, Emil Voráček eds, Prague 2019, pp. 171–184.
- **SEIDEL 2018:** Max Seidel, "Adolph Goldschmidt (1863–1944)", in *I conoscitori tedeschi tra Otto e Novecento*, Francesco Caglioti, Andrea De Marchi, Alessandro Nova eds, Milan 2018, pp. 349–366.
- **SEKANINA 2004:** Milan Sekanina, *Kdy nám bylo nejhůře? Hospodářská krize 30. let 20. století v Československu* [When Were We Worse? The Great Depression of the 1930s in Czechoslovakia], Prague 2004.
- **SENA CHIESA 2009:** Gemma Sena Chiesa, "La capsella e il suo decoro. Il liguaggio delle immagini fra devozione cristiana e tradizione imperiale", in *Il tesoro di San Nazaro. Antichi argenti liturgici dalla basilica di San Nazaro al Museo Diocesano di Milano*, Gemma Sena Chiesa ed., Milan 2009.
- **SERRANO COLL 2015:** Marta Serrano Coll, "André Grabar (1896–1990). The Novel Conception of Iconography", in *Rewriting the Middle Ages in the Twentieth Century*, vol. III: *Political Theory and Practice*, Julia Pavón Benito ed., Turnhout 2015, pp. 197–221.
- **SHASHLOVA 2020:** Ekaterina I. Shashlova, "Russian Philosophers in France in the Interwar Period: A Review of the Studies of Emigrant Philosophers", in Foletti/Palladino 2020.
- **SIMMEN 1998:** Jeannot Simmen, *Kasimir Malewitsch – das schwarze Quadrat. Vom Anti-Bild zur Ikone der Moderne*, Frankfurt a. M. 1998.
- **SKÁLOVÁ 1991:** Zuzana Skálová, "Das Prager *Seminarium Kondakovianum*, später das Archäologische Kondakov-Institut und sein Archiv (1925–1952)", *Slavica Gandensia*, 18 (1991), pp. 21–49.
- **SLÁDEK 1994:** Zdeněk Sládek, "Prag: Das 'russische Oxford'", in *Der grosse Exodus. Die russische Emigration und ihre Zentren 1917–1941*, Karl Schlögel ed., Munich 1994, pp. 218–233.
- **SLÁDEK/BĚLOŠEVSKÁ 1998:** *Dokumenty k dějinám ruské a ukrajinské emigrace v Československé republice (1918–1939)* [Documents on the History

of Russian and Ukrainian Emigration in the Czechoslovak Republic (1918–1939)], Zdeněk Sládek, Ljubov Běloševská *et al.* eds, Praha 1998.

- **SMIRNOVA 1999a:** *Drevnerusskoe iskusstvo. Vizantija i Drevnjaja Rus'. K 100-letiju Andreja Nikolaeviča Grabara (1896–1990)* [Old Russian Art. Byzantium and Kievan Rus'. For the 100th Birthday of Andrej Nikolajevič Grabar], Engelina S. Smirnova ed., Saint Petersburg 1999.
- **SMIRNOVA 1999b:** Engelina S. Smirnova, "Andrej Nikolaevič Grabar i voprosy russkoj kul'tury v ego naučnom nasledii", [Andrej Nikolaevič Grabar and Problems of Russian Culture in His Scholarly Heritage], in Smirnova 1999a, pp. 76–82.
- **SMRČKOVÁ 2009:** Jitka Smrčková, *Přínos profesora N. P. Kondakova pro výzkum ikon* [The Benefit of Professor N. P. Kondakov in the Field of Research on the Icon], Prague 2009, [online: https://is.cuni.cz/webapps/zzp/download/120005807, accessed 16.07.2019].
- **SOMERSET/WATSON 2015:** *Truth and Tales: Cultural Mobility and Medieval Media*, Fiona Somerset, Nicholas Watson eds, Columbus 2015.
- **SONIČEVA 1995:** N. E. Soničeva, "Georgij Vladimirovič Vernadskij", in *Istoriki Rossii XVIII–XX vekov*, vol. 2, Moscow 1995, pp. 107–116.
- **SPIESER 1991:** Jean-Michel Spieser, "Héllénisme et connaissance de l'art byzantin au XIXe siècle", in *Hellenismos, quelques jalons pour une histoire de l'identité grecque*, Conference proceedings (Strasbourg, 25–27 October 1989), Leiden [i.a.] 1991, pp. 337–362.
- **SPIESER 2000:** Jean-Michel Spieser, "Du Cange and Byzantium", in *Through the Looking Glass. Byzantium Through British Eyes*, Robin Cormack, Elizabeth Jeffreys eds, Aldershot 2000, pp. 199–210.
- **SPIESER 2007:** *Présence de Byzance*, Jean-Michel Spieser ed., Gollion 2007.
- **SPRINGER 1886:** Anton Springer, "Introduction", in Nikodim P. Kondakov, *Histoire de l'art byzantin: considéré principalement dans les miniatures*, Paris 1886–1891, pp. 1–14.
- **SPRINGER 2006:** Matthias Springer, "Völkerwanderung", in *Reallexikon der Germanischen Altertumskunde,* 2nd ed., vol. 32, Berlin / New York 2006, pp. 509–517.
- **STRADA 1998:** Vittorio Strada, "Icona e anti-icona: armonia e caos nella spiritualità russa", in *Il mondo ed il sovra-mondo dell'icona*, Sante Graciotti ed., Venice 1998, pp. 71–81.
- **STRUVE 1996:** Nikita Struve, *Soixante-dix ans d'émigration russe 1919–1989*, Paris 1996.
- **STRZYGOWSKI 1901:** Josef Strzygowski, *Orient oder Rom. Beiträge zur Kunstgeschichte der spätantiken und frühchristlichen Kunst*, Leipzig 1901.

- **STRZYGOWSKI 1928:** Josef Strzygowski, "Die mit Flechtbändern verzierte Platte vom Wawel", *Seminarium Kondakovianum*, II (1928), pp. 53–59.
- **SVAČINA 1937:** *Bude se na nás dívat: život v soukromí, smrt a pohřeb presidenta Osvoboditele* [He Will Be Watching Us: Private Life, Death and Burial of the President Liberator], Rudolf Svačina ed., Prague 1937.
- **SVITÁK 1990:** Ivan Sviták, *The Unbearable Burden of History: The Sovietization of Czechoslovakia*, vol. 1: *From Munich to Yalta*, Prague 1990.
- **TAROUTINA 2018:** Maria Taroutina, *The Icon and the Square: Russian Modernism and the Russo-Byzantine Revival*, University Park, PA 2018.
- **TASSI 2007:** Ivan Tassi, *Storia dell'io. Aspetti e teorie dell'autobiografia*, Rome/Bari 2007.
- **TAUCHEN 2015:** Jaromír Tauchen, "Law in the Protectorate of Bohemia and Moravia", in *Plundered, But By Whom? Protectorate of Bohemia and Moravia and Occupied Europe in the Light of the Nazi-Art Looting*, Proceedings of an international academic conference (Prague, 21–22 October 2015), Prague 2015, pp. 43–56.
- **TEJCHMANOVÁ 1991:** Světlana Tejchmanová, "Politická činnost ruské emigrace v Československu v letech 1920–1939" [The Political Activity of Russian Emigration in Czechoslovakia in the Years 1920–1939], *Sovetskoe slavianovedenie*, 6 (1991), pp. 24–36.
- **TEJCHMANOVÁ 1993:** Světlana Tejchmanová, *Rusko v Československu. Bílá emigrace v ČSR (1917–1939)* [Russia in Czechoslovakia. White Emigration in Czechoslovakia], Prague 1993.
- **TELLENBACH 1982:** Gerd Tellenbach, "Kaiser, Rom und Renovation: Ein Beitrag zu einem großen Thema", in *Tradition als historische Kraft. Interdisziplinäre Forschungen zur Geschichte des früheren Mittelalters (Festschrift Karl Hauck)*, Mandred Balzer ed., Berlin [i.a.] 1982, pp. 231–253.
- **TENIŠEVA 1930:** Maria K. Teniševa, *Emal' i inkrustatsiia* [Enamel and Inlaid Work], Prague 1930.
- **THIERRY 2005:** Nicole Thierry, "André Grabar et l'Orient", *Comptes rendus des séances de l'Académie des Inscriptions et Belles-Lettres*, CXLIX/3 (2005), pp. 1111–1115.
- **TOLL 1943:** Nicholas P. Toll, *The Excavations at Dura-Europos, Final Reports*, vol. 4,1,1: *The Green Glazed Pottery*, with technological notes by Frederick R. Matson, New Haven 1943.
- **TOLL 1946:** Nicholas P. Toll, *The Excavations at Dura-Europos, Preliminary Report of the Ninth Season of Work, 1935–6. Part II: The Necropolis*, New Haven 1946.
- **TOLL' 1928:** Nikolaj P. Toll', *Koptskie tkani Chudožestvenno-promyšlennogo muzeja v Prage* [Coptic Fabrics from the Museum of Applied Arts in Prague], Prague 1928.

- **TOLL' 1936:** Nikolaj P. Toll', "L'art parthe comme l'un des éléments de la formation du style byzantin", in *Actes du IVe Congrès International des Études Byzantines*, vol. 2, Sofia 1936, pp. 207–209.
- **TOMAN 1995:** Jindřich Toman, *The Magic of a Common Language. Jakobson, Mathesius, Trubetzkoy, and the Prague Linguistic Circle*, Cambridge, MA / London 1995.
- **TOMASI 2008:** Michele Tomasi, "De la collection à l'histoire: sur la genèse et la structure de l'Histoire des arts industriels au Moyen Âge et à l'époque de la Renaissance de Jules Labarte", in *Histoire de l'histoire de l'art en France au XIXe siècle*, Roland Recht, Philippe Sénéchal, Claire Barbillon, François-René Martin eds, Paris 2008, pp. 255–266.
- **TOMASI 2009:** Michele Tomasi, "Labarte, Jules", in *Dictionnarie critique des historiens de l'art actifs en France de la Révolution à la Première Guerre mondiale*, Philippe Sénéchal, Claire Barbillon eds, Paris 2009, [online: https://www.inha.fr/fr/ressources/publications/publications-numeriques/dictionnaire-critique-des-historiens-de-l-art/labarte-jules.html?search-keywords=Labarte, accessed 09.06.2020].
- **TORBAKOV 2008:** Igor Torbakov, "Rethinking the Nation: Imperial Collapse, Eurasianism, and George Vernadsky's Historical Scholarship", *Kennan Institute Occasional Papers*, 302 (2008), pp. 1–21.
- **TOUGHER 2019:** *The Emperor in the Byzantine World. Papers from the Forty-Seventh Spring Symposium of Byzantine Studies*, Shaun Tougher ed., London / New York 2019.
- **TRUBECKOJ 1930:** Nikolaj S. Trubeckoj, "Das 'Münchener slavische Abecedarium'", *Byzantinoslavica*, II (1930), pp. 29–31.
- **TRUBECKOJ 2005:** Nikolaj S. Trubeckoj, *Russland-Europa-Eurasien: Ausgewählte Schriften zur Kulturwissenschaft*, Vienna 2005.
- **TUNKINA 1995:** Irina V. Tunkina, "N. P. Kondakov: obzor ličnogo fonda" [N. P. Kondakov: Panorama of His Personal Resources], in *Archivy russkich vizantinistov v Sankt-Peterburge*, Igor P. Medvedev ed., Saint Petersburg 1995, pp. 93–119.
- **TUNKINA 2001:** Irina V. Tunkina, "N. P. Kondakov po neizdannym vospominanijam B. V. Varenke. 1917–1920 gody" [N. P. Kondakov in the Unpublished Memoirs of B. V. Varenke. Years 1917–1920], in *Nikodim Pavlovič Kondakov, 1844–1925. Ličnost', naučnoe nasledie, archiv. K 150-letiju so dnja roždenia* [Nikodim Pavlovič Kondakov, 1844–1925. Personality, Academic Legacy, Archive. On the Occasion of the 150th Anniversary of His Birth], Moscow 2001, pp. 56–62.
- **USPENSKIJ 2012:** Boris Uspenskij, "Europe as Metaphor and Metonymy (in Relation to the History of Russia)", in Boris Uspenskij, Victor Zhivov,

"Tsar and God" and Other Essays in Russian Cultural Semiotics, Marcus C. Levitt ed., Boston 2012, pp. 175–190.

- **VASILIEV 1937:** Alexander A. Vasiliev, "The Opening Stages of the Anglo-Saxon Immigration to Byzantium in the Eleventh Century", *Annales de l'Institut Kondakov*, 9 (1937), pp. 39–70.
- **VEBER 1993:** Václav Veber *et al.*, *Ruská a ukrajinská emigrace v ČSR v letech 1918–1945*, vol. 1, Prague 1993.
- **VEBER 1994:** Václav Veber *et al.*, *Ruská a ukrajinská emigrace v ČSR v letech 1918–1945*, vol. 2, Prague 1994.
- **VEBER 1995:** Václav Veber *et al.*, *Ruská a ukrajinská emigrace v ČSR v letech 1918–1945*, vol. 3, Prague 1995.
- **VEBER 1996:** Václav Veber *et al.*, *Ruská a ukrajinská emigrace v ČSR v letech 1918–1945*, vol. 4, Prague 1996.
- **VELMEZOVA 2007:** Ekaterina Velmezova, *Les lois du sens: la sémantique marriste*, Bern 2007.
- **VELMEZOVA 2010:** Ekaterina Velmezova, "Les linguistes russes à l'épreuve de l'émigration: quelques pistes pour une future recherche sur les contacts russo-tchèques dans le domaine de la linguistique", in Foletti 2010, pp. 53–63.
- **VENTURI 1936:** Lionello Venturi, *History of Art Criticism*, New York 1936.
- **VERLINDEN 1932:** Charles Verlinden, "Review of: Kantorowicz 1927", *Revue belge de Philologie et d'Histoire*, 11/1–2 (1932), pp. 262–264.
- **VERNADSKIJ 1913:** Georgij V. Vernadskij, "O dviženii russkich na Vostok" [On the Movement of Russians to the East], *Naučnyj istoričeskij žurnal*, 1/2 (1913), pp. 52–61.
- **VERNADSKIJ 1927a:** Georgij V. Vernadskij, "Mongol'skoe igo v russkoi istorii" [The Mongolian Yoke in Russian History], *Evraziiškii Vremennik*, 5 (1927), pp. 153–164.
- **VERNADSKIJ 1927b:** Georgij V. Vernadskij, *Načertanie russkoj istorii*, vol. 1, Prague 1927.
- **VERNADSKIJ/KALITINSKIJ 1926:** Georgij V. Vernadskij, Alexander P. Kalitinskij, "Otčet o rabotach Seminarija imeni Kondakova (Seminarium Kondakovianum) v Prage za pervyj god ego suščestvovanija" [Report on the Works of the Seminar Named after Kondakov (Seminarium Kondakovianum) in Prague in the First Year of Its Existence], in *Recueil d'études dédiées à la mémoire de N. P. Kondakov. Archéologie, histoire de l'art, études byzantines*, Prague 1926, pp. 297–298.
- **VERNADSKY 1926:** George V. Vernadsky, "Nikodim Pavlovič Kondakov", in *Recueil d'études dédiées à la mémoire de N. P. Kondakov. Archéologie, histoire de l'art, études byzantines*, Prague 1926, pp. I-XXX.

- **VERNADSKY 1931:** George V. Vernadsky, *Lenin: Red Dictator*, New Haven / London 1931.
- **VERNADSKY 1933:** George V. Vernadsky, *A History of Russia*, New Haven / London 1933.
- **VESELOVSKIJ 1873:** Alexander Veselovskij, *Sravnitel'naja mifologia i ejo metod* [Comparative Mythology and Its Methodology], Moscow 1873.
- **VON SEE 1994:** Klaus von See, *Barbar, Germane, Arier. Die Suche nach der Identität der Deutschen*, Heidelberg 1994.
- ***VYSTAVKA* 1913:** *Vystavka drevne-russkago iskusstva ustroennaja v 1913 godu v'oznamenovanie čestvovanija 300-letija carstvovanija Doma Romanovych'* [The Exhibition of Ancient Russian Art Organized for the Occasion the Festivities of the 300th Anniversary of Rule of the House of Romanov], Moscow 1913.
- **VZDORNOV 1986:** Gerold I. Vzdornov, *Istorika Otkrytija i izučenija russkoj srednevekovoj živopisi, XIX věk* [Discovery and Study of Medieval Russian Painting, the Nineteenth Century], Moscow 1986.
- **VZDORNOV 2006:** Gerold I. Vzdornov, "Nikodim Pavlovič Kondakov, V zerkale sovremennoj vizantinistiki" [Nikodim Pavlovič Kondakov. In the Mirror of Contemporary Byzantine Studies], in Gerold I. Vzdornov, *Restavracija i nauka. Očerki po istorii otkrytija i izučenija drevnepusskoj živopisi*, Moscow 2006, pp. 291–306.
- **WAETZOLD 1921-1924:** Wilhelm Waetzoldt, *Deutsche Kunsthistoriker*, 2 vols, Leipzig 1921–1924.
- **WARD-PERKINS 1966:** John B. Ward-Perkins, "Memoria, Martyr's Tomb and Martyr's Church", *The Journal of Theological Studies*, 17/1 (1966), pp. 20–37.
- **WEINGART 1922-1923:** Miloš Weingart, *Byzantské kroniky v literatuře církevně slovanské. Přehled a rozbor filologický. Část I. a II.* [Byzantine Chronicles in Church Slavonic Literature. Philological Overview and Analysis. Part I and II], Bratislava 1922–1923.
- **WEITZMANN 1936:** Kurt Weitzmann, "Das Evangelion im Skevophylakion zu Lawra", *Seminarium Kondakovianum*, VIII (1936), pp. 83–98.
- **WEITZMANN 1948:** Kurt Weitzmann, *The Joshua Roll: A Work of the Macedonian Renaissance*, Princeton 1948.
- **WENGER 1996:** Antoine Wenger, "Pie XI et l'Union soviétique", in *Ratti* 1996, pp. 893–907.
- **WES 1990:** Marinus A. Wes, *Michael Rostovtzeff, Historian in Exile. Russian Roots in an American Context*, Stuttgart 1990.
- **WHARTON 1990:** Annabel J. Wharton, "Rereading *Martyrium*: The Modernist and Postmodernist Texts", *Gesta*, 29/1 (1990), pp. 3–7.

- **WINOCK 1996:** Michel Winock, *"Esprit" Des intellectuels dans la cité 1930-1950*, Paris 1996.
- **WINTER 1942:** Eduard Winter, *Byzanz und Rom im Kampf um die Ukraine. 955-1939*, Leipzig 1942.
- **WOLF 1990:** Gerhard Wolf, *Salus populi Romani: die Geschichte römischer Kultbilder im Mittelalter*, Weinheim 1990.
- **WULFF 1929:** Oskar Wulff, "Der Ursprung des kontinuierden Stils in der russischen Ikonenmalerei", *Seminarium Kondakovianum*, III (1929), pp. 25-40.
- **ZAORAL 2013:** Roman Zaoral, "Karel VI. Schwarzenberg. Student, spolupracovník a mecenáš Kondakovova ústavu" [Karel VI Schwarzenberg. Student, Collaborator and Patron of the Kondakov Institute], in *Schwarzenbergové v české a středoevropské historii*, Zdeněk Bezecný, Martin Gaži, Martin C. Putna eds, České Budějovice 2013, pp. 547-556.
- **ŽEBELEV 1924:** Sergey A. Žebelev, "ΟΞΥΣ ΤΑ ΠΡΑΓΜΑΤΑ", in Aa.Vv. 1924, pp. 31-38.
- **ZHIVOV 2012a:** Victor Zhivov, "Cultural Reforms in Peter I's System of Transformations", in Boris Uspenskij, Victor Zhivov, *"Tsar and God" and Other Essays in Russian Cultural Semiotics*, Marcus C. Levitt ed., Boston 2012, pp. 191-238.
- **ZHIVOV 2012b:** Victor Zhivov, "The Myth of the State in an Age of Enlightenment and its Destruction in Late Eighteenth-Century Russia", in Boris Uspenskij, Victor Zhivov, *"Tsar and God" and Other Essays in Russian Cultural Semiotics*, Marcus C. Levitt ed., Boston 2012, pp. 239-258.
- **ZIMMERMANN 1999:** Volker Zimmermann, *Die Sudetendeutschen im NS-Staat. Politik und Stimmung der Bevölkerung im Reichsgau Sudetenland (1938-1945)*, Essen 1999.
- **ZIMMERMANN 2003:** *The Art Historian: National Traditions and Institutional Practices*, Michael F. Zimmermann ed., Yale 2003.

INDEX OF NAMES

INDEX OF PLACES

COPYRIGHT RULES

PHOTOGRAPHIC CREDITS

FIGS 1, 4, 25, 26, 29: private collection; **FIGS 2, 3:** from Ivan Foletti, *From Byzantium to Holy Russia. Nikodim Kondakov (1844–1925) and the Invention of the Icon*, Rome 2017, figs 5, 38; **FIGS 5–7, 18:** © Wikimedia Commons; **FIGS 8a–b, 9:** from Maria Taroutina, *The Icon and the Square: Russian Modernism and the Russo-Byzantine Revival*, University Park, PA 2018, pp. 62, 181; **FIG. 10:** © Arkhivy Rossiyskoy akademii nauk, http://arran.ru/?q=en/node/68; **FIGS 11, 17:** from Nikolay Andreyev, *A Moth on the Fence: Memoirs of Russia, Estonia, Czechoslovakia, and Western Europe*, Catherine Andreyev ed., Patrick Miles transl., Surbiton 2009, p. 113, fig. 13; **FIGS 12, 15, 19a–b, 38:** © Ústav dějin umění Akademie věd České republiky, Praha; **FIG. 13:** from Francesco Lovino, "Communism vs. *Seminarium Kondakovianum*", *Convivium*, IV/1 (2017), pp. 142–157, fig. 3; **FIG. 14:** from Kateřina Iberl, "Natalie Grigorjevna Jašvilová: sloup Seminaria Kondakoviana", *Parrésia*, 5 (2011), pp. 323–333, p. 325; **FIGS 16, 27a–c:** from *Seminarium Kondakovianum*, I (1927), III (1929), V (1932); **FIG. 20:** from Paul Muratoff, *Trente-cinq primitifs. Collection Jacques Zolotnizky*, Paris 1931, pl. IV; **FIGS 21–23, 34:** © Archives du Collège de France, Paris; **FIG. 24:** from *Byzantinoslavica*, I (1929); **FIGS 28a–b:** from André Grabar, *L'empereur dans l'art byzantin. Recherches sur l'art official de l'Empire d'Orient*, Paris 1936; **FIG. 30:** from Ernst Kantorowicz, *Kaiser Friedrich der Zweite*, Berlin 1927; **FIG. 31:** from Steven Luckert, Susan Bachrach, *State of Deception: The Power of Nazi Propaganda*, Washington, D.C. 2009; **FIGS 32a–c:** © La Documentation française. Photo Présidence de la République; **FIG. 33:** © Archives ECPA; **FIGS 35a–b:** from André Grabar, *Martyrium. Recherches sur le culte des reliques et l'art chrétien antique*, 2 vols, Paris 1946; **FIG. 36:** from *Cahiers archéologiques*, I (1945); **FIG. 37:** from Zuzana Frantová, Kristýna Pecinová, "The Icon of Old Brno: A Reconsideration", *Opuscula Historiae Artium*, 62 (2013), pp. 62–75, p. 63, fig. 1.

PARVA Convivia • 8

BYZANTIUM OR DEMOCRACY? KONDAKOV'S LEGACY IN EMIGRATION: THE *INSTITUTUM KONDAKOVIANUM* AND ANDRÉ GRABAR, 1925–1952

Ivan Foletti & Adrien Palladino

Printing & binding: Quatro print, a.s., Heršpická 6, 639 00 Brno.
Paper: Via Laid Natural 270 g/m^2, Munken Pure 120 g/m^2.
Typeface: Hermann by W Foundry.

First edition, Brno–Rome 2020, 216 pages.
Number of copies: 500.

info@earlymedievalstudies.com
info@viella.it

www.earlymedievalstudies.com
www.press.muni.cz
www.viella.it